JESUS THE WARRIOR?

JESUS THE WARRIOR?

HISTORICAL CHRISTIAN PERSPECTIVES & PROBLEMS ON THE MORALITY OF WAR & THE WAGING OF PEACE

by

W. MICHAEL SLATTERY

MARQUETTE
UNIVERSITY
PRESS

© 2007
Marquette University Press

ISBN-13: 978-0-87462-730-5
ISBN-10: 0-87462-730-3

Library of Congress Cataloging-in-Publication Data

Slattery, W. Michael (William Michael), 1945-
  Jesus the warrior? : historical Christian perspectives & problems on the
morality of war & the waging of peace / by W. Michael Slattery.
    p. cm. — (Marquette studies in theology ; #53)
  Includes bibliographical references and index.
  ISBN-13: 978-0-87462-730-5 (pbk. : alk. paper)
  ISBN-10: 0-87462-730-3 (pbk. : alk. paper)
  1. War—Religious aspects—Christianity. I. Title.
BT736.2.S53 2007
241'.6242—dc22

                                                                    2007016282

COVER DESIGNED BY JOSH HARVEY.

© 2007 Marquette University Press
Milwaukee, Wisconsin 53201-3141
All rights reserved.
www.marquette.edu/mupress/

♾The paper used in this publication meets the minimum requirements of the
American National Standard for Information Sciences—
Permanence of Paper for Printed Library Materials, ANSI Z39.48-1992.

MARQUETTE UNIVERSITY PRESS
MILWAUKEE

The Association of Jesuit University Presses

TABLE OF CONTENTS

Introduction   7

Chapter 1: The Rationale, Causes & Reasons for War & Inter-Group Lethal Conflict-Resolution   13

Chapter 2: War & Inter-Group Lethal Violence in the Hebrew Scriptures   31

Chapter 3: Treatment of War & Non-Violence in the Christian Scriptures   53

Chapter 4: Early Christian Approaches to War & Peace (from Apostolic Through Late Patristic Period   77

Chapter 5: The Morality of War & Inter-Group Lethal Conflict-Resolution: Recent Christian Perspectives Regarding the Problem of Just War Rationale   107

Chapter 6: Understanding War & Violent Conflict-Resolution: the Christian Problem of Living in the Twenty-First Century   159

Chapter 7: Practitioners & Models of Christian Morality with Respect to Violence and War   187

Chapter 8: How to Live Today as a Christian with the Morality of War   223

Appendices   235

Bibliography   247

Index   255

INTRODUCTION

In the apostolic and early Christian communities, the followers of the Christ were proscribed from bearing and using weapons and instruments that threaten and inflict physical violence and no leader of the early Church nor patristic writer approved or encouraged participation in any army or militia, be it that of Rome, revolutionary forces, or other local or national power.[1] Following and despite supposedly Kephas' use of the sword in cutting off the ear of servant of the high priest, a violent act condemned by Jesus while he himself was being unjustly arrested (Mt. 26:51-53, Mk. 14: 47; and Lk. 22:49-51), the early Christians sought to emulate and realize the teachings and practices of Jesus in loving service and peace-making even in the face of persecution.

By the fourth century CE, though, with the cessation of persecution of the Christians and recognition of Christianity as an acceptable religion under direction of the proconsul Galerius in 311, the acceptance of Christian symbols by the still un-baptised Constantine (reign of 306-337 CE) the following year in the historic battle at the Milvian Bridge, issuance of the Edict of Milan announcing universal religious tolerance in 313 CE, and later recognition of Christianity as the sole religion of the state in 381 CE under the emperor Theodosius I, Christian attitudes towards military service and war began to change noticeably from non-acceptance to approval. What changed Christian thinking on the use of violence and war as an acceptable means of dispute resolution? Were the thinking and practices of the apostolic and early Church and the patristics merely idealistic or was the ethical and moral understanding of military force and war only further developed in line with the new status of Christians as part of ruling state? Was the moral interpretation of Jesus teachings by the early

---

1 Richard McSorley, SJ, *New Testament Basis of Peacemaking* (Center for Peace Studies: Washington, DC, 1979), pp. 71-72. See hereafter statements by Justin Martyr (c. 100-165 CE), Clement of Alexandria (c. 150-215 CE), Iraneus of Lyons (c. 130-200 CE) Tertullian (c. 160-225 CE), Origin (c. 185-254 CE), Eusebius of Caesarea (c. 260-340 CE), Cyprian of Carthage (c. 258 CE), Lactantius (late third and early fourth century CE), etc.

Church just an expedient way of surviving as a threatening minority in a Jewish culture amid a foreign controlling empire of Rome? How did these Christian view the role of government and the state and what is an appropriate moral understanding and application for us today? What were the positions of Jesus, as can best be determined from hermeneutical and exegetical interpretation of the scriptures, toward the use of military and violent physical force and toward the exercise of security and rule of government? Had the early Christians simply misinterpreted the teachings and practice of Jesus, only to be corrected by later Christian followers? Were the apostolic and early Christian communities actually pacifists and is this mistaken interpretation? Were the teachings and practices of Jesus actually advocating non-violence and opposition to war or have such understanding mistook other texts that seem to counter this? Did the teachings of Jesus on violence and war contradict the practice of war in the Hebrew scriptures? How did the early Christians understand the image of God as warrior and the bellicosity of the Hebrews in the Hebrew scriptures and rationalize their opposition to war and military force? Is the vindictive image of God in the Hebrew scriptures as viewed by Marcion misaligned with the image of God held by Jesus? What were the rationale, intent and the appropriate understanding of the just war argument that was later developed initially by and further expanded by ethicists and theologians? These and related questions will be pursued in this paper. Further, we shall analyze the ethics and appropriateness of just war theory in contemporary society. Have ecclesial and clerical leaders from the Middle Ages until today undermined and perverted early Christian interpretation on the morality of war, or refined the criteria for military engagement? If the teachings and practice of Jesus on the practice of violence and military force are ambiguous or ambivalent, what moral and ethical treatment in that regard is appropriate today?

In pursuing answers to the aforenoted barrage of questions, we shall draw upon sources that seek to define the causes and treatment of war and military force, but only to provide a cursory understanding in order to grapple with the moral and ethical issues therein. In this regard, we shall consider the definition of war (inter-group inter-group lethal conflict)[2] and physical violence and briefly explore the causes and effects of war from aspects related to political, social, economic, ethnic, psychological, religious, etc. issues.[3] Because this paper specifically treats the moral and ethical aspects of war, we shall concentrate and develop our understanding therein, but need to establish a basic understanding of the causes and dynamics of war and violent conflict-resolution.

Any interpretative approach to Christian response to war and military force must begin with the approach applicable in the Hebrew scriptures and the theological understanding therein. We shall confine our research to the work of twentieth century Hebrew scriptures biblical scholarship.[4] In contrast, the Christian scriptures, particularly that of the canonical Gospels, presents positions that appear contradictory in themselves or opposing the apparent acceptance of war in the Hebrew scriptures.[5] We shall explore these in depth, especially from the moral

---

2 McSorley, p. 3, uses this definition upon which we shall further expand in the next section.

3 The underlying research for this perusal of the causes of war stems from basic research in political science, international relations, nation-building and revolution, and political development. We shall avail work undertaken by Kenneth Waltz, Samuel Huntington, Harry Eckstein, James Dougherty and Robert Pfaltzgraff, Jr., Sigmund Freud, William James, Daniel Levinson, Edward Tolman, Robert Park, Herbert Spenser, Alexis deTocqueville, Raymon Aron, Morris Janowitz, Amitai Etzioni, Peter Berger, Chalmers Johnson, Karl von Clausewitz, Mao Tse-Tung, Kalman Silvert, and Quincy Wright.

4 The basis of this analysis will rely on works dealing with the understanding and treatment of war, its morality and the understanding of Yahweh's relationship to war in the Hebrew scriptures. Therein, the basis of reference will use works by Susan Niditch, TR Hobbs, Gerhard vonRad, Millard Lind, Peter Craigie, Patrick Miller, Bruce Birch Walter Brueggemann, and even Max Weber's sociological analysis of the religious cohesion of the Hebrew confederacy (*Bund*) based on a War God and Johannes Pedersen's work on the psychic unity of Israelites engaging in cultic rites related to war.

5 We shall base our analysis on the works undertaken by John H. Yoder, Richard Hays, and Richard McSorley. We will expand on this through analysis of and hermeneutical interpretation of various Christian Scrip-

perspective of peace making. The position of Jesus regarding war and physical violence and moral judgments issued by the patristic writers until the early fifth century will be explored in depth.[6]

In consideration of the differences on the morality of war and violence between those elicited and demonstrated by the early Church and its treatment by Christians in the twentieth century and thereafter, it behooves us to explore the theoretical applications of just war concepts and Christian reaction to such violence today as well as the morality of war itself.[7] In conclusion, this paper will analyze and evaluate the practices of the contemporary Church in exercising the morality of war and peace, or its accommodation to ruling powers in their practice of international relations.

The underlying assumption of this paper focuses on the teachings and activity of Jesus who did not preach, teach, or direct his followers to engage in bellicose and aggressive way of living, but rather

---

ture sayings related to the condemnation of violence or assumed condoning of war as a permissible means of conflict resolution with the assistance of commentary provided by Bruce Vawter, Joseph Fitzmyer, Carroll Stuhlmueller, John L. McKenzie, and Raymond Brown. In order to grasp the teachings and activity of the historical Jesus to substantiate the above, we will utilize studies by John Meier, John Dominic Crossan, and Christological interpretation by Marcus Borg, Jon Sobrino, Juan Segundo, et al.

6 The patristic writings of Justin Martyr, Cyprian of Carthage, Clement of Alexandria, Origen, Tertullian, Athenagoras, et. al. as well as cotemporaneous writings of Lactanius, Hippolytus, et al. will be quickly reviewed along with historical commentary provided by Flavius Josephus and the Christian Apologist Minucius Felix. The problem of Marcion will be critiqued and the Christian dilemma on war as dealt by Augustine will be introduced and will be expounded in a later section.

7 We shall rely on Augustine's "City of God" and Michael Walzer's work dealing with just war theory, the moral analysis of Stanley Hauerwas and Richard Hay, the papal social encyclicals and pronouncements of various Roman Catholic bishops' conferences, positions pronounced at the second Vatican Council of the Catholic Church which deal with the issues of war and violent conflict-resolution, and the writings of Roland Bainton, Joseph Allen, James Douglass and Gerhard Lohfink.

emphasized the importance of tolerance, love in the positive sense,[8] non-retaliation, stressing forgiveness, and emphasizing the doing of justice and liberating the oppressed, *marginales*, weak, outcast, foreigners, and handicapped. By his way of living and his teachings, clearly Jesus believed in non-violence and avoided physical conflict. Thus, war and physical violence in conflict resolution runs not just contrary to Jesus' teaching and way of living, but can be construed to be never condoned by Jesus. We will also hypothesize that Jesus' image of, relationship with, and realization of God differs from that characterized in the Hebrew scriptures (Exodus, Judges, Joshua, etc.) while not denying the power and intervention of God on behalf of the weak and oppressed. The teachings of Jesus, while contested by some as ambivalent or ambiguous regarding the morality of war, cannot be construed to condone violence and war as a means of conflict resolution and more than strongly direct Christian believers to exercise a way of living contrary to violent and inter-group lethal group interaction in war and conflict resolution. Although the Church frequently speaks out of both sides of its mouth and often its leadership fails to show leadership in following the apostles and early patristics in living the teachings of Jesus, prophetic elements continue to call it back to its roots and demand that it exercise the moral integrity demanded by Jesus of his followers.

---

8 Jesus' teaching of "Do unto others as you would have them do unto you" is a positive spin on the teaching of an ancient Hebrew scholar, Hillel, to "do not do to others what you would not want them to do to you."

CHAPTER I

THE RATIONALE, CAUSES & REASONS FOR WAR &
INTER-GROUP LETHAL CONFLICT-RESOLUTION

Between 1100 and 1925 CE, roughly 35.5 million persons died in wars on the European continent and the British Isles, of which nearly 38% were in the First World War (8.4 million soldiers and about five million civilians). During the twentieth century, though, between 165 million and 258 million persons died in 165 declared wars. In the Second World War alone, 17 million soldiers and 34 million civilians died, or at least one third of the fatal war casualties of the twentieth century. During the US engagement in Vietnam alone, more than three million Vietnamese died in contrast to the deaths of 54,000 interventionist, US military personnel. Increasingly, civilians comprise more than 75 percent of deaths in wars of the twentieth century.[1] Mention of the deaths of about 200,000 civilians in each of two nuclear blasts for Hiroshima and Nagasaki and of the more than 200,000 deaths in the fire bombings of Tokyo in 1944 is unneeded.[2] With the US' first invasion of Iraq (under United Nation auspices) that occurred in 1991, while only several hundred US soldiers died, unofficial reports indicate that well over 100,000 Iraqi soldiers were killed, particularly on the Basra Road. After that war, UNESCO reported that by 1998 more than 600,000 Iraqi children, because the

---

1 This data is attributed to a speech delivered by Bishop Thomas Gumbleton, auxiliary bishop of the Roman Catholic diocese of Detroit, at an award ceremony of St. Norbert College, Green Bay in the fall of 2003.

2 It should be noted that at least in the case of the Hiroshima bombing, Hiroshima was third on the list of targets for the day. Yokohama, a city of roughly four million at that time, was first and Nagoya, a city whose population was approaching two million, was second, but due to overcast cloud cover and other weather conditions were scratched in favor of Hiroshima. If the bombs dropped on Hiroshima and Nagasaki been delivered to their primary targets, civilian casualties would in all probability have been even more horrendous.

US-led sanctions refused to allow refurbishment of the demolished Iraqi water treatment facilities following the 1991 war, became fatalities. In response to this situation, then Chief of Staff Collin Powell stated that he had no interest because his concern pertained to lost US military and Madeleine Albright, then US ambassador to the UN, declared in an interview for US Public Television that this was the price of war (that Saddam Hussein extracted).[3] The most recent war of international interest, the US-led invasion and occupation of Iraq beginning in 2003, certainly substantiates the claim that civilian, not military personnel suffer more deaths, not to mention casualties and the destruction of infrastructure, personal capital, and natural resources, with the deaths of roughly 600 US soldiers compared to more than 11,000 Iraqis by the summer of 2004.[4]

---

3 UNESCO publication. Powell's comment was quoted by unnamed news sources and Albright's interview was aired in the fall of 2003. The US Army Corp of Engineers had reported at the end of the 1991 Iraqi War that, with failure to allow restoration of these water facilities, no less than one-half million Iraqi children could be expected to die due to disease etc., not to mention deaths that would be induced on the aged, weak and infirm. While some would quibble over definitional technicalities, how can anyone but declare this to be other than partial genocide with the intentional death of so many youth?

4 Iraqbodycount.net. One should note that both the US-led coalition and the provisional Iraqi government under US direction have prohibited and forbad the tabulation, publication, and reporting of deaths and casualties of Iraqi civilians. This has resulted in this independent organization of reporting civilian deaths in Iraq since mid-2003. Nevertheless, it reported that 7,350 civilians died in the two months of the US-led invasion prior to May 1, 2003 and that their data reveal that between 9,148 and 11,005 were reported killed by mid-year.

Innumerable examples of military objectives disregarding civilian casualties could be listed, be they the fire bombing of Dresden in 1944, the rape of Nanking by the Japanese at the start of WW II, the bombings of Rotterdam, London, etc. by the Nazis, the incidents of My Lai and other Vietnamese villages, etc., but we only wish to stress that the proportion of civilian deaths and casualties both is rising numerically and percentage-wise and runs counter to the statements and rationalization that advanced weapons are more technologically developed and will reduce civilian casualties. Revolutionary and insurgency violence counter-

What fundamental reasons and causes can then induce, lead or force people into war and other inter-group lethal types of conflict resolution?[5] It behooves us to explore the very causes and objectives of war if moral judgment of war and inter-group lethal means of conflict resolution are to be exercised morally and understood from a Christian perspective.[6]

---

ing overwhelming more powerful forces can be expected to magnify civilian deaths and casualties. Evaluation of the effectiveness of the military tactics of superior force, in fact, has proved to undermine the objectives of demoralizing the local populace, but merely has resulted in greater support by the local populace for their local, ethnic leaders in the face of heightened bellicose activity.

It is important to note that, unlike fighting and tactical methods of previous times, both militaries and insurgents increasingly must wage conflict within urban centers rather than on open battlefields because power resides in control of industry, transport, infrastructure, and the hearts and minds of the local populace and because urban warfare remains the only strategically viable means for less well-equipped military or insurgent forces to struggle against forces armed with better, more technologically developed, faster, and more powerful weaponry and the forces or means to deliver such.

5 We are not investigating events that precipitate war or inter-group lethal violence against groups, but hunting for more basic causes. The reader should note that this section focuses on the causes and means of war from the standpoint of scholars and writers who themselves recognize war as one means of conflict-resolution, without necessarily considering such the ideal, but accepting it as realistic. No comment on the morality of such causes is here offered.

6 Bernard Lonergan's *Insight* (Toronto: University of Toronto Press, 1992) and *Method in Theology* (Toronto: University of Toronto Press, 1990) provide direction for applying epistemology to morality. Based on Lonergan, at least five acts are required for being a moral person: the moral person must (a) first accumulate data, facts and knowledge, (b) next categorize this information logically, (c) evaluate and discern this information, (d) make judgment on this information and its implications, and (e) act according to the judgment on the evaluated data. See for further development of this idea: Russell B. Connors, Jr. and Patrick T. McCormick, *Character, Choices, and Community: The Three Faces of Christian Ethics* (New York: Paulist Press, 1998) p. 4-7, 35-53, and 174-199 and

Inter-group lethal conflict erupts and war is embarked upon by leaders and groups or peoples for a host of reasons. In a political sense, war is the extension of politics, an instrument of policy with political motives, and a political act in itself.[7] "War is therefore an act of violence intended to compel our opponents to fulfill our will." (Clauswitz, 1972, 208) Politics involves the decision-making and active process of allocating scarce resources.[8] War itself can be viewed as a decision-making process that utilizes physical coercion and inter-group lethal threat or terror that results in the same effectiveness as war itself by playing upon psychological influences, that are linked to and become a form of violence; it can also be understood to be means of negotiation, that does not restrict decision-making of choices to oral or logical dialogue. Clausewitz honestly deemed the use of and role of law, either national or international, as hardly worth mentioning as a

---

Richard M. Gula, SS, *Reason Informed by Faith: Foundations of Catholic Morality* (New York: Paulist Press, 1989) pp. 28-32.

We have no intention, although it may be enlightening for future and more detailed analysis, either to analyze the utility of war as a means of conflict resolution or to review the various types of war and inter-group lethal conflict. Such is not the purpose of this paper. Let it be said that, generally speaking, the types of war and inter-group lethal conflict considered hereafter entail an array of violent conflict resolution from inter-group lethal combat to guerrilla warfare, domestic and international terrorism, conventional warfare between states, nuclear war, etc. Further, while the morality of specific weaponry may be debated, it is not the intent of this paper to analyze such because the focus resides on the morality of war and inter-group lethal conflict themselves. Similarly, this paper will not evaluate the appropriateness or morality of the rules of war, law or governmental orders related to war.

7 Karl von Clausewitz, Gen., "The Nature of War," excerpted from Clausewitz's *On War* (Barnes and Noble, Inc) in Robert L. Pfaltzgraff, Jr. (ed.), *Politics in the International System* (Philadelphia: JB Lippincott Company, 1972), pp. 208-210. Gen. Clausewitz was the Prussian Chief of Staff and Director of the General War Academy in Berlin in the early 1800s. His seminal thinking on war is used by all students of military training and international relations.

8 David E. Apter, *Choice and the Politics of Allocation* (London: Yale University Press, 1971), p. 10.

restriction to violence and war because law effectively fails to impair or hardly deter the exercise of power when political forces and rationale coalesce to foment war. Mao Tse-tung has similarly expressed that politics comes out of the barrel of a gun, the effective implication of Clausewitz's dictum; Mao took this thinking further and applied this thinking within domestic contexts to revolution, inclusive of guerrilla warfare, which he characterized as the "seizure of power by armed force, the settlement of the issue by war, ... the central task and the highest form of revolution."[9]

What are the scarce resources that politics, inclusive of war as an inter-group lethal means in that process, allocates and for which it wages inter-group lethal conflict? These resources are not restricted to natural resources such as water, food such as fish and grains, commodities, raw materials such as coal, bauxite, iron ore, etc., but also include humans, in terms of numbers because of their expertise and skills, and technology. The allocation process for which wars are fought may also entail the means of production: hydro-, thermal, or nuclear electrical plants, smelters, foundries, manufacturing plants or factories, refineries, food processing plants, warehouses and storage facilities, etc.; it includes transport systems such as railways and air rights and related delivery equipment (ships, aircraft, locomotive and freight cars, over-the-road trucks and trailers, etc.).

What, then, brings leaders, parties, political groupings, societies, etc. to engage in threatening and bellicose acts of war to attain political objectives through forcing one's will upon other political groups? Are there other reasons for engaging in inter-group lethal violence besides, as Clausewitz indicated, getting one's enemies to do one's will? Exemplary reasons of such include vengeance or revenge for unwanted acts committed upon oneself or one's group, extermination or genocide, distraction of the local populace from domestic dilemmas, relief from constituent pressure, the breakdown of political order and dilution of legal means of redress, frustration-aggression phenomena, intellectual stimuli, restriction on upward mobility, etc. These also must

---

9 Mao Tse-tung, "Problems of War and Strategy," in *Selected Works*, I (Beijing: Foreign Languages Press, 1964) and reprinted in M. Rejai, (ed.) *Mao Tse-tung on Revolution and War* (Garden City, NY: Anchor Books, 1970), p. 61.

be considered. Essentially, the issue of aggression and what causes it will help explain the reasons and causes of war and inter-group lethal violence.

Change, be it social, political, ethnic, religious, economic, psychological, etc., acts as an important factor that stimulates and induces war, particularly if such change is radical, eccentric, and rapid, and either the status quo shifts precipitously or the limits of toleration of oppression are reached. Education, that is self-education and realization of new possibilities that if sought after, facilitates this change. Change alone, though, cannot completely be causation in war. It is important to review, then, other causes of war. Quincy Wright suggests that causes for war can be attributed to scientific, historical, and practical reasons and that, to understand the nature and morality of war, it behooves one to realize that war has technological, legal, sociological, and psychological aspects. From a behavioral standpoint, anthropological aspects must also be added. Let us consider these causes and aspects in greater depth. By scientific, Wright infers that there are at work forces, interests, controls, and motives in international and domestic relations which effect power. He describes the conditions attributed to fomenting war as follows, using the term scientific more from the standpoint analogous to the physics of power and interest, and analogous to mathematics because it is to some extent numerically calculable, especially with regard its probability. He identifies the causes of war:

> (1) to the difficulty of maintaining stable equilibrium among the uncertain and fluctuating political and military forces within the state system; (2) to the difficulty of utilizing the sources and sanctions of international law so as to make it an effective instrument for determining the changing interests of states, the changing values of humanity, and the just settlement of international disputes; (3) to the difficulty of so organizing political power than it can maintain order in a universal society, not threatened by other societies external to itself; and (4) to the difficulty of making peace a more important symbol in world public opinion than particular symbols which may locally, temporarily, or generally favor war.[10]

10   Quincy Wright, *A Study of War* (Chicago: University of Chicago Press, 1964), p. 105. Quincy Wright worked in the Navy Department, the State Department, and as a judge at the Nuremberg Tribunal.

He concludes that these conditions make appraisal difficult and unlikely. This approach is based, though, on a rationale that is explicable through natural law and is premised on deterministic thinking.

Historical causes analyze past historical events and ferret out processes and patterns of change; they seek to "demonstrate causes by drawing from a detailed knowledge of the antecedents of a particular war, events, circumstances, and conditions which can be related to the war by practical, political, and juristic commonplaces about human motives, impulses, and intentions." (Wright, 1964, 106) While similar to a mathematical analysis of the probability of war, this form of analysis remains just as difficult and unlikely.

Practical causes of war seem to concentrate on the nature of free will and individual arbitrary decisions arising from complex relationship between individual ambitions, desires, purposes, animosities, aspirations, and irrationalities. One should advise caution on this approach also because waging war involves many people and systemic structures in modern society is not easily relegated to individual arbitrariness. Proponents of this type of analysis attribute the causes of war to:

> (1) Men and governments find themselves in situations where they believe they must fight or cease to exist, and so they fight from necessity. (2) Men or governments want something—wealth, power, social solidarity—and, if the device of war is known to them and other means have failed, they use war as a rational means to get what they want. (3) Men and governments have a custom of fighting when their culture requires fighting in the presence of certain stimuli, and so in appropriate situations they fight. (4) Men and governments feel like fighting because they are pugnacious, bored, or the victims of frustrations or complexes, and accordingly they fight spontaneously for relief or relaxation. (Wright, 1964, 107)

From a technological perspective, war arises when tension from pressure and resistance cannot be tolerated any longer in a world or regional balance of power. Each power is viewed as a war-machine in itself. War is essentially and critically related to a larger physical system and the balance of powers therein, and erupts theoretically only with dis-equilibrium. Law and morality, however, pose difficulty in this simplistic analysis.

As noted above regarding the complexity of decision-making in governmental systems with regard to war in modern societies, "states go to war by means of constitutional procedure in order to defend themselves" (or to wage war unilaterally or preemptively), "to resist injustice, to fulfill a duty, to enforce a right, to vindicate national honor, or to implement policy," states Wright. (Wright, 1964, 109) States or opposing groups go to war deliberately and generally with not too little reflection, particularly in the form of law for established governments.

Contrarily, but not denying the above, states and their peoples go to war for many latent, subconscious or unconscious reasons that support, if not supercede in reality, the legal and constitutional causes of war. Leaders of such states not infrequently manipulate this underflow of emotional-based reasoning and exploit such for their own objectives. The recent US-led invasion of Iraq adequately demonstrated the clever use of the fear of international terrorism to inflame national war sentiment. In such situations, government statements remain little more than hollow propaganda. War, then, may be interpreted as a conflict of cultures.

Psychologically, culture relies on images, myths, and ideals that are held by individuals.[11] Wars are clashes between individuals holding various psychological myths, images, and values that such individuals perceive to be in conflict and contradictory.[12] Culture and its symbols represent nothing more than the collective formulation of desires (desires that lead to war were termed "inordinate ambitions" by Wil-

---

11 See William James, "The Moral Equivalent of War," in Leon Bramson and George W. Goethals (eds.), *War: Studies from Psychology Sociology Anthropology* (New York: Basic Books, 1968), p. 21-22.

12 A wonderful incident during the WW I reminds us that these myths can be debunked when men realize their common humanity which their distorted perceptions have hidden. In this incident that occurred on Christmas day, the German and Allied forces on their own in the trenches of France put their weapons down and played a friendly game of football (soccer). As a result, when Christmas evening came, they were no longer able to be bullied by their commanding officers to re-engage in inter-group lethal battle. Sadly, the troops in the trenches had to be replaced to commence inhumane hostilities. US Public Television has shown a creative animation of this historical event.

liam James)[13] and intentions of individual psyches. Opinions to characterize perceived enemies and to wage inter-group lethal hostilities,
arising from individual psyches, may result in a collective decision to
do battle. Wright astutely notes the possibility for manipulation of
such, something all the more possible in mass-media societies with
concentrated control.

> The fact that opinions rather than conditions induce political
> action, the ease with which opinion can be manipulated by special
> interests, and the presence of irrational drives of adventure, per-
> secution, escape, and cruelty account for the usual irrationality of
> war and for the relatively slight correlation of its occurrence with
> any definable population or economic changes. The tendency for
> individuals to concentrate their loyalties upon a concrete group and
> to concentrate their aggressive dispositions upon an external group
> makes it possible that an incident in the relations of the two groups
> will acquire a symbolic significance and stimulate mass reactions
> which may produce war.[14]

Further, incompatible desire to dominate, either by leaders or by
collective groups within states, may stem from hostile attitudes
and lead to war through progressive intensification of psychologically based hostility.

William James and William McDougall consider war as a primal act
descending from man's animal heritage. Although seen as meaningless
in its destruction, pillage, and reversion to uncivilized methods of
resolving inter-group conflict, both acknowledge that society portrays
it as a stage for laudatory human virtues (i.e., love of glory if that
can be considered a virtue) and for what is considered manly virtues
from which social progress is reputed to evolve. Although McDougall
claims that the pugnacity of nations is being reduced by industrial
and intellectual rivalry through emulation (i.e., selection of the fit and
elimination of the less fit),[15] the data on war in the twentieth century
noted at the beginning of this section seem to refute this rationale.

---

13 James, "The Moral Equivalent of War," p. 24.

14 Wright, *A Study of War*, p. 113.

15 William McDougall, "The Instinct of Pugnacity," in Bramson and
   Goethals' *War*, pp. 42 and 43. D.O. Hebb and W.R. Thomson refute

Sigmund Freud poses a different twist on the psychological cause of war, namely that war, a social phenomenon, and aggression, a personal phenomenon, are different manifestations of the same drive system, namely, the control of the balance of life and death in evolutionary development.[16] E.F.M. Durbin and John Bowlby postulate that repressed discipline drives aggression (possessiveness, strangeness, frustration, etc.) underground in order to reduce anxiety.[17] Harry Stack Sullivan, on the other hand, carries this line of thought further and considers aggression as the result of inability of men to communicate their fears and anxieties.[18] Erik Erikson sees "war arising as a consequence of profound social ambiguities" and is "an alternative to the 'totalistic' nature … of achieving personal wholeness."[19] The manner in which the individual (or, for that matter, the state) deals with itself is the way in which it deals with the rest of society. Thus, Erikson, by extrapolation, perceives that aggressive and inter-group lethal interaction exercised by states, is the manner that they deal with themselves.[20] Without question, the formation and role of the psyche

---

the James' and McDougall's claim regarding the animal nature in man as the cause of pugnacity and war, but rather attribute such to the human traits of group-inter-group lethal violence in animals, whose attribute they claim characterize the complexity of the primate. Time, space, and expertise restrict further development of this argument in this paper.

16   Sigmund Freud, "Why War?," an open letter to Albert Einstein published by the League of Nations Institute of Intellectual Cooperation, and included in Bramson and Goethals, *War*, pp. 71-80.

17   E.F.M. Durbin and John Bowlby, "Personal Aggressiveness and War," in Bramson and Goethals, *War*, pp. 81-103.

18   Harry Stack Sullivan, "Toward a Psychiatry of Peoples," Bramson and Goethals, *War*, p. 111.

19   Bramson and Goethals, *War*, p. 68.

20   In considering the US, this would certainly seem to be the case since the mid-twentieth century. For example, the US has the highest murder rate amongst industrialized nations, 0.7% or 18,000 for a population exceeding 260 million, and has engaged in more military conflicts [(exceeding 60 according to the Stockholm International Peace Research Institute (SIPRI), *Arms Trade with the Third World* (New Jersey: Humanities Press, 1973) and SIPRI, *World Armaments and Disarmament: SIPRI Yearbook*

and personality, particularly authoritarian personalities and especially in totalitarian societies, of individual leaders and their collective grouping bear tremendous influence in bringing people to war, something which the work of Erickson and Daniel Levinson clarify.

A voluntaristic consideration of the cause of war explains that war is caused by a group seeking to remove or emasculate obstructive powers through violent means in order to achieve group policy with regard to particular interests, objectives, or ends. One must conclude, as does Wright, that the image which governments, states, cultures, or groups hold of themselves as peace-seeking is distorted, but not recognizable, to the states waging war. The US-led invasion and occupation of Iraq fails to present an exception. Just how much ethnic, racial or religious prejudice can be attributed to underlying causes of war can be debated.

Turning from psychological analysis of the causes of war to sociologically based approaches, Darwin significantly effected social interpretation from Karl Marx, Emile Durkheim, Thomas Malthus, *et al.* to more contemporary thinkers. Even the computer modeling and projections undertaken by the Club of Rome and Club of 77 driven by the work of the Dutch Finance Minister Jon Tubergin of the early 1970s forecasted, as did Malthus previously, that overuse and eventual elimination of scarce resources by the human species combined with over-population and increasing detrimental effects of pollution would lead societies and peoples to ever greater levels of internecine strife and increasingly abject impoverishment.[21] Sumner, following the seminal work of Durkheim, highlights a different approach to Darwinist struggles of the fittest that emphasizes the cohesiveness of societies in promoting identity and in struggles against other societies or groups, but not necessarily evolving into intra-group competition.

1973 (New Jersey: Humanities Press, 1973)] since WW II. One must acknowledge that the existence of valid reasons other than the excuse of combating communism and acting as the hegemonistic policeman and power broker of the world for US bellicosity.

21   William Graham Sumner, "War," Bramson and Goethals, *War*, p. 209 promotes a similar analysis which he terms the competition of life, distinguished from the struggle for existence which focuses on agrarian-type difficulties confronting the vicissitudes of nature.

The closer and the more powerful neighboring or opponent groups are, the greater the tendency to engage in conflict and war; with the corollary, the weaker or the more distant such groups, the less likely may be the outbreak of war, but the greater the tendency toward disintegration of the aforenoted cohesion. The motives for inducing war, however, reside in causes related to hunger, love, vanity and fear of superior powers, claims Sumner.[22]

Park raises an interesting question, that has moral consequences, on whether war should be conceived as a social institution or as a biological process (in line with Darwin's thinking), fatally rooted in human nature itself and depicted as resulting in the inevitable, and social process.[23] The deterministic aspect of the biological interpretation of war not only is fatalistic, but disregards the power of the human will to decide its own fate and effect its own destiny. Margaret Mead, in contrast then, concludes that war is an invention, not a biological necessity.

Whatever the type of government, societies maintain standing armies and reserve forces because of the possibility of aggression and war itself.[24] Although de Tocqueville comments that all countries are subject to war, it would seem more correct to state that there is potential for subjection to threat, war, and aggression. Switzerland, even during WW II, was not attacked, but was threatened to be attacked and prepared to counter such. While one would expect the militarist driving influence in garrison states to instigate and perpetuate war, de

---

22 *Ibid.*, p. 212. Sumner hypothesizes correctly that the greater and more powerful an existing military, the more likely the opportunity for it to engage in war to test its weaponry and to exercise what they identity. "By making warfare more efficient and more terrible, modern technology has made war itself our number one social problem," asserts Robert E. Park, "The Social Function of War," ," Bramson and Goethals, *War*, p. 229. This echoes the theme emphasized at the beginning of this section. While under such circumstances, peace is all the more desirable, unfortunately, it has not made war the less inevitable.

23 Park, p. 230. See also Bronislaw Malinowski, "An Anthropoligical Analysis of War," ," Bramson and Goethals, *War*, p. 247-251.

24 Alexis de Tocqueville, "On War, Society, and the Military," Bramson and Goethals, *War*, p. 329.

Tocqueville perceived most astutely, however, that democratic societies also have strong tendencies for their militaries to constantly engage in battle as a means of promoting their own interests and upward mobilization, something reflective of the democracies in Greece as well as the Western democracies; but democratic societies, nevertheless, protest and contend their interest and desire for peace.[25]

---

25 One needs to be conscious, however, that often non-veteran elites (who usually are the best educated, come from wealthiest families, and possess multiple and skilled abilities) administering militaries in democratic societies are more adventuresome in engaging in war for various purposes and interests than the officers and soldiers under them, military personnel who have seen and understand the terrible effects of war. Plutocratic tendencies and the influence and interests of major corporations, be they strictly domestic or global, assume enormous interests aligned with the governing elite, or vice versa.

One may substantially argue against de Tocqueville's conclusion when given the assumed role of the US in the world after WW II. Although the leadership and citizens of the US proclaim this society to be the beacon of democracy and peace loving, it has been warring or involved in conflict situations almost incessantly during this same period, for a host of reasons, much of which may be attributed to defense of its self- and economic interests no matter how far extended or removed from its actual territory. The claim of de Tocqueville that democratic societies find more interest and propensity in supporting peace and avoidance of war may also be disputed given the history of the latter half of the twentieth century, particularly in light of the many wars associated with newly formed nations and democracies. However, his analysis of democratic societies seems to bear ever more applicable relevance to the extent that democratic societies are increasingly interlinked through globalization of corporations which promote increasing mutual interest among competing elites.

Nevertheless, de Tocqueville correctly analyzed the results of democratic states frequently engaged in war: "War does not always give over democratic communities to military government, but it must invariably and immeasurably increase the powers of civil government; it must almost compulsorily concentrate the direction of all men and the management of all things in the hands of the administration... All those who seek to destroy the liberties of a democratic nation ought to know that war is the surest and the shortest means to accomplish it." de Tocqueville, "On War, Society, and the Military," p. 333.

Harry Eckstein has documented the following causes for violence, rebellion, and revolution in internal wars that facilitate the understanding of the causes of war, particularly internal wars. Contrary to popular belief, poverty does not precipitate revolution, nor can it be proved that rapid economic progress foments unrest leading to internal war or that major economic disruption after long-term growth seems to result in such.[26] Other plausible hypotheses causing internal war that are listed in detail by Eckstein are summarized herebelow for general consideration.

1. Intellectual factors such as: Failure of the governing regime to adequately perform political socialization; inability of society to integrate or clarify conflicting myths; unrealizable social values and corrosive social philosophies; alienation of intellectuals such as in Colombia and the Philippines in the 20th century.

2. Economic factors in addition to those cited above, such as: Severe imbalances between production and distribution of goods.

3. Factors related to social structure such as: Inadequate recruitment into elite strata despite a growing pool of eligible candidates as often occurs in economically underdeveloped societies; unmanageable anomie resulting from rapid social mobility and political disorientation (e.g., Japan of the 1920s); frustration from inadequate social mobility resulting in social stagnation; and sudden appearance of new social classes,

4. Political factors such as: Estrangement of rulers from society; ineptness of governing by ruling elite or their decay and corruption coupled with increasing strength of non-elite; undermining of the legitimacy of government; divisions among the governing classes; responding to oppressive government; active subversion that result in disorientation, impediment to elite rule, and formation of new political groupings; and excessive toleration of alienated groups.[27]

---

26 Harry Eckstein, "On the Causes of Internal Wars," Eric A. Nordlinger (ed.), *Politics and Society: Studies in Comparative Political Sociology* (Englewood Cliffs, NJ: Prentice-Hall, 1970), pp.291-292. Trotsky also surmised that, if poverty precipitated revolution and unrest, peasants and lower classes would always be at war.

27 For more detailed description of the above, kindly see Eckstein, "On the Causes of Internal Wars," pp. 291-300. For a more in-depth sociological analysis of revolution, kindly see Seymour Martin Lipset, *Revolution and Counterrevolution: Change and Persistence in Social Structure*

Social structures themselves can induce war and leadership based on such. In Dwight Eisenhower's farewell as president, he cautioned future leaders and policy formation of the US to be wary of the increasing military-industrial complex. A mutual support mechanism therein fosters increasing belligerence and economic profiteering whereby the military engages in war which stimulates the economy in the need for churning out war materiale and the military-related businesses needed for the continuation of war and conflict in order to extend their increasing profitability, a truly vicious circle.[28] Contrary to the optimistic thinking of Herbert Spencer and Auguste Compte, the sociologist Raymond Aron does not conclude that industrialization leads to refocusing national interests on work, militarization, and democratization and, thus, peaceful inter-state relations. He fails to note, however, that the modern military-industrialized states tend to interact more peacefully amongst each other, creating effectively hegemonistic interests and mutual objectives, but do not reduce war-like relations with underdeveloped states, the locus of hegemonistic control of natural resources and markets for end products of industrialization.[29] This hegemonism in many respects closely resembles a new iteration of neo-imperialism.

(London: Heinemann, 1969), particularly Chapter Three on Values and Entrepreneurship in the Americas.

28   For more detailed consideration of this characteristic of modern industrial states, kindly see Herbert Spencer, "The Military and the Industrial Society" and Harold D. Lasswell, "The Garrison State," in Bramson and Goethals, *War*, pp. 299-327. Spencer never imagined that the negative relationship would ensue between modern industrial societies and their military systems, but Lasswell paints a grim picture of such. Whether Eisenhower ever read either of these two works is unknown. Certainly Lasswell's sociological and political astuteness with regard to the central power and influence of the military is born out, but he mistook the function of non-military elites focused on industrial and economic centrality becoming the directors of military incursions, that military elites considered risky and opportunistic, not too short of resembling plutocratic governments.

29   Raymond Aron, "War and Industrial Society," Bramson and Goethals, *War*, pp. 359-402. Neo-imperialism and hegemonism need not be restricted to the Axis powers of the second world war, Germany and Ja-

In modernizing societies, particularly in developing countries, where identities associated with estate, caste, class, region, religion, or ethnic origin begin to pale as importance is placed on the nation-state, nationalism, the role of military elites in development and mobilization assume enormous importance and influence, often resulting in attitudes blindlessly supportive of war, but also in furthering solidarity among diverse groups, particularly with mass citizen armies, because of the social and psychological alienation and anomie that ensue with modernization and the search of a new identity.[30] War-making in contemporary society relies heavily on highly and professionally trained leaders and soldiers, even in cases of revolution or modern terrorism.[31] By nature, military elites are motivated heavily by status and its achievement. Military elites, trained for war and for creating through subordination the maintenance of social order, become

---

pan, but these powers certainly follow modern historic classical models of Britain, France, Spain, etc. and recent iterations can be seen in the US.

30   Kindly see Morris Janowitz, "The Military in the Political Development of New Nations," and Chalmers A. Johnson, "Civilian Loyalties and Guerrilla Conflict," Wilson C. McWilliams (ed.), *Garrisons and Government: Politics and the Military in New States* (San Francisco: Chandler Publishing Co., 1967), pp. 67-98. The understanding of Earnest Hemingway that the struggle and brotherhood in the Spanish civil war gave its participants meaningful identity in life cannot be overlooked. The Long March and political development in China under the Communist with Mao Tse-tung as its leader, and the further attempt to perpetuate the revolution led by the Red Guard, India under Jawaharlal Nehru and Defense Minister Gen. Chavan following the defeat by China , Pakistan similarly under Gen. Ayub Khan, the influence, initially of Gen. Nasution, and role of the military in Indonesia upon Pres. Soekarno which eventually resulted in his overthrow and assumption of leadership by Gen. Suharto, Gen. Ne Win in Burma and the role of the military in attempting modernization, etc. amply demonstrate the important, though, questionable role served by the military and its elites in modernization. In all cases, the military negatively undermines industrial development, to the extent, that investment in weaponry and military expenses are proportionately increased.

31   Morris Janowitz, "Military Elites and the Study of War," Bramson and Goethals, *War*, p. 346- 351.

entwined with war-making in their thinking. This phenomenon, though, is not limited to modernizing or developing societies. Industrialized societies, as indicated above, also find meaning in the role of military advancement and empowerment, resulting in emphasis on the centrality of understanding the function and importance of the state, particularly nationalism. One necessarily must ask whether the rise of such militarist power and its accompanying nationalism brings identity because of the hollowing of traditional religious understanding.

Other factors not directly referenced above, such as entangling alliances (related either to hegemony or ideology) and either the manifest or latent forms of nationalism supported by militarism, have also been important causes of war. Social factors like polarization and group stereotyping, particularly related to ethnic, national, religious, and economic treatment, may lead to prejudice and ideological rationale for supporting or inducing war, but without recognizing the possibility of political lag, cognitive dissonance, mistaken identification, or the ability of targeted objects to satisfactorily respond to change.

From the standpoint of military analysis, arms control itself, or lack thereof, may serve as a cause for hostile behavior resulting in war. The twentieth century is replete with examples of insufficient arms control stimulating the emergence of war. Ineffective arms control certainly facilitated numerous inter-group lethal eruptions among the super-powers and their client states and can be attributed as causing increased hostility.

In conclusion, it is safest to analyze that a host of factors cause war. Probably not one of them is dominant in every or most cases. The causes of war remain difficult to assess and understand. At the least, one may acknowledge that war is caused by psychological influences on an individual leadership and group or national level, by sociological forces related to group and ethnic dynamics, by limitations of the rule of law internationally or the complications and manipulation of law domestically, by the unchecked acquisition of arms and failure to maintain perceptive balance of armed threat, by misunderstood and misused moral argument, by human limitations of language and cultural symbols, by economic and political objectives that may be connected to obtaining and controlling scarce resources, their processing and distribution, by exploitation of leaders fostering national identity, particularly in developing countries, by militarism and nationalism under the guise of patriotism, by religious rationale in theocratically purist groups, by war itself as a self-perpetuating institution, by ineffective political decision-making in societies that leave no alternative for solution to intense and difficult dilemmas, and a by a host of unmentioned reasons. The cost of war today has become increasingly wasteful in terms of use of financial capital, and more so with respect to loss of human life, most of which are non-combatants. Suffice it to be noted that war is not easily understood.

CHAPTER 2

WAR & INTER-GROUP LETHAL VIOLENCE IN THE HEBREW SCRIPTURES

"Me don' understand politics, me don' understand big words like 'democratic socialism.' What me say is what de Bible say, but because people don' read de Bible no more, dey tink me talk politics. Ha! It's de Bible what have written and it strong, it powerful." Bob Marley

If internecine relationships between societal groups have been common phenomena from pre-historical times to today, from a religious standpoint, what do the Hebrew or Christian scriptures relate about this aspect of human behavior and how are we to interpret these scriptures?[1] Review of the Hebrew scriptures shall be restricted hereafter to the Law (Torah), consisting of the Pentateuch, the Prophets, and the Writings, categorization as per Hebrew thinking, not the Christian canon.[2] No analysis of the recount, interpretation, or morality related to war in the Mishnah or the Talmud shall be directly used, although such may be enlightening with further review.

---

1 It, unfortunately, exceeds the scope of this paper to consider comparative religious interpretation of inter-group lethal group violence in non-Christian and non-Hebrew scriptures. Such would not only be interesting, but would facilitate inter-religious dialogue to understand such interpretation and tradition in other religions.

2 The Prophets have been divided into Former and Latter Prophets: Former Prophets include Joshua, Judges, Samuel, and Kings and the Latter Prophets refer to Isaiah, Jeremiah, Ezekiel, and the twelve minor prophets, inclusive of Amos, Malachi, Joel, Jonah, etc. The Writings contain: Psalms, Proverbs, Job, Ruth, Canticle of Canticles, Lamentations, Ecclesiastes, Esther, Daniel, Ezra, Nehemiah, and Chronicles. See James C. Turro and Raymond E. Brown, SS, "Canonicity," Raymond E. Brown, SS, Joseph A. Fitzmyer, SJ and Roland E. Murphy, O.Carm. (eds.), *The Jerome Biblical Commentary* (Englewood Cliffs, NJ: Prentice-Hall, 1970), pp. 518-521.

HEBREW SCRIPTURES

> *... Joshua said to the people, "Now shout, for the Lord has given you the city and everything in it. It is under the Lord's ban.... "They observed the ban by putting to the sword all living creatures in the city: men and women, young and old, as well as oxen, sheep, and asses. (Joshua 6:16-17, 21)*
>
> *Samuel said to Saul: "This is what the Lord of hosts has to say: '... Go now, attack Amalek, and deal with him and all that he has under the ban. Do not spare him, but kill men and women, children and infants, oxen and sheep, camels and asses.'" (1 Sam: 15:1,3)*[3]

By contemporary standards, the murder in war of civilians, women and children, elderly, etc., i.e., non-combatants, would have to be considered immoral, particularly if done indiscriminately. That the Hebrew scriptures depict God, the Lord, commanding such would seem unfathomable and contrary to the perception of an all-loving, all-caring, omnipotent and personalized (but not anthropomorphized) power. Nevertheless, the aforenoted two passages cannot be considered irregular or exceptional in those scriptures.

No little consternation confronts the reader of the Hebrew scriptures with regard to war and the engagement of peace than the apparent

---

3 Scripture quotations and references for both the Hebrew and Christian scriptures hereafter will use the translation in The New American Bible (New York: Catholic Book Publishing Co., 1992).

  Gerhard von Rad, *Holy War in Ancient Israel* (Grand Rapids, Michigan: Wm. B. Eerdmans Publishing Co, 1991), translated by Marva J. Dawn and John H. Yoder from *Der Heilige Krieg im alten Israel* (Gottingen: Vendenhoeck & Ruprecht, 1958) relying on works by Martin Noth and Albrecht Alt, notes that the story of Joshua defeating the Canaanite in the famous story of the collapse of Jericho, as well as the story of the defeat of the Canaanites at Ai, was historically inaccurate because the destruction of the great walls of Jericho occurred in the 15th century bce, well before the time of Joshua of the house of Joseph. (See also John L. McKenzie, SJ, *Dictionary of the Bible* (New York: Bruce Publishing Company, 1965), pp. 457-458 and Peter J. Keaney, "Joshua," . Brown, Fitzmyer, Murphy, O.Carm. (eds.), *The Jerome Biblical Commentary*, pp. 123-124 and Dominic M. Crossan , OSM, "Judges," *Jerome Biblical Commentary*, pp. 150-151.

vindictiveness and violence of war engaged by the Hebrews and on their behalf, if the reader considers peace and brotherly/sisterly love one of the principal hallmarks of religious objectives. The Hebrew scriptures, however, are replete with images otherwise, particularly beginning with Exodus and followed by Deuteronomy, Judges, Joshua, Samuel, Kings and the different perspective of Hebrew national identity from the book of Chronicles.

It is an anachronism to term "holy" the action of war, the very acts of inter-group lethal, physical violence engaged intentionally, systematically and institutionally, not to mention the barbarity of killing itself. Nevertheless, the ancient Israelites often, but not always, undertook holy war as a means of religious sanctification of their chosen state and relationship with their perceived God. How does one interpret and rationalize the holiness of war, if such can be considered? Ben Ollenburger, citing Julius Wellhausen, concludes: "Ancient Israel as a people of God was a military camp, and its God was a warrior. War was at the heart of Israel's religion and thus of its identity."[4]

The memorable event of the Exodus from Egypt under a life of enslavement through a journey to a promised land flowing with milk and honey and offering freedom as a people covenanted with God is sprinkled throughout both the Hebrew and the Christian scriptures. The early Israelites, prior to reaching that Promised Land, were a people living in a tent, eating with staff in hand and girded and shoed in readiness to move and engage in battle. Thus, from the Exodus from Egypt (c. 1440 bce) onward, the Israelites were a people engaged in conflict both to reach, create, and expand their homeland against opposing forces more powerful than themselves and to fashion themselves into

---

4 Ben C. Ollenburger, "Gerhard von Rad's Theory of Holy War," in von Rad, *Holy War in Ancient Israel*, p. 3. Wellhausen in his *Prolegomena to the History of Ancient Israel* (Cleveland: World, 1957), p. 321, cited by Ollenburger, pp. 3-4, insightfully notes that prophets lacked this delight with the practice of war: " … the heroes of Israelite legend show so little taste for war, and in this point they seem to be scarcely a true reflection of the character of the Israelites as known from their history"(321). Ollenburger continues, "Of these heroes—the patriarchs—he (Wellhausen) says, 'Brave and manly they are not, but they are good fathers of families, a little under the dominion of their wives, who are endowed with more temper'(320)."

a political nation. War became a way of life for them, but was in fact a way of life for the people of the Mideast region for eons.

What made the war conducted by the ancient Israelites holy, a term not used in the Hebrew scriptures, but in fact recognized by the Hebrews as such? Let us consider what made the conduct of inter-group lethal and institutionalized conflict in the form of war thought to be holy or sanctified in itself by briefly reviewing the seminal works of key thinkers and theologians focused on this subject.

T.R. Hobbs has summarized the common traits of "holy war" as described by Gerhard von Rad in his seminal work on the same subject.[5] These traits are as follows and should be kept in mind when interpreting the understanding toward and morality of war in the Hebrew scriptures:

1. "The blowing of a trumpet as the announcement of the holy war;
2. The naming of the army as the 'people of Yahweh';
3. The sanctification of the participants;
4. The sacrificing of an offering and /or the consultation of Yahweh;
5. The announcement of victory by Yahweh 'I have given … into your hands';
6. The announcement that Yahweh 'goes out' before the army;
7. The claiming of the war as 'Yahweh's war' and the enemy as 'Yahweh's enemy';
8. The encouragement not to fear, because the enemy will lose courage;
9. The war-shout;
10. The fear of Yahweh among enemy troops;
11. The practice of the 'ban', the slaughter of all enemy men, women and children;
12. The dismissal of the troops with the cry 'To your tents O Israel.'"

---

5 See T.R. Hobbs, *A Time for War: A Study of Warfare in the Old Testament* (Wilmington, Del.: Michael Glazier, Inc., 1989), pp. 203-204 and Gerhard von Rad, *Holy War in Ancient Israel* , especially pp. 41-73.

That holy war in the Hebrew scriptures focused on the centrality of YHWH (*i.e.*, Yahweh) in the lives of the ancient Israelites cannot be understated. Nevertheless, the acquisition of land, particularly with regard to the promised land, through revolt, centuries of absorption, tribal conflict, indigenization, organized attack by militias, tribal warrior bands, or army cannot be overlooked as a key motivation and would appear lesser in predominance to defense of such territory in the face of threats from the Egyptians, Assyrians, Persians, Babylonians, etc. While the victory or defeat depends on the status of the relationship of the Israelites to YHWH, as Millard Lind stresses, one must also consider the use of intelligence, technological advancement of weaponry, tactical and strategic prowess, mental attitude of combatants, and preparedness for war. Nevertheless, the Israelite enactment of war or its termination relies on the guidance and will of their God. Religion, which includes culture, cult, rite, myth, tradition, symbolism, and belief, is the core to understanding, but not necessarily agreeing with, the Israelite perception of war and inter-group lethal conflict.

THE COVENANT AND ROLE OF YAHWEH IN HEBREW WARS

It is not unnatural to consider that every point of the ancient Israelites' lives is closely linked to their covenanted relationship with their perceived God, inclusive of inter-group lethal war in attempting to arrive at and make a Promised Land their own. This differs little, if at all, from the religious interpretation of life from other peoples of those times, Egyptian, Assyrian, etc. To speak of war, then, in ancient Israel is to speak of religion and the Israelites' relationship with God, and vice versa. The covenanted relationship involved the formation of a federation of individual and independent groups (as in the twelve tribes of Israel) and the ensuing inter-relationship among them, centered on worship and cultic rites, a form of amphictyony.[6] Friedrich Schwally perceptively identified this corporate worship in a sacrificial cult as the context whereby ancient Israel conducted war, thereby making it

---

6 von Rad, *Holy War in Ancient Israel*, p. 51, astutely asserts: " ...we can indeed consider holy war as an eminently cultic undertaking—that is, prescribed and sanctioned by fixed, traditional, sacred rites and observances."

holy war—"an activity undertaken by Israel as the army of Yahweh
in defense of the federation (covenant), over which Yahweh was sovereign."[7] Thus, God, or possibly better stated, the God perceived by
the ancient Hebrews, was naturally understood as the God who led,
protected, and fought with and for them as their warrior. Moses and
the political leaders of the Hebrews were merely the agents of Yahweh,
but necessary for God to act in history.[8] Not dissimilar to practices of
other cultures of those times, the ancient Israelites perceived their God
as core to their very existence and survival in a harsh world. It behooves
the reader of the Hebrew scriptures to understand this perception of
Yahweh as the warrior within the context of their era.[9]

---

7 Ollenburger, p. 5.

8 Bruce Birch, *Let Justice Roll Down: The Hebrew Scriptures, Ethics, and
   Christian Life* (Louisville, Kentucky: Westminster/John Knox Press,
   1991), pp. 126-128.
      Solomon and many of the kings thereafter consolidate power and
   engage in political intrigue, which thereby divert the understanding of
   Yahweh's role, but not for the prophets who continue to see Yahweh, not
   the majesty and power of the king, as key to expansion and continuation of the state of Israel, contrary to the covenant of the federation or
   league of the tribes of Israel. Birch, *Let Justice Roll Down*, pp. 224-228.
   Max Weber, who influenced Gerhard von Rad, astutely surmises that the
   prophets railed against the Davidic and successive royalty when they were
   shut out of the centrality of leadership, effectively de-militarized from
   the cultic ritual of sanctifying Israel's holy wars. They, thereby, became
   ideologists and advocated the importance and centrality of Yahweh's role
   in Israel's history and the ultimate, dominant and underlying force in
   securing Israel's destiny in war, effectively diluting the power and role of
   human leadership in war-making.

9 I am grateful for an understanding of this point to Julianne Claassens. One must remember, though, that while the carrying of the Ark
   into battle sociologically differed little from the practices of the Hebrews'
   neighbors, the early Israelites never viewed their leaders as divine nor
   their actions, inclusive of directives in war, as divine and causing victory
   in battle. Only Yahweh was divine and scripturally only through the efforts of Yahweh was victory in battle attained, provided the covenanted
   followers of Yahweh did not stray from their relationship with God. This
   final point makes the Israelite interpretation of history and war somewhat akin to magic, not religion, i.e., where the negative outcome of war,

Although Schwally contended that it was the pietistic interpretation of history, a retroactive interpretation to previous historic events, that emphasized the importance and centrality of the covenanted relationship with Yahweh and the role played by Yahweh in the formation and existence of Israel, inclusive of war, writers such as Millard Lind explain and emphasize a very different hermeneutical and theological interpretation of the role of Yahweh in Israel's wars. What is crucial, contends Lind, is the important realization that it is Yahweh who wages and miraculously wins the battle, not the human agent(s), i.e., the Israelites.[10] Thus, for example, Yahweh directs Gideon to reduce the

---

namely loss, is attributed to the sins of the ancient Israelites against their covenant with Yahweh, but victory is proof that Yahweh has fought for them and they have not jeopardized the outcome. Schwally termed this violation of covenant obligation as "collective liability" of the confederation of Hebrews. Thus, even wars against confederation members were seen as holy wars. Johannes Pedersen viewed the need for psychic unity in war-making in early Israel. Where breach of covenant obligation existed, psychic unity became deficient and, thus, could be the contributing cause to loss in war. The psychic unity or unity of soul should probably be interpreted within the context of a faith reliant upon Yahweh as the critical warrior in holy war.

T.R. Hobbs also adopted an interpretation of war analogous to Claassens when he considers the ethics of war and the ban in the Hebrew scriptures. See T.R. Hobbs, *A Time for War*, pp. 17 and 211. Hobbs notes that the act of war was not problematic for the ancient Israelites (nor does it seem to be for contemporary Israelites either); killing another human in battle was not a matter of right and wrong, or good or evil—these are value terms unrelated to actions of nations in armed conflict. War was a social institution and part of the way of living in ancient Israel, claims Hobbs.

10   Millard C. Lind, *Yahweh Is a Warrior: The Theology of Warfare in Ancient Israel* (Scottdale, Pennsylvania: Herald Press, 1980), pp. 49-50. Lind relates the importance of Yahweh's deliverance of the Hebrews from the Egyptians through a military victory at the Red Sea wherein all the Egyptians pursuing the Hebrews were drowned. This powerful act of Yahweh was accomplished without the Hebrews even fighting their pursuing Egyptian forces—a clear and demonstrative act that Yahweh, not the Israelites themselves, determine the victorious outcome of battle and war. This theme shall be considered hereafter. That God favors the side of the

number of his forces and, in doing so, Gideon conquers (Jgs. 7:1-22).[11]
Gerhard von Rad, however, considers as a key to understanding the

> weak, the marginal, the outcast or minorities, and the helpless is shown in
> the Exodus paradigm. Susan Niditch, *War in the Hebrew Bible: A Study in
> the Ethics of Violence* (New York: Oxford University Press, 1993), p. 149
> notes:
>
>> Like the ideology of the ban as God's justice, the ideology of non-
>> participation belongs not to the powerful able to impose their
>> will but to the disenfranchised who identify with the powerless
>> Judeans, their wives and children, who stand trembling in fearful
>> anticipation of their destruction by invading enemies. One response
>> to such powerlessness is to imagine taking up arms in a righteous
>> cause and with God's help utterly eliminating the evil and unjust
>> enemy in open combat (i.e. the ideology of the ban as God's justice,
>> another is to imagine striking at the enemy less completely and
>> more covertly through trickery and deception, employing the tools
>> of the assassin (the ideology of tricksterism). 2 Chronicles 20 and
>> the other miracle war accounts with which it shares a trajectory
>> offer another option to those who lack political, economic, or social
>> power, divine intervention. Only this option does not encourage
>> the waging of war, by urging its adherents to wait for God. War is
>> safely set on 'the sacred shelf' ... out of Israel's reach.
>>
>> Taken as a whole, the various threads we have explored in 1 and
>> 2 Chronicles—the elimination of certain references to David's
>> cruelty, the genealogical treatment of the conquest that leaves out
>> the ban, the emphasis on Solomon's status as a leader of peace
>> allowed to build God's holy dwelling on earth, the positive value of
>> Israel's helplessness, a helplessness that encourages God to assume
>> the role of rescuer, and the emphasis on victory in war as divinely
>> sent miracle, the most dramatic examples of which commands
>> no human to fight at all—reveal a late biblical tradition groping
>> toward peace. The Chroniclers build upon sentiments and images
>> available in earlier biblical tradition but combine them to make a
>> breakthrough toward an ideology of peace.

11 Judges 7 relates how Gideon with 32,000 men was directed by Yahweh
    to twice reduce the number of soldiers to eventually 300 men who de-
    feated the Midianites, Amalekites, and all the Kedemites, "as numerous
    as locusts."

    2 Chronicles 20: 4-17 relates a similar approach to understanding that
    the cause of victory in war is not the human agent but the intervention

practice of holy war in the cult of the covenanted relationship between Yahweh and the Hebrews, a covenant whereby the Hebrews jealously treated Yahweh as their God and the only god, and Yahweh acted jealously on behalf of the oppressed and weaker Israelites to make them God's chosen people and gave them a homeland of cultivable land.

DIFFERENT INTERPRETATIONS OF HEBREW WARS
BY VON RAD, LIND, ET AL.

Unlike Lind et al., von Rad views the basis for the development of the holy war to be situated initially in the cultic tradition of holy war during the time of judges, not with the Exodus.[12] He states with regard to the song of Deborah (Judges 4: 14-16 and 5:2 and 9, specifically) that "the song, in its marveling at the event, declares something important: in this event the tribes experienced themselves as 'Israel'—that is, as a unity led and protected by Yahweh. More accurately, they unexpectedly experienced that their cultic bond with Yahweh also had far-reaching consequences on the political level."[13] Von Rad also contends, as footnoted above, that the concept of holy war later became a sanctifying rationalization—the effective spiritualized ideology—of previous Israelite history of war written into literature, not just practiced and lived, by the Priestly or Deuteronomic theologian

of Yahweh, as declared by Jahaziel for King Jehoshaphat to encounter the Moabites and Ammonites.

12   Von Rad, *Holy War in Ancient Israel*, p. 72.

13   *Ibid.*, p. 59. Von Rad explains that 1 Samuel 11, telling how Saul, the last of the epoch of judges and by whom one individual of the tribe of Benjamin arose as leader of holy war in defense of the covenant, launched a holy war against the Ammonites in defense of one of the remotest exposed outposts, Jabesh in Gilead,and later the Philistines (1 Sam 14). Under Saul, all wars were holy wars, wherein miraculous natural events occurred by the grace of Yahweh to win the day.

  Not all of Israel's wars were holy wars, because they were undertaken not in the name of Yahweh, not in sacral alliance among the tribes, not in defense of the amphictyony, nor with the miraculous power of Yahweh dominating the human endeavor or the spirit of Yahweh descending upon the Israelites. (It should be noted that the theory of amphictyony is no longer considered tenable by most scholars, though we acknowledge von Rad's use of it in his thinking.)

in contrast to the Yahwist (J) interpretation when the prophets no longer interpreted and justified holy war for Israel but the kingship with a then institutionalized modern army, in contrast to the tribal militias of the purported amphictynony, that determined the politics of war.[14] In the Deuteronomic tradition, von Rad concludes that, while the wars of ancient Israel were defensive in nature on behalf of the amphictyony, they were re-interpreted as wars of religion and the Deuteronomic writers revived the ancient tradition. In fact, von Rad asserts that the prophets, in antagonistic opposition to the post-Davidic royalty that had adopted institutionalized warfare, interpreted many pre-Davidic conflicts as holy war (or Yahweh war), but Lind counters that the use of such thinking, though not the term, was used by prophets prior to David (1000 -962 bce). For Weber, though he was a sociologist pursuing the study of Jewish society, Pedersen, Schwally, and von Rad, the synergy between Yahweh's intervention and the conduct of human faithful, not just as agents in the thought of Lind but as minor factors in the act of war, effectively made war holy because of the linkage between religion and politics.[15] T.R. Hobbs counters, though, that the term "holy war" is mistaken and misleading and should more appropriately be titled "Yahweh war" because, amongst other reasons, the Hebrew scriptures do not use the term holy war whose origin appears to be Greek, and, approximating the interpretation proffered by Millard Lind, the Israelites or their federation embarked on war in the name of YHWH.[16]

14 Von Rad, *Holy War in Ancient Israel*, pp. 96-102. The Priestly theologian reacted to the profaning of history through royal diminishment of holy war during the Solomonic enlightenment and the centrality of the royalty seeking self-aggrandizement. For a brief and reliable understanding of the Yahwist tradition in the Hebrew scriptures, see Eugene H. Maly, "Introduction to the Pentateuch," *Jerome Biblical Commentary*, p. 3. The Yahwist tradition can see victory coming out of defeat and its emphasis of covenant does not come from Sinai, but from Abraham.

15 This statement certainly generalizes the commonality of thinking between these authors who clearly expressed nuances of different interpretations on how the concept and practice of holy war evolved, but for the sake of brevity we are forced to restrain our explanation hereabove.

16 Hobbs, *A Time for War*, see pp. 204-205. Citing G.H. Jones, "Holy War or Yahweh War," *VT* 25 (1975), pp. 642-658, Hobbs advances that

In contrast with the above interpretation, Rudolf Smend offers the explanation that the existence of a dialectical relationship between war and peace ensued in ancient Israel. The major judges, of whom he considered Moses the first in the Exodus event, were prophetic, charismatic, and dynamic war leaders and were followed alternately by minor judges who promoted the covenanting relationship with Yahweh, the foundation of which was at Sinai, and who oversaw static periods. Thus, the war of Yahweh (as originated with the Exodus) preceded holy war that was a result of the amphictyony. Smend explained this phenomenon within the context of inter-tribal relations between the Rachel Tribes of Joseph and Benjamin, who bore and promoted the war tradition and the Leah Tribes of Judah etc. who represented the covenant tradition.[17] Fritz Stolz presented an explanation of holy war even more contestable to that of von Rad et al. by asserting that the confederation did not even exist until the kingship of David, that wars prior to Saul were merely individual or independent tribal wars, that the concept of holy war was devoid of reality and based on myth because it contrasted divine power with total human powerlessness, and that this concept of war had its base in Deutoronomic interpretation of the post-exilic Jerusalem temple, from which Isaiah, Hosea, *et al.* found their sustenance, but the original thinking of which was derived from pre-Israelite (non-Hebrew) cult of Jerusalem inherited

---

Yahweh War interpreted as holy war is the result of literary development of the Hebrew scriptures that seek to produce uniform interpretation that is actually imperialistic but have religious character while lacking correct historical interpretation.

Hobbs also contends, "One thing is certain, throughout Israel's history warfare was a given, a fact of life, and it was viewed as an appropriate means for settling disputes between peoples. Israel, like her neighbours, went to war motivated by ' ... the perceptions by statesmen of the growth of hostile power and the fears for the restriction, if not the extinction, of their own.'"(p. 225, wherein Hobbs cites M. Howard, *The Causes of Wars* [2nd ed.] (Cambridge, Mass: Harvard University Press, 1983), p. 18.)

17 Rudolf Smend, *Yahweh War and Tribal Confederation* (translation of *Jahwekrieg und Stammerbund: Erwagugun zur altesten Geschichte Israels*) (Nashville: Abingdon Press, 1970), pp. 28 ff.43-75, 98-108, and 120-135.

by David. Stolz accepted, though, that the Israelites believed that
Yahweh fought as a warrior for them in their defense.[18]

Beginning with Genesis 14 in which Abram undertakes a military
rescue of his nephew Lot, although it remains unclear whether an
actual battle occurred even though Abram "pursued" and "defeated"
the kings and kidnappers, the Hebrew scriptures embark upon numerous accounts and interpretations of violent and inter-group lethal
events related to Israel. (See for example particularly Deuteronomy,
Joshua, Judges, 1 Samuel, 2 Kings, and Chronicles.) The author of
Genesis 14 appears to be equating Abram and Hebrew leaders with
the neighboring warrior kings, but ascribing an ethic of engaging only
in inter-group lethal combat as a defense for righting injustice and
unrelated to any war-profiteering.

THE BAN IN HEBREW SCRIPTURES

Deuteronomy 20, on the other hand, presents a provocative case of
total annihilation of Israelite enemies (Hittites, Amorites, Canaanites,
Perizzites, Hivites, and Jebusites) who, prior to the Israelite immigra-
tion, had occupied and resided on the land that Israel claimed was
being given to them by their God. This is the ban oft referenced in the
Hebrew scriptures. Under the ban, every living enemy of Israel—all
men, women, children, inclusive even of living animals—was to be
put to the sword, unlike the possible negotiated peace with Israel's
enemies outside of this land where all the men were killed and the
women, children, and livestock were placed in forced slavery, when
the Israelites fought and beat them.

How can one interpret the harshness of the ban? Certainly, not all
war undertaken and defended in the Hebrew scriptures encompasses
the ban. There is an ascending scale of accepted violent and inter-group
lethal behavior rising from revenge, raid, feud, capture of property
(wives for the Benjamites in Judges 21), ritualized melee in the battle
for Jericho (Josh. 6) in miracle accounts (also Ex. 17, Josh. 8 and
10, 1 Sam 7, 2 Chron. 20, etc.) wherein Israelites fight and inflict
annihilating death on enemies losing territory, state-sponsored wars

---

18   See Fritz Stolz, *Jahwes und Israels Kriege* (Zurich: Theologischer Verlag,
     1972) as referenced and reviewed by Lind, *Yahweh Is a Warrior*, pp. 28-29
     and Ollenburger, "Gerhard von Rad's Theory of Holy War," pp. 24-29.

led by Israel's kings through institutionalized militaries (mercenary or otherwise) in defensive or offensive exercises for political goals, and the enactment of the ban in various inter-group lethal conflicts (e.g., Num. 21:2-34; Deut. 2:30-35, 3:6-7, 7:2-6, 12-15 and 23-26, and 20:10-20; Josh 6:17-21, 7:11-20, 8:24-29, 10:28-40, and 11:11-14; 1 Sam 15:3-19; 22:19).[19] Susan Niditch suggests the following perspectives to understand the practice and ethics of the ban. As an *herem* (*hrm*)—i.e., making sacred, inviolable, consecrating for destruction, setting aside and sacred for God or God's priests, a sacrifice for God—the ban was undertaken by the early Israelites as means to sacrifice everything or part of one's possessions, inclusive of booty and human life, for YHWH (Lev. 27:28). Even human life was not to be spared, redeemed or ransomed.[20] It is "God's due." (See 1 Kings 20.) Certainly, such thinking typified early Mid-Eastern culture with the sacrifice of even one's own children and first-born (Gen. 22), not just one's conquered peoples. It was thought by people of those times that even human sacrifice or offering to the deity, inclusive of YHWH, was pleasing to the deity.[21] Examples of such are found not just with the Israelites, but also with the Mesha Inscription of the Moabites. The Israelites and Mid-eastern peoples of that period would make vows and promises of exchange to their god for favors that they sought (winning the battle or war for the sake of land, property or tribe) or in thanksgiving for victory.

Was the ban to be interpreted mythologically or metaphorically? Probably neither interpretation is applicable because it represents a real world practice of that period. Nevertheless, Niditch describes the mentality of the ban in the post-Exilic imagery of a banquet celebrating the total eschatological defeat of all Israel's enemies wherein YHWH

---

19   Susan Niditch, *War in the Hebrew Bible*, pp. 16-17.

20   Niditch underscores the rationale of the Israelites for killing any and all living things in inter-group lethal war as "the devotion of conquered humans to God …Only this definition explains the ban's emphasis on killing humans."

21   Nevertheless, other scripture writers adopt a condemning stance on human sacrifice: Lev. 18:21, 20:2-5; Deut. 12:31, 18:10; Jer. 7:30-31, 19:5, Isa. 57:5; Ezek. 20:25-26. See Niditch, *War in the Hebrew Bible*, p. 45.

makes a sacrificial meal of the slain enemy, not totally unlike the celebration by Marduk in the *Enuma elish*.[22] (See Jer. 46:10;[23] Ezek. 38-39; and Isa. 34:5.) Thus, the ban is portrayed by scripture writers as sacrificial and oblatory and much to the chagrin and consternation of biblical scholars the enactment of the ban is condoned or directed by YHWH (or better interpreted, as described by respective scripture writers, as under the guidance of YHWH). Even while the writer of Jeremiah, particularly chapters 46-49, presents oracles against the nations to the exclusion of Babylon which was identified as being the agent of YHWH and, thus, acceptable to Israel and Israel's submission to Babylon, the scripture turns the tables on Babylon in chapters 50 and 51, and justifies and necessitates vengeance of the Lord and war upon Babylon in retribution for destruction of the temple in Jerusalem—an enactment of the ban.[24]

The Israelites also undertook the ban as a means of exacting justice for righting a wrong of themselves or others upon themselves.[25] Niditch alerts scripture scholars to the importance of reform related to justice while simultaneously justifying war with the ban as being fought for a justly and Godly cause:

22   Niditch, *War in the Hebrew Bible*, pa 38-39.

23   Walter Brueggemann, *A Commentary on Jeremiah: Exile and Homecoming* (Grand Rapids, Mich.: William B. Eerdmans Publishing Co., 1998), p. 420, notes that, "(p)erceiving the world theologically, they (i.e., the Israelites) were able to discern that when a nation violates the larger dynamic of the political process which has a coherent moral purpose, trouble comes." As a result, according to Jeremiah and other prophets, Israel or other actor states assume the role of agent of YHWH to enact the will of YHWH and bring justice. Brueggemann continues, regarding the purpose of this eschatological battle, "It is that God may avenge God's own foe." (p. 428.) Because Egypt has opposed YHWH, "God will take up the whole of the Egyptian army as a bloody 'sacrifice'."

24   Brueggemann, *A Commentary on Jeremiah*, pp. 461-483.

25   Niditch, *War in the Hebrew Bible*, p. 57, supplements this view by noting, "These (Deuteronomic writers) are the writers for whom the ban becomes not a means of gaining God's favor through offering human booty, but a means of gaining God's favor through expurgation of the abomination, through justly deserved punishment of the subversive enemy, external to the people Israel or internal."

The Deuteronomic writers, supporters of the Josianic reform,
consider the ban a means of rooting out what they believe to be
impure, sinful forces damaging to the solid and pure relationship
between Israel and God."[26]

As such, the ban is held by these writers somewhat askance and not
entirely justified in itself, but only acceptable from the standpoint of
sacrificial action while simultaneously relating to the imposition of
divine judgment. Justice in the implementation of the ban can also
be considered from the standpoint of righting any abomination of sin
or turning away from the covenant with YHWH in the case of Israelites themselves, particularly Israelites engaging in idolatry.[27] Niditch
also asserts, "In the Hebrew scriptures, the ban as God's justice is an
ideology of those who consider themselves disempowered and beset,
politically, economically, and culturally."[28]

The ban is assumingly never to be associated with lawless and
chaotic slaughter of innocent creation, of soldiers running amuck of
order and discipline, although it is difficult to imagine how killing can
be considered anything other than a breakdown of social order and
whole, personal well being. Deuteronomy 20:1-20 describes in detail
the code of exercising war and the ban, discriminating when, how and
to what extent the ban is to be applied. In Deut. 20:1-8, clearly the
author emphasizes that the importance of waging inter-group lethal

---

26 Niditch, *War in the Hebrew Bible*, p. 56.

27 *Ibid.*, pp. 62-63. See also (a) Josh. 7 for the story of ban-like retribution on Achan who used the herem for his own and, therefore, must be
destroyed with all his family and possessions as reparation and (b) Deut.
13:12-18 wherein the ban in war is used as a defense of faith in supporting YHWH's judgment.

Niditch clearly explains the reason for employment of the ban with
regards to relations with foreigners and the effect of idolatry. " ... the
demand that the people of the land be banned (Deut. 7:2) and not be
pitied ("to pity" being the opposite of the ban) is accompanied by orders
that no connections are to be made with the foreigners and no treaties,
for treaties lead to intermarriage, and intermarriage to the worship of the
foreign spouse's god—to contamination of the specially chosen, sacred
people ... " (p. 65).

28 Niditch, *War in the Hebrew Bible*, p. 74.

conflict depends totally on YHWH; moreover, every cause or reason to avoid participation in war seems almost to be acceptable, but, if after pleading with one's adversary for peace, meaning their submission to the Israelites' terms, no acceptance is reached, then the Israelites may exact the ban. Nevertheless, there lurk monumental dangers in the application of the ban. One may with little difficulty question the xenophobic nature of the rationale of applying the ban with justification for its use rooted in the fear of being tainted by contact with non-Israelites who worship gods other than YHWH (Deut. 13 and Josh 22) and the hypothetical result of abomination of the people of YHWH. True, in the Deuteronomic tradition, Israel considered itself fraught with danger and threatening social forces that could undermine its social and cosmic order and, thus, sought a radical purifying means to rid itself of any of these threats, as expressed in the ideology of the ban. This code of conduct of war in Deut. 20 and 22 may likewise be interpreted as ritualistic military discipline, particularly justifiable in a closed society in the eyes of the scripture writer.[29] Niditch capture the essence of the ban as a war ideology on behalf of enforcing justice when she states:

> … the ban-as-God's-justice ideology actually motivates and encourages wars implying that wars of extermination are desirable in order to purify the body politic of one's own group, to eradicate evil in the world beyond one's group, and to actualize divine judgment. In the ban as God's justice a sharp line is drawn between us and them, between clean and unclean, between those worthy of salvation and those deserving elimination. The enemy is thus not a mere human, an offering, necessary to win the assistance of God, but a monster, unclean, and diseased. The ban as God's justice thus allows people to accept the notion of killing other humans by dehumanizing them and the process of dehumanization can take place even within the group during times of stress, distrust, and anomie.[30]

---

29   In Deuteronomy, Israel is commanded to kill all males in enemy towns outside of the land claimed by Israel and take all women, children and livestock as booty, but in towns within the land claimed by Israel the Israelites under the ban are to annihilate "anything that breathes." (Deut. 20:16-18)

30   Niditch, *War in the Hebrew Bible*, p. 77. One cannot help but compare the similarities of this understanding presented by Niditch with those

That the fear and loathing of what is culturally, politically, ethnically, or religiously unknown and thus not understood remain at the heart of the ideology of justifying war, ban or otherwise, and cannot be underemphasized. The xenophobia has captured the minds and hearts of a people and thwarted any rational interrelationship or dialogue, particularly related to unprovable beliefs.

Lest one think that the ban was absolutely condoned by writers of the Hebrew scriptures, Niditch suggests that it should not be considered as acceptable sacrifice or as righteous justice. She identifies Judges 19-21 as texts that raise issue with the ethics of the ban and seem to call for another ideology of war. Hosea 1 similarly criticizes Jehu for excesses in the slaughter of Joram and Ahab's Baal-worshiping wife, Jezebel (who persecuted the prophet Elijah), Ahaziah of Judah, Ahab's sons, and all Baal supporters (2 Kings). Further, despite the expediency of the war ideology employed in Deuteronomy, 2 Samuel, 1 and 2 Kings, or Joshua, the authors of the post-exilic 1 and 2 Chronicles in their rewrite of Israelite history appear to be conscious of unwonted and tyrannical violence in slaying all under the ban, eliminating Israel's enemies so they will not have to be reencountered, and the acquisition of booty and property. The cruel, vengeful, and rapacious killing of physically and socially weak members of society and the accumulation of wealth through warring conquest seemed to bother the writers of 1 and 2 Chronicles, insinuating criticism of the negative aspects of the ban and war.[31]

While Joshua and Deuteronomy may have applied the ban and the ideology of war for a tribe, not yet brought into a unified state

international political leaders justifying war against peoples who share different world views. This exploration of the justification of war shall be pursued later in this work.

31   Employing the war ethic as an underdog, i.e., engagement in guerilla warfare, permits the abandonment of any code of war by those out of power and foregoes any sense of guilt in the killing of another human, thereby not necessitating any purification. For examples of this ideology of war through tricksterism in the Hebrew scriptures, see Gen. 34 for treatment related to the rape of Dinah, Judges 13-16 for the story of Samson, Judges 4 and 5 for Jael's violence, and Judges 3 for Ehud's slaying of Eglon in righteousness for Israel's oppression. See also Niditch, *War in the Hebrew Bible*, pp. 106-122.

but still leading through a federation (*bund*) of tribes, Numbers (31) presents an institutionalized approach to war and the ban.[32] Therein, Numbers premises the enactment of war and the ban under a stratified society with priestly leadership, inclusive of the organized military, and monarchal or post-monarchic rule. Further, under the priestly leadership of Numbers 31, some enemy, particularly virginal girls, are spared the ban because of the need for wives, utility as chattel, and the issue of religious purity. In the end, however, the abomination for which the ban sought eradication ultimately falls on the priests and the soldiers who must seek atonement for the abomination that they themselves become because of the killing of another human. "The cause is holy, the war is ritualized, but the killing defiles."[33]

Not all of the writers of the Hebrew scriptures condone or accept war even. Some of the prophets criticize the violent actions of the Israelites or express longings for peace. Johannes Pedersen and some other biblical scholars, however, note that peace for the Israelites does not necessarily mean refrain from violent conflict.[34] Peace implies harmony amongst friends and experiencing victory in battle (1 Chron. 22; 2 Chron. 13, 14, and 26). This approach to an understanding of peace differs little from the concept of the *Pax Romana* or the *Pax Americana*

---

32 Hobbs, *A Time for War*, p. 21, comments perceptively with regard to a publication of the late Peter Craigie, "War, Religion and Scripture," published in *The Bulletin of the Canadian Society of Biblical Studies*, 1986, that the consideration of war in the Hebrew scriptures viewed from the standpoints of (a) a modern and institutional nation state and (b) religion as a free-standing institution is inappropriate, as Craigie has done because the culture of ancient Israel "is dominated by concepts of kinship/belonging, and intimately bound up with kinship is the religious ideology of the people." On pp. 33-41, Hobbs, similar to the earlier analysis presented by von Rad, stresses that the importance of interpreting the rationale for the ancient Israelites to engage in war relies heavily on the social composition of the confederation of tribes, which are based on households, in a pre-nation-state of Israel or Judah. It was the federation of tribes that sought to defend its identity and struggle to create its very well-being that served as a cause for engagement in war.

33 Niditch, *War in the Hebrew Bible*, p. 89.

34 Johannes Pedersen, *Israel: Its Life and Culture* (London: Oxford University Press, 1940), vol. 1, p. 311.

(which should really be understood as the *Bella Americana*). Thus, Isa. 2:4 and Mic. 4:3, although seeming to be an idealistic termination of tension and conflict wherein swords are beaten into plowshares and spears into pruning hooks while nation shall not war against other nations and offspring shall be uninstructed in war-making, appears to clearly advocate true peace and avoidance of hostility. Jer. 43:11-12 demonstrates that peace comes with violent conquest and submission of one's enemies. Hos. 1:4 likewise condemns excesses in war while Numbers 31 requires purification following war because of the abomination and defilement of the military in killing other creation. Amos 1-2 critiques warring practices and the expediency of war as a political act whether practiced or perpetrated by Israel, Judah, or their pagan neighbors, but stops short of outright condemnation of the practice of violent and inter-group lethal force of war-making even though it justifies YHWH's punishment for the crimes of war.

AVOIDANCE OF WAR AND MORAL TREATMENT OF WAR
IN THE HEBREW SCRIPTURES?

How do the Hebrew scriptures teach avoidance of war? Jeremiah (22:13-17) turns the hearts and minds of the Israelites toward the way of seeking God through the manner in which we live. Thus, to know God is to do justice and righteousness, to vindicate the poor and the needy. The *ptochos*, or the people in Christian scriptural thought who do not have what is necessary to subsist, must be subsidized and provided for in terms of jobs, food, clothing, shelter, etc., or, if not, injustice leads to conflict and the avoidance of peace.[35]

> He shall judge between the nations
> and impose terms on many peoples.
> They shall beat their swords into plowshares
> and their spears into pruning hooks;
> One nation shall not raise the sword against another,
> Nor shall they train for war again. (Isa. 2:4 and Mic 4:3)

The aforenoted scripture in Isaiah and later repeated almost verbatim by Micah would seem to offer a scriptural approach that seeks the

---

35   Robert McAfee Brown, *Unexpected News: Reading the Bible with Third World Eyes* (Philadelphia: The Westminster Press, 1984), p. 99.

culmination of eternal peace and the absence of inter-group lethal and violent conflict. This verse is frequently repeated as the ultimate hope and longing for peace in the Hebrew scriptures. It behooves the reader, however, to use caution regarding this interpretation because much of the rest of Isaiah remains bellicose and anything but peaceful. Both Isaiah (Isa. 34:2-8) and Deutero-Isaiah (Isa. 49:26) present harsh and violent acts of YHWH in searing judgment of Edom as the avenger of Zion and on behalf of the liberation of Israel. Thus, although the authors of both Isaiah and Deutero-Isaiah seek some form of peace without inter-group lethal and violent conflict, they accept YHWH's just vindication of prior persecution while simultaneously acknowledging the execution of justice for the oppressed and the poor (Isa. 54 and 55) with the reward being peace and happy fulfillment of long-endured oppression. In the fourth song of the suffering servant, Deutero-Isaiah presents, contrary to the thinking of the Targums and other Jewish thought, a model of expiatory suffering, inclusive of receiving inter-group lethal violence, whereby the suffering recipient is rewarded with peace, power and glory.[36]

In consideration of the aforenoted review of the treatment of war in the Hebrew scriptures, one must question what were the Israelites' or the scripture writers' moral evaluation of the acts of war and inter-group lethal violence, inclusive of the ban. T.R. Hobbs best surmises this when he notes "the act of war was *not* a problem for the ancient Israelites. The Old Testament is full of examples of warfare and there is no evidence to suggest that warfare *per se* is regarded as even a necessary evil. It is taken for granted as a part of life."[37] With regard to Gen. 34 when the sons of Jacob killed all in deceit, Hobbs notes further that the motivation for Jacob's reaction to this killing " … is not 'right and wrong' or 'good and evil', as though these were absolute values. Rather the motivation is defense of honour." (Hobbs, 1989, 17) Killing another human being in inter-group lethal conflict is merely taken for granted by the writers of the Hebrew scriptures. As noted above, some of the scripture writers accept the dehumanizing aspects of inter-group lethal violence in war, but, as Niditch

36   Carroll Stuhmueller, "Deutero-Isaiah," *The New Jerome Biblical Commentary* (Englewood Cliffs, NJ: Prentice Hall, 1990), pp. 341-342.

37   TR Hobbs, *A Time for War*, p. 17.

emphasizes, expedience rules and the moral acceptance of such is not deeply questioned.

Treatment of foreigners and perspectives on foreign peoples indicate partially the thinking and interaction vis-à-vis war or peace. Who are foreigners but people who differ in thinking, culture, religion, custom, ethnic or tribal identity, language, political structure, etc. from the attributes and characteristics of one's own group. Although the afore-noted review demonstrated that Israel's relationship with foreigners was often bellicose, it belies a seemingly contradictory stand adopted by many of the prophets. The prophets such as Jeremiah et al. clearly showed openness and more than fairness to the foreigner, because they were conscious that Israel was a foreigner once in a strange land. The prophets counsel that the foreigner should be treated as a guest and not a pariah. Jeremiah treats the foreigner in the same manner as that of the *anawim* (*ptochos* in Septuagint Greek), the marginalized and most oppressed in society and demands that preferential deference and treatment be granted those who are different and alien in society:

> Only if you thoroughly reform your ways and your deeds; if each of you deals justly with his neighbor; if you no longer oppress the resident alien, the orphan, and the widow; if you no longer shed innocent blood in this place, or follow strange gods to your own harm, will I remain with you in this place … (Jer. 7:5-7)

In conclusion, we may observe the following principal tenets on the treatment of war and lethal violence in the Hebrew scriptures. The earlier scriptures of Exodus, Joshua, Judges and I and II Samuel implicitly accept the use of war and refrain from moral questioning of its validity because they essentially accept that war is conducted at the behest and direction of YHWH. It is YHWH who delivers the enemies of the Israelites into defeat and it is YHWH who is the actual warrior; the Israelites are merely the agents or instruments for enactment of the will of YHWH. That the practice of the brutal ban was employed by the Israelites at the direction of YHWH cannot be contested in terms of scriptural interpretation, but to what extent it was realized remains somewhat questionable. Certainly, cotemporaneous neighbors, tribes, and nations of the Israelites utilized such practice and, therefore, it would not seem unthinkable that Israel employed the same. Such barbarity, from a contemporary perspective, must be assessed from the perspective of those times and, as such, one can surmise that the ban represented the sacrifice of all the valuable assets, i.e., living beings, to one's God in return for winning the battle. It cannot be overlooked that the *bund*, the federation of Israelite tribes, was in a process of seizing and defending land for themselves, and expanding thereon, particularly after the Davidic reign. I and II Chronicles and some of the prophets represented a more humane approach to treatment of and relations with non-Israelites. They, particularly early Jeremiah and to some extent Isaiah and Micah, appeared to advocate a more reasonable approach to orderly relations with foreigners, inclusive of conquerors, and could be interpreted as better representatives of peace.

CHAPTER 3

TREATMENT OF WAR & NON-VIOLENCE
IN THE CHRISTIAN SCRIPTURES

Clearly, the treatment of war and organized inter-group lethal physical violence in the Christian scriptures, particularly in the sayings and activities of Jesus primarily, and in Acts and the various letters, distinctively differ from much, but not all, of the treatment and interpretation of the same in the Hebrew scriptures. While the position of Marcion in the second century regarding the vindictive God of the Hebrew scriptures in contrast to the perceived God of Jesus resulted in his excommunication, Marcion's contentions are not totally lacking in substantive support for a different ethical interpretation toward war and warrant reconsideration because the gospel representation of Jesus' sayings and mode of life differ sharply from the aforenoted treatment of war in the Hebrew scriptures.

Before entering into a review of the Christian scriptures regarding the treatment of war and organized inter-group lethal violence therein, it behooves one to question as an entry point and object of analysis whether these scriptures clearly delineate any ethical or moral judgment with regard to such. Although T.R. Hobbs strongly suggests that the treatment of war by the Christian scriptures is ambiguous and ambivalent, something to be explored herebelow, to the contrary, any review of the life, purported words, and actions of the Jesus of Nazareth and their interpretation by the scripture authors would seem otherwise and in clear opposition to inter-group lethal institutional violence in the form of war.[1]

One might question what meaning does the historical Jesus of Nazareth bring to his world and times as well as does this Jesus offer us anything different with regard to ethical and moral thinking on war and organized inter-group lethal violence. If, as T.R. Hobbs and others contend, the understanding of Jesus' words and deeds with respect to

---

1 TR Hobbs, *A Time for War*, pp. 231-233.

the war or inter-group lethal violence is ambivalent or ambiguous and that the religious thought of Jesus is rooted in the Hebrew scriptures, then one may conclude that Jesus has nothing to offer in this regard and, in fact, Jesus' understanding of such would not have been too dissimilar from that reviewed above. However, incontestably Jesus came to give a new commandment, a new law, that superseded the inadequacies of the old law under the old covenant—namely, the new commandment of love, something totally different than the focal mentality of the Hebrew scriptures, but intricately dependent upon and interwoven with the necessity for justice.[2] John Dominic Crossan identifies the following as words, translated as per below, that actually came from the historical Jesus, amongst others, in contrast to sayings that Jesus disciples or authors of the Christian scriptures attribute to him.[3] These sayings of Jesus are critical to understanding the position of Jesus with regard to war and we shall pursue them further in greater

2 One cannot help but to recall the criticism of G.K. Chesterton with regard to the problem of Christianity, "It is not that it has failed and found to be wanting, but that it is difficult and untried." Mohatmas Gandhi's critique is just as salient, "I like your Jesus, but you Christians do not know him." Martin Luther King wisely warned that an attack on justice anywhere is an attack on justice everywhere. Finally, Pastor Martin Niemoller of the German Confessing Church in 1939 lamented that,

> First they came for the *Jews* and I did not speak out—because I was not a *Jew*. Then they came for the *communists* and I did not speak out—because I was not a *communist*. Then they came for the *trade unionists* and I did not speak out—because I was not a *trade unionist*. Then they came for *me*—and there was *no one left* to speak out for *me*.

Quoted in an iterated form by James Burl Hogins and Gerald A. Bryant, *Juxtaposition* (Palo Alto, Cal.: Science Research Associates, 1971), p. 23. Similarly, a German Lutheran theologian who was tried and convicted of treason by the Nazis for his opposition to their rule but would never admit to his guilt, was found to have a note in his pocket when the Nazis killed him. The note only said that he was guilty of having failed to speak out earlier.

3 John Dominic Crossan, *The Historical Jesus: The Life of a Mediterranean Jewish Peasant* (San Francisco: Harper, 1992), p. xix.

detail later in this chapter, but highlight them as the core premise for analyzing war in the Christian scriptures.

> Love your enemies and pray for those who abuse you. (Lk. 6:27; Mt. 5:44)
> (Offer no resistance to one who is evil.) If any one strikes you on the right cheek, turn to him the other also; and if any one would sue you and take your coat, let him have your cloak as well; and if any one forces you to go one mile, go with him two miles. (Mt. 5:39-41 and Lk. 6:29)

With regard to the reign of God, Jesus intentionally places, as the motive and objective for his active public ministry during the final year and one-half to two years of his historical life, the centrality of the good news of love, its preaching and practice.[4] What does the reign of God mean for Jesus? The reign of God does not differ from the enactment of love and the liberation over the rule of sin and oppression. For Jesus, this love necessitates a clear preferential election for walking with the economically poor and oppressed in the struggle to overcome everything that encompasses the enslavement of humanity under sin. The reign of God necessitates the follower of Jesus to contravene common sense; certainly, the Beatitudes cannot be accepted as a common-sense way of acting in this world, unless one believes in the promise of an eschaton and hope in a future humanity that requires the believer to facilitate that development according to the interpreted will of God.

---

4 Jon Sobrino, "Central Position of the Reign of God in Liberation Theology," in Jon Sobrino and Ignacio Ellacuria, eds., *Systematic Theology: Perspectives from Liberation Theology* (New York: Orbis Books, 1996), pp. 38-74. Sobrino identifies the reign of God as the central concept in liberation theology because the reign of God focuses on the totality of God and the particular historicization of that totality which works out the immanent, but not yet transcendent, liberation over the rule of sin. For liberation theology and Christians, the objective of the reign remains nothing other than the salvation and the concretization of love; it can be mistakenly interpreted as the utopia for the poor, but the utopia to which all Christians are called by Jesus to work to realize.

"Which is the first of all the commandments?" Jesus replied, "The
first is this: 'Hear, O Israel! The Lord our God is Lord alone! You
shall love the Lord your God with all your heart, with all your
soul, with all your mind, and with all your strength.' The second
is this: 'You shall love your neighbor as yourself.' There is no other
commandment greater than these." The scribe said to him, "Well
said, teacher. You are right in saying, 'He is One and there is no
other than he.' And 'to love him with all your heart, with all your
understanding, with all your strength, and to love your neighbor
as yourself' is worth more than all burnt offerings and sacrifices."
And when Jesus saw that [he] answered with understanding, he
said to him, "You are not far from the kingdom of God." (Mark
12: 28-34)

Unlike in the Hebrew scriptures, the reign of God, or as the aforenoted
text translates the "kingdom of God," becomes the fulfillment of love
of God through the love of more than love of neighbor; it requires
that the disciple treat others more than as a mere neighbor and, in
fact, as a brother or sister of the same Father or Mother God. Contrary to the terminology used in Christian tradition which relies on
triumphalistic theology and subscribes to military, if not militaristic,
and political-power symbols such as army of God, soldiers of Christ,
king, kingdom, throne, reign, battle, etc., the reign of God (*basileia*)
presented by Jesus through the Christian scriptures differs radically.[5]
The teachings, life and life style, and discipline of Jesus, contrarily,
are best portrayed as service and servant, love to one's own death for
redemption of others, justice on behalf of the oppressed, poor, marginalized and outcast, etc. This reign of love contradicts the common

---

5 The triumphalistic model of the Church as an institution with quasi-
imperial reign was subscribed for centuries, until severely criticized at the
second Vatican Council. This approach to reign was reinforced (a) by re-
formative attacks on the institutional Church and its practices made jus-
tifiably by Luther and the reformers and (b) in defensive Church response
to the applicable criticism raised in the Enlightenment. See Avery Dulles,
SJ, *Models of the Church* (New York: Doubleday, 1987), pp. 34-39.
The Matthean gospel uses the term "kingdom" 55 times, "kingdom of
heaven(s)" 32 times, and "kingdom of God" 4 times. See John P. Meier,
A Marginal Jew: Rethinking the Historical Jesus, Vol. 2, "Mentor, Message,
and Miracles" (New York: Doubleday, 1994), p. 274.

sense adopted by today's Christians in industrialized societies and elite status in "non-Christian" societies.

The eschaton, the reign of God, as viewed in the Christian scriptures and witnessed in the primitive and early Church should be interpreted as something that is "already but not yet." The Christian followers of Jesus in the apostolic period seemed to believe that Jesus would soon return, but even within several decades after Jesus' passing, Paul, amongst other Christians, clearly demonstrated that that belief had changed, even for himself in contrast to his position in First Corinthians. They began to understand even within the first century that the eschaton, the new age, had begun but its finality had not yet arrived.

Early Christians considered that they as disciples of Jesus were called to a peaceful life as part and parcel of integrating the Christian message into their very existence.[6] Some Christians today, inclusive of the

6 Arne Rasmusson, *The Church as Polis: From Political Theology to Theological Politics as Exemplified by Jürgen Moltmann and Stanley Hauerwas* (Notre Dame, Ind.: University of Notre Dame Press, 1995), p. 305, notes that the Sermon on the Mount cannot be considered as addressed to individuals in isolation, but must be applied by individuals in community. In citing Hauerwas, Rasmusson emphasizes two key points. First, the early Christians did not consider themselves as pacifists, but interpreted the peaceful life as integral to their discipleship. They, however, accepted and engaged in peaceful means of non-violent resistance. Thus, Hauerwas states in "The Sermon on the Mount, Just War and the Quest for Peace," *Concilium*, No. 1, 1988, p. 39: "When the Sermon [on the Mount] is divorced from this ecclesial context it cannot help but appear as a 'law' to be applied to and by individuals. But that is contrary to fundamental presuppositions of the Sermon that individuals divorced from the community are incapable of living the life the Sermon depicts. They understand the Sermon as an ethic for individuals is to turn the Sermon into a new law with endless legalistic variations. The Sermon is only intelligible against the presumption that a new eschatological community has been brought into existence that makes a new way of life possible. All the so-called 'hard sayings' of the Sermon are designed to remind us that we cannot live without depending on the support and trust of others."

Second, Rasmusson interprets the thinking of Hauerwas with regard to resistance, and non-resistance. Rasmussen notes that Hauerwas reasons the following: (1) Jesus' life was about confrontation with the powers that enslave people, but the means of confrontation differ from those used by

Catholic bishops, seem to believe that the early Christians changed their thinking with regards to non-violence when they realized that the final stage of the eschaton would not occur shortly. This misunderstanding fortified the shift to a natural-law acceptance and justification of war and violence in an imperfect world. This clearly contradicts the thinking of the early Church as seen herein where Christians realized that they were living in the final times, although the final stage of such was not clearly understood, and that non-violence was an essential way of living the teachings of Jesus, or, as Stanely Hauerwas defines it, that non-violence was "not first of all an 'ethic' but a declaration of the reality of the new age."[7]

With respect to those whom one considers antagonistic or hostile to oneself in the sense of threatening or even a lethally offensive enemy, Jesus commands difficult action: "Love your enemies and pray for those who persecute you" (Mt. 5:44) and "Do not resist one who is evil." (Mt. 5:39) This love mandated by Jesus is not directed at just

---

the powerful. (2) The love of Jesus and that required for the baptized are one and they are anything but impartial and disinterested because they relate to the kingdom. (3) If Jesus' teaching can be interpreted as being pacifist, then such begins with the way the community lives and interacts; the non-violence that Jesus calls for arises from Christian convictions and practices. Rasmusson, *The Church as* Polis, pp. 305-306.

Hauerwas emphasizes that the early followers of Jesus came to realize that the making of this kingdom required their taking part in the life of Jesus, particularly the death and resurrection, and being conscious of the change in history. "Jesus directs our attention to the kingdom, but the early followers rightly recognized that to see what that kingdom entailed they must attend to his life, death, and resurrection, for his life reveals to us how God would be sovereign. Therefore to learn to see the world eschatologically requires that we learn to see the life of Jesus as decisive for the world's status as part of God's kingdom." Stanley Hauerwas, *The Peaceable Kingdom: A Primer in Christian Ethics* (Notre Dame, Ind.: University of Notre Dame Press, 1983), p. 83.

7 Stanley Hauerwas, *Should War Be Eliminated?* (Milwaukee, WI: Marquette University Press, 1984), p. 51. One cannot fail to note the similarities of thinking of this approach to eschaton and the radical and real living out of the one's Christian faith in the patristic period with positions advocated by reknown liberation theologians.

one's friends and those who love us, but necessitates non-reciprocating love even toward one's enemies. Reciprocity is not a caveat for the Christian's love. Contrary to the thinking of many contemporary Christians, it is impossible to love and pray for one's enemies and then engage them in inter-group lethal violence. Reinhold Niebuhr, for example, a respected moralist and theologian, interprets the aforenoted Matthean guidance of Jesus as an impossible ideal, something that cannot be put into practice on this earth but is only applicable in another eschaton.[8] That Christians have and continue to act in this manner, though, remains the scandal of Christianity. Jesus does not ask discipleship that is easily subscribed to or enacted. To truly love according to the commandment of Jesus is not facilely accomplished. Jesus never inflicts suffering or death upon others, but accepts suffering with love, even to death on a cross. This Matthean teaching of Jesus must be interpreted totally within the context of the Sermon on the Mount wherein the Matthean Jesus underscores the critical teachings and practices of Jesus with the antitheses that emphasize the Jesus-like response.[9] (See Mt. 5:21-24, 5:38-42, and 5:43-45.)

What underlies the core teaching of this new commandment? Richard McSorley correctly directs us to the humanistic basis of Christianity, namely the nearly infinite value of the human person.[10] Whether considered from either an humanistic or theological perspective, this

8 See Reinhold Niebuhr, *An Interpretation of Christian Ethics* (New York: Seabury, 1979), pp. 91and 116 and Reinhold Niebuhr, *Moral Man and Immoral Society* (New York: Charles Scribner Sons, 1932), pp. 179-180.

9 When the Matthean Jesus instructs his followers to non-violent re-action in the face of injury or death, as in " … if anyone strikes you on the right cheek, turn the other also … " the import of which is not about judicial reproach or legal recourse. Scriptural commentators such as Robert Guelich have attempted to explain this saying as reference to a courtroom treatment. Richard B. Hays, *The Moral Vision of the New Testament: A Contemporary Introduction to New Testament Ethics* (San Francisco: Harper, 1996), pp. 325-326, counters that this interpretation totally misses the point of Jesus' teaching and makes no sense given the totality of the gospel's message and adds that the teaching of Jesus in this regard "eschews retaliation and defense of self-interest."

10   Richard McSorley, SJ, *New Testament Basis of Peacemaking* (Washington, DC: Center for Peace Studies, 1979), pp. 12-13.

infinite value of the person remains paramount. War and inter-group
or individual lethal violence dehumanizes the oppressor or transgressor,
whether sanctioned by rule of law or not.

For the sake of understanding the Christian perspective on the
morality of war, it behooves us to review briefly the purported or
interpreted statements of Jesus, as witnessed in the canonical scriptures,
on this topic, to the extent that they exist, or statements and actions
of Jesus that would indicate Jesus' interpretative thinking with regard
to the issue of war, lethal inter-group violence, and weapons and war
material, inclusive therein of statements often used to interpret Jesus'
thinking regarding this topic.

The key to Jesus' teaching can be found in the Beatitudes (Mt. 5:
3-11, Lk. 6: 20-26) and Matthew's description of the last judgment
(Mt. 25:31-46). Which persons do the beatitudes call blessed? In Matthew, in a more expansive and inclusive description than that found
in Luke who contrasts the blessed with the woes cast upon those presently at ease and wealthy in worldly leisure, the blessed are those who
are poor [(*ptochos*) in spirit], who mourn, who are meek, who hunger
and thirst for righteousness (i.e., act in moral conduct in conformity
with the will of God), who are merciful, who are clean of heart, who
are the peacemakers, who are persecuted for the sake of righteousness, who are insulted and persecuted because of Jesus himself. The
specific reference in Mt. 5:9 to peacemakers does not mean as in the
philosophy of the Hebrew scriptures "one who produces prosperity,"
but, rather, refers to those who reconcile quarrels. Reconciliation is
the Christian office of the Gospels, and, in fact, the title of genuine
Israelites.[11] But, if reconciliation is the meaning of peacemaker, then
belligerence and lethal violence and war cannot be interpreted in any
way as peacemaking. In the Sermon on the Mount, what is meant
for Jesus' disciples—who are to be a city on the mountain-top, a light
for the world to see as establishment of God's new order, Mt. 5:38-
48—provides the fundamental guidance to create this new order.

What concretely does the Gospel mean by "to thirst for righteousness" and "may suffer persecution for the sake of righteousness?"
What is the moral conduct required to conform to the will of God?

---

11 John L. McKenzie, "The Gospel According to Matthew," *The Jerome
    Biblical Commentary*, p. 70.

The judgment of the nations in Matthew 25 succinctly provides this answer in clear and simple language:

> Come you who are blessed by my Father. Inherit the kingdom pre-
> pared for you from the foundation of the world. For I was hungry
> and you gave me food, I was thirsty and you gave me drink, a
> stranger and you welcomed me, naked and you clothed me, ill and
> you cared for me, in prison and you visited me. Then the righteous
> will answer him and say, "Lord, when did we see you hungry and
> feed you, or thirsty and give you drink? When did we see you a
> stranger and welcome you, or naked and clothe you? When did we
> see you ill or in prison and visit you." And the king will say to them
> in reply, "Amen, I say to you, whatever you did for one of these least
> brothers of mine, you did for me." (Mt. 25:34-40)

Righteousness then is the preferential care and treatment of the marginalized and oppressed. It is the antithesis of peace, the thesis of war, that further marginalizes, impoverishes, enslaves, demeans, and dehumanizes the human living conditions, human spirit and personal integrity. Jesus himself captures his own fate as one persecuted for the sake of righteousness and those who follow him can expect to suffer the same fate. (Mt. 16:24-26.)

JESUS & THE USE OF PHYSICAL & LETHAL VIOLENCE

The only action of Jesus entailing physical force that could be consid-ered violence relates to the overturning of the tables and seats of the moneychangers and commercial traffickers and the driving, from the outer courts of the temple (the court of the Gentiles), of those engaged in the business of selling animals and doves for sacrifice in the form of a temple tax on all males aged 19 and over and exchanging money for their purchase. (See particularly Mt. 21:12 and Jn. 2:14.) John's account, written more than one-half century after the historical Jesus, describes Jesus making a whip out of cords to be used in this act of expulsion; Matthew's story, more proximate to the public life of Jesus and relying on Mark's rendition of 11:15-19 but reordered in different chronological sequence, mentions no act of creating a whip.

The question confronting us, then, raises the dilemma of whether Jesus engaged in violent physical activity, while acknowledging that no lethal violence was employed. John Dominic Crossan presents us with the answer to this apparent difficult question on Jesus possible use of physical violence against other persons. Crossan, recognizing this action and its related saying undertaken by Jesus, insists rightfully that this story must be interpreted in light of Mark's and Thomas' gospels and that the intent of these writers focuses on Jesus' symbolic destruction of the temple itself and its cult. There was nothing wrong in buying and selling animals and doves for sacrifice because all Jews were required to make some sin-offering (Lv. 5:7) and some form of money exchange was required because Roman coins were not permitted to be used in support of the temple. What the synoptic Gospel writers are describing does not concern any act of physical violence, but the symbolic act of destroying the very meaning of the Jewish temple, namely, the fiscal, sacrificial, and liturgical operation of the temple, to be replaced by the new commandment of Jesus to love one's God and one's fellow human beings and clearly ties this with the symbolic story of the Jesus cursing the barren fig tree.

John also links this symbolism more clearly with the destruction of Jesus' body in his death and crucifixion and ends this story with the discussion of the destruction of the Jerusalem temple that took 46 years to construct (Jn. 2:14-22).[12] John P. Meier concurs with this interpretation, but indicates that the treatment of worship in the temple for every Gospel source (Q, Mark, John, etc.) was one of "unperturbed acceptance."[13] Edward J. Malley, SJ explains this story as "an eschatological act in the spirit of Mal. 3:1-3, 8-9, which came to be interpreted as the Messianic purification of the temple (Ez. 40-48) ... Jesus' action is seen as an exercise of his Messianic authority, symbolizing God's judgment against the abuses of the temple."[14]

---

12   Crossan, *The Historical Jesus*, pp. 355-360.

13   John P. Meier, *A Marginal Jew: Rethinking the Historical Jesus*, Vol. 3 (New York: Doubleday, 2001), pp500-501. Meier delineates the difference between Jesus' thinking on the temple and that of the theology of Qumran which forbade entry or worship in the temple because it was defiled and envisioned after a future purification an eschatological temple for use, while Jesus accepted the actual temple as a place willed by God for worship.

14   Edward J. Mally, SJ, "The Gospel According to Mark," *The Jerome Biblical Commentary*, p. 47. John L. McKenzie, "The Gospel According

While the synoptic writers apparently focused on Jesus' wrath at the dishonesty of the Temple traffickers, in John the wrath is directed at the Temple institutions themselves.[15]

How does one explain the use of the whip of cords rendered only in John's story? Was this for use against the commercial practitioners in the outer courts or for driving the livestock out of the temple itself? Bruce Vawter, CM interprets this instrument symbolically as demonstrative of Jesus' authority, similar to the interpretation of John L. McKenzie, and, second, as necessary to drive the animals (sheep, calves, etc.) if, in fact, they were numerous.[16] One cannot overlook the extreme importance of symbolism and refined theology in the Gospel of John; the whip of cords is nothing more than symbolic of messianic authority against a corrupt religious regime.

If one takes the story literally, though mistaken as it may be, Mark and Matthew clearly have Jesus exercising physical violence against the tables and seats of the commercial traffickers, not against the traffickers themselves. In no place in the canonical or apocryphal accounts of the gospel story of Jesus can we find Jesus exercising physical violence against persons. To do so runs diametrically counter to the message of love and respect lived by Jesus. It is difficult to imagine that Jesus, who never attacks or belittles specific individuals for their failings and sins, would or could engage in a violent and physical attack on the very physical persons themselves. Thus, it behooves the reader to

to Matthew," *The Jerome Biblical Commentary*, p. 99 explains this purification of the temple with a further twist by noting that this was Jesus' direct confrontation with the Jerusalem hierarchy.

15 The paraphrasing and collation of Is. 56:7 and Jer. 7:11 by Mark and Matthew equate the commercial activity in the temple to that of a den of thieves, i.e., evil-doers, who hide their activity under the auspices of the temple operation. Some have interpreted this den of thieves also to mean revolutionaries. McSorley, *New Testament Basis of Peacemaking*, p. 25, explains that Jesus' description of the outer court of the temple as a den of thieves concerned the only part of the temple that was open to Gentiles, i.e., non-Jews, was in fact excluded to them by this commercial activity. By Jesus' driving this activity outside the temple, the Jerusalem temple was once again open to all peoples, not just Jews.

16 Bruce Vawter, CM, "The Gospel According to John," *The Jerome Biblical Commentary*, p. 429.

be conscious that this story of the cleansing of the temple deals not with physical violence but with the symbolic destruction of the temple and the death of Jesus whereafter a new locus of worship centered on one's treatment of fellow humans and worshiping one's God wherever is intended by the Gospel writers. To read the story literally totally misses the point of the scripture writers.

The only time that Jesus, one of his followers, or a bystander attempts to make use of a weapon intended for maiming or killing another person, Jesus strongly remonstrates (Mk 14:47, Mt 26:51-54, Lk. 22:49-51, Jn.18:10-11 in the story of a sword being drawn in the garden at the arrest of Jesus). Raymond E. Brown clearly states that, according to Matthew, Luke and John, this text was written for the benefit of the early Christian community who themselves were being persecuted, arrested and killed, and that Jesus disapproves of resorting to violent and lethal activity even when so confronted.[17] This "sentiment is harmonious with Mt. 5:39, where Jesus forbids his followers to answer violent action by violent action, and with (Mt.) 10:39, which encourages them to be willing to lose their lives for his sake.... (A)nd v. 52b goes beyond the do-not-return-violence principle, for it warns that in the divine plan violence by a human being will be punished by equal violence," states Brown.[18] That one of the disciples, as told by Matthew and Luke, but left unidentified in Mark, or that Simon Peter as told by John's Gospel, lashed out at the

17   Raymond E. Brown, *The Death of the Messiah: From Gethsemane to the Grave: A Commentary on the Passion Narratives in the Four Gospels*, Vol. 1 (New York: Doubleday, 1994), pp. 274-275.

18   *Ibid.*, pp. 275-276. Brown reinforces his contention that this thinking is more than the Matthean presentation of Jesus, but infers that it pervades the Christian community and its understanding of Jesus' teaching and arises from Jewish moral teaching of Gen. 9:6, "Whoever sheds the blood of a fellow human being shall by a human have his own blood shed." Brown references but does not concur with Kosmala ("Matthew") who "has argued for a different source, namely the Aramaic targum of Isa 50:1, which has added the image of a sword to that passage in the Hebrew Bible: "All you (that kindle a fire, (that) take a sword, go fall in the fire that you have kindled and into the sword that you have taken. From my Memra [personified Word] you have this: You shall return to your destruction." (p. 576)

servant of the high priest is presented by these three Gospel accounts as a misunderstanding of what a disciple of Jesus should do, something that remains consistent throughout the Passion story from the Mount of Olives scene. (Brown, 1994, 267) The misunderstanding concerns the issue that the kingdom or rule of Jesus is not of this world and the living out of Christian identity is not directed to advance the motives and objectives of worldly aspirations. The Matthean Jesus makes a general poetic (chiastic) assertion about the use of the sword (or weapon) even in self-defense that "For all who take the sword, by the sword will perish," (Mt. 26:52) because, according to Matthew, the scriptures must be fulfilled.

That Jesus' followers had and used a weapon would seem out of character from the understanding of the exegesis noted above. Given that all the canonical gospels report this incident vouches for its authenticity. Certainly, it was commonplace for men during that period to carry such weapons to defend themselves against wild beasts—and the company did wander the countryside before arriving at Jerusalem—and possibly even against robbers, etc. At the very least, that such weapons were held and used by the disciples of Jesus only demonstrates that, as aforenoted in the previous paragraph, they still did not get it with regard to the teaching of Jesus. Nowhere in the Acts of the Apostles nor thereafter in any of the epistles of Christian scriptures can we find that the followers of Jesus use or hold lethal weapons. In fact, Paul exhorts the Corinthians to practice non-violence as Jesus did. The disciples in the apostolic period got it![19]

One may question whether this approach of the early apostolic and patristic Church merely was adopted by Jesus' followers because they were numerically an insignificant minority and armed resistance even in the face of unjust oppression and lethal violence would undoubtedly prove futile. Certainly, there were increasingly opportunities to rebel in organized fashion against Roman legions, their Palestinian

19 "For, although we are in the flesh (*sarx*), we do not battle according to the flesh, for the weapons of our battle are not of flesh but are enormously powerful, capable of destroying fortresses." (2 Cor. 10:3-4) Paul's weapons and battles are not constrained to sexual and worldly causes, but involve something far greater, but they do not entail lethal weapons that destroyed the physical.

surrogates, or temple authorities, as the Zealots and Sicarii amassed armed resistance that ultimately failed to overthrow oppressive powers in the apostolic period and later as invading tribes attacked the Roman imperial armies. While this hypothetical question may spur debate, it fails to understand and appreciate the fundamental meaning of the teachings of Jesus that his followers came to understand very early in the apostolic period, particularly in light of the death of one whom they believed to be God. (Mt. 26:53-56.)

JESUS & THE USE OF LETHAL WEAPONS

The Christian scriptures, in several places, also report Jesus speaking about swords, i.e. lethal weapons that are for use in exercising physical violence. Luke, for example, has Jesus at the Last Supper instructing his fellow table-sharers to sell their cloak and buy a sword, if they lack one (Lk. 22: 36). The intent of Luke herein is twofold—first, to prepare the reader for the use of the sword by a disciple in the later arrest of Jesus and, second, to demonstrate that the disciples of Jesus still do not understand what Jesus was about and the preparation for any situation does not involve possession and use of lethal weapons even for self-defense. This interpretation is confirmed two verses later when Jesus, in frustration at the disciples' continued inability to understand his message and purpose, effectively rebukes his followers by saying "Enough of that!" when they offer that they are prepared and have two swords.[20]

---

20 Brown, *The Death of the Messiah*, pp. 270-271, explains the herme-
    neutics of this language as follows and cites Joseph Fitzmyer's interpreta-
    tion. "The response of the disciples that they have in their possession two
    swords shows that they have (mis)understood literally. The disciples' mis-
    understanding leads Jesus to use the phrase *hikanon estin. Hikanos* means
    "sufficient, enough, fitting." 'It is fitting' would be a highly ironic rendi-
    tion, equivalent to 'That's the way you normally misunderstand.' More
    characteristic of the Lucan Jesus would be resignation: 'That's enough.'
    One must be wary not to translate the phrase as if Jesus were saying that
    two swords were enough for the task .... Fitzmyer (Luke 2.1434) insists
    correctly 'the irony concerns not the number of the swords but the whole
    mentality of the apostles.'" Brown further comments on the interpreta-
    tion of the text that "One may add that they have not been the only ones
    to misunderstand: This text has been (mis)used as a general declaration

People seeking justification in purported, but misunderstood, Christian morality for use of weapons and engaging in lethal conflict often cite Mt. 10:34 that Jesus has come not to bring peace, but the sword. The meaning of this Matthean verse lies in division caused by Christians living according to Jesus' message such that people oppose the Gospel, its application and those living according to the Gospel. For the early Christian community in the apostolic period, deep division immediately arose with relations to Jews. Jesus, of course, is the messenger of peace, not of discord and division, but reaction to the message results in division, even within families, although opposition to the Christian message arises not just among non-Christians but also from the non-Christian baptized who fail to understand the true meaning of Jesus' message. This theme can be found in Simeon's statement to Mary in Lk. 2:34-35 which harks back to Mi. 7:6 that foretells the sad state of division even amongst family wherein some members are following the word of God and trusting in that God.[21] Mt. 10:34, ("Do not think that I have come to bring peace upon the earth. I have come to bring not peace, but the sword.") does not infer that Jesus condones the use of weapons and lethal violence, as Christians have so often abused others in misinterpretation of this text, but, as seen in the two verses immediately following, show the discord amongst not only Christians, but amongst those closest by even family ties, when Jesus' true followers are rejected for their faithfulness.[22] Thus, all these scriptural verses are not meant by their Christian authors to

of the right of Christians to bear arms; as support for the right of the medieval papacy to exercise both material and spiritual power (two swords); and as a proof that Jesus encouraged armed revolution!"

The correct hermeneutic of this verse concerning selling one's cloak for purchase of a sword is Jesus' warning for his followers to be prepared for anything, but not that they acquire and hold weapons in self-defense.

21 McKenzie, "The Gospel According to Matthew," p. 81, states regarding the interpretation of these verses, "Then the disciple has no choice except to prefer the new community to the community of blood."

22 Luke avoids any misunderstanding of seeming to condone use of lethal weapons, by noting that belief in Jesus does not bring peace, but is a cause of division even amongst family. (Lk. 12:51.)

be taken literally with regard to using lethal weapons, but are mere figurative speech.[23]

JESUS RELATIONSHIP WITH SOLDIERS & THE ISSUE OF SOLDIERY

Some commentators interpret Jesus' acceptance of soldiers and Jesus' non-confrontational interaction with them as his willingness to acknowledge and accept the ultimate purpose of military activity, to attain or maintain a desired status even through the use of organized lethal force—something absolutely contrary to the teachings and life of Jesus, though. In the story of the centurion coming to implore Jesus to help his ailing servant, Jesus heals the servant because of the marvelous faith of the centurion, one who, though he does not share in the worship of the God of the Hebrews, is to be included amongst the other improbable social outcasts accepted in the kingdom of heaven with the tax collectors, prostitutes, beggars, etc. Similarly, the centurion at the foot of the cross of Jesus is the one who recognizes Jesus as truly the son of God, that is the truly just one who is persecuted and suffers non-violently for the sake of others. "The role of soldiers in the New Testament narratives, however, must be seen in proper context: precisely as Roman soldiers, they serve to dramatize the power of the Word of God to reach even the unlikeliest people."[24] None of the writers of the Christian scriptures directly condemn the Roman soldiers for their military service, but seek to show that even those engaged in the despicable positions and professions, not necessarily voluntarily, can still be receptive to the grace of God and can become believers. All these soldiers come in humility and recognize their limited worth in the face of God.

Cornelius, the Roman centurion who became the first Gentile convert to the new Christian religion, is not required to renounce his military service (Acts 10:1-11:18).[25] Neither Jesus nor his disciples implicitly

---

23   Brown, *The Death of the Messiah*, p. 269.

24   Richard B. Hays, *The Moral Vision of the New Testament: A Contemporary Introduction to New Testament Ethics* (San Francisco: Harpers, 1996), p. 335.

25   Richard J. Dillon and Joseph A. Fitzmyer, SJ, "Acts of the Apostles," in *The Jerome Biblical Commentary*, p. 188, suggests that Cornelius was probably a half-convert to Judaism, similar to other Roman legionnaires

accept war or lethal violence, i.e. soldiery, simply because they accept soldiers. They accept those whose faith brings them to accept God and recognize Jesus. Analogously, Jesus accepts prostitutes, but not prostitution, associates with extortionists, tax-collectors working for foreign occupiers, but does not condone their practices, and praises the good thief, but does not promote thievery.

THE ROLE OF GOVERNMENTAL AUTHORITY IN WAGING WAR & JESUS' POSITION ON VIOLENCE

One may question whether Jesus implicitly accepts military activity, meaning the act of war, policing operations, and the threat of employing lethal organized force because of the Markan account (Mk. 12:13-17; cf. also Mt. 22:15-22) that seems to portray Jesus as accepting the rule of civil government in any form, inclusive of occupation and rule by a foreign army as was the case of the Roman legions ruling Palestine and Jerusalem. The story in Mark has often been interpreted that Jesus accepted paying tribute or taxes to civilian powers and recognizing civilian governments while demanding the paying of homage only to God for the things related to God. Such interpretation distorts the meaning of these scriptures, though. With regard to relations with governments, inclusive of conscription and participation in armed force, Carlos Bravo offers a more appropriate translation of Mark 12:17. "Render to Caesar this idolatrous coin which is a blot upon Israel and give to God what belongs to him, which is the government of the people, unjustly held in Caesar's power."[26] This translation coincides to some extent with the scriptural commentary of Edward J. Mally who notes that "In view of the belief that God's kingdom would come imminently and all earthly kingdoms would disappear, Jesus' saying is

who "accepted ethical monotheism of the Jews, attended their synagogue services, but did not keep the whole Mosaic Law, and usually were not circumcised." Moreover, the basic story behind the story emphasizes that God shows no partiality between any person, Jew or Gentile, but accepts anyone who "fears" God and acts uprightly is acceptable to God.

26 Carlos Bravo, "Jesus of Nazareth, Christ the Liberator," Jon Sobrino and Ignacio Ellacuria (eds.), *Systematic Theology: Perspectives from Liberation Theology*, (Maryknoll, NY: Orbis Books, 1993), p. 117. N.T. Wright concurs in this hermeneutical interpretation of this text.

less a statement of principle about loyalty to Church and state than a pronouncement about the relative insignificance of Rome's political power compared to God's kingdom."[27] The context for this pericope of Mark (12:13-17), used also as a source by Matthew (22:15-22) and Luke (20:20-26) and independently by Thomas (100), is seen within a series of disputes between Jesus and Jewish religious groups, but the historical veracity of this incident remains highly dubious.[28] That the Pharisees were aligned with Herodians presents an highly unusual alliance. This could only be explained by the Pharisees, who tolerated collaboration with Rome but sought to impose capital punishment on Jesus, becoming partners with the Herodians. The Herodians were followers of Herod Antipas and represented more nationalistic factions opposing Roman rule, but for protection of Herod's rule sought to execute Jesus as Herod had done to John the Baptist because he presented a potential threat of popular uprising. The combination of these two groups is unusual at best. Thus, this whole pericope must be understood within the context posed by Mark of Jewish religious authorities seeking to thwart the popularity of Jesus and deter the undermining of their own religious authority. Bravo's analysis of Jesus' position on Roman rule seems appropriate. "It is evident that Jesus rejects Roman rule, which goes against the exclusive Reign of Yahweh. The burden of the tribute is not only unjust, but it is also intolerable because it appertains to the cult of the emperor,"[29] the emperor whose image was on the Roman coins and who was considered a god opposing the Christian understanding of God and the kingdom of the Christian God. The synoptic writers in this pericope effectively criticize even the payment of tribute to Caesar because Roman rule makes the

---

27   Mally, "The Gospel According to Mark," *Jerome Biblical Commentary*, p. 48. Mally supplements this exegesis by highlighting the change in Christian thinking at the time Mark was written some 35 years later, "Expectation of an imminent end of the world had abated among Christians, and Jesus' pronouncement was reinterpreted as sanctioning the principle that a man's loyalty to civil authority need not contradict his obedience to God" with special pertinence to Christians under Nero's persecution.

28   Meier, *A Marginal Jew: Companions and Competitors*, vol. 2, pp. 334, 561-563.

29   Bravo, "Jesus of Nazareth, Christ the Liberator," p. 120

Kingdom impossible—"the religious power which has kidnapped the freely-giving God of the covenant and put in God's place a deity of laws, merits and purifications." (Bravo, 1993, 119) The final analysis pertaining to the participation in state power as exercised in military activity with the potential for lethal combat runs diametrically counter to the Kingdom of God and the teachings of Jesus.[30] Thus, this pericope is a criticism of even state power that detracts the Christian's focus from fulfilling the will of God, particularly with regards to Roman control that Jesus judges to be unjust.

The Zealots, Their Use of Revolutionary Violence, & Jesus

Do the number of Zealots amongst Jesus' followers and in the early Christian community not undermine this apparent non-violent posture of Jesus and his teachings? This seems to pose a dilemma and probably incited numerous debates within the primitive Christian communities. As a group, the Zealots can be considered both as puritanical nationalistic revolutionaries, especially several decades after the death of Jesus, along the line of unsuccessful followers of the Maccabees and as a coalition of bandit groups, many originating from and supported by the peasantry.[31] During the public life of Jesus, Zealots were not known to be engaged in violent revolutionary activity, though; this development only materialized at the first Jewish war in 66 ce. John L. McKenzie places their origin at a revolt against the census of Quirinius about the time of the birth of Jesus. Given the aforenoted explanation of Jesus' viewpoint on Roman rule and the payment of taxes to Rome, the Zealots would in many ways find affinity in their

30   The centrality of Jesus' message that he was about making and bringing the kingdom of God was not exceptional for his time. The Zealots looked for a kingdom in the form of a return to the grandeur and centrality of focus on God within an Israelite state and they attempted several time during the first century ce to bring about that kingdom. The Essenes, as witnessed in the documents at Qumran, also looked forward to establishing a kingdom, a renewal of covenant with God, totally focused on centrality of YHWH in their lives within an ascetical and quasi-hermit setting. See Stanley Hauerwas, "Jesus and the Social Embodiment of the Peaceable Kingdom," John Berkman and Michael Cartwright, eds., *The Hauerwas Reader* (Durham, NC: Duke University Press, 2001), p. 117.

31   Crossan, *The Historical Jesus*, p. 213.

thinking and as a result identify with Jesus because they believed (a) in
the messianism of the Hebrew scriptures, but from the standpoint of
recovering Jewish independence, (b) in the worship only of YHWH,
and (c) in their conviction that acceptance of foreign domination by
the Romans and payment of taxes (with Roman denominated coins)
was blasphemy.[32] Clearly, the occasional use of harassment, violence,
and murder by some Zealots in forcing fellow Jews to retain strict
separation from Gentiles and their way of living was unacceptable to
Jesus. John the Baptist seems, according to Flavius Josephus, to have
associated with the Zealots and then to have broken from their violent,
nationalist fanaticism that eventually evolved from political rebellion
into social revolution by 67 ce wherein both sacerdotal and aristocratic
leadership was destroyed. That Jesus, a follower of his mentor John,
had numerous Zealot followers was probably to be expected and in no
way contradicts the underlying message of love and non-violence. It
should be noted, though, that Simon the Zealot (actually the Cananean)
was probably not a member of the Zealot group as many scripture
scholars have inferred.[33] That some Zealots were followers of Jesus
need not imply that Jesus supported the violent aspects of Zealots'
nationalism or puritanical radicalism, something opposite what Jesus
represented. The Zealots, like the Pharisees, sought to purify Jewish
political and religious institutions, but, different from the Pharisees,
were willing to use violent and lethal means. On the other hand, the
primitive Christian community certainly must have wrestled with the
issue of the occupying Romans and the means of eradicating such
two and three decades after Jesus' death, given the number of Zealots
following the newly developing Christian community. The Christian
community disassociated itself from the Zealots and their revolution
against Roman rule from 66 ce and thereafter precisely because Jesus
taught and lived non-violence, rejected retaliation, exhorted love of

---

32   McKenzie, *Dictionary of the Bible*, p. 947.

33   Meier, *A Marginal Jew*, vol. III, pp. 205-208 makes a convincing case that
     Simon was merely zealous in the practice of the Mosaic law and insistent
     that his fellow Jews observe this law to the extent that Jews separate Is-
     rael from idolatrous practices, but Simon would have had to drastically
     change his life and his sectarian thinking to be all inclusive in openness
     to accepting the coming of the kingdom for all peoples.

one's enemies, and made killing absolutely contradictory to his message of the good news of a kingdom not of this world.[34] Thus, the problem of violent and lethal warfare promoted by the Zealots did not confront the historical Jesus, but certainly was an issue three decades later for Jesus' followers.

Jesus, the Recipient of Lethal Violence & Model for Dealing with Violence

Although we have examined Jesus' position with regards to the use of lethal violence upon others, nothing has been reviewed concerning the receptivity of violence. The Jesus who neither accepted nor exercised violence being employed upon another person was willing to receive and be subject to violence, even lethal violence upon himself in his death on a cross as a criminal who was purported to threaten the state and the local religious powers. The primitive Church, using Jesus as their model, cautioned their followers that this was the difficult path of Jesus which they should or might follow. "From the days of John the Baptist until now, the kingdom of heaven suffers violence, and the violent are taking it by force."[35] (Mt. 11:12) Jesus, in seeming acceptance of self-victimization, viewed himself at the end of his life as becoming the target of opponents of the good news of his message of

---

34   For a description of the Zealots and their revolutionary activity in the 60s ce, see Flavius Josephus, *Jewish War* 2.425-451 and 486-490 and for an analytical study of the Zealots in these wars see Crossan, *The Historical Jesus*, pp. 212-218. In some respects, the Zealots of the 60s ce resemble many traits associated with puritanical peasant movements stimulated by foreign occupation, such as the Khmer Rouge. The violence unleashed by the Zealots lay hidden within their puritanical anger at being occupied or against the failure of their religious leadership to subscribe to puritanical rigidity. The Zealots became notorious for carrying daggers hidden within their clothing and for assassinating both Roman occupiers and Jews whom they thought sympathized or collaborated with the Roman rulers, thereby acquiring the sect name of Sicarii (stabbers) by the Romans about the time of the first Jewish war.

35   Crossan, *The Historical Jesus*, p. xv and xx, indicates that this and the following pericope relating the story of the vineyard owner who sends his son to his tenants who kill the son rather than repay the owner with some of the fruit of the vineyard, as words that Jesus actually spoke.

justice, peace, love and reconciliation in the parable of the son sent to
the vineyard tenants only to be rejected and killed. (Mt. 21:32-42 and
Luke 20:9-17, with some alteration, rely on Mk. 12:1-12 for relating
this pericope.) Although some scripture scholars interpret this parable
as a theology of and formulation by the primitive Church because
of its heavy allegory, many scholars like Crossan today acknowledge
that this parable was used by Jesus, but has been embellished with
allegory by the primitive Church, particularly in light of the Gospel
of Thomas, No. 65, wherein the parable is told without the detailed
allegory.[36] Thus, not only Jesus, but also the early Church accepted
that, in following the will of God, one must be ready for and accept
the possibility of being the recipient of lethal violence.

Despite the potential for being the target of (lethal) violence, Jesus
neither teaches nor tolerates retaliation. Unlike the Hebrew scriptures,
that intended to moderate vengeance whereby punishment should
not exceed the injury received (Lev. 24:20-21) or the admonishment
to judges to "show no pity" (Deut. 19:18b-21), Jesus forbids even
proportionate retaliation and instructs his followers (who happen to
be the powerless and the victims of the powerful) not even to resist the
evil doer.[37] The followers and community of Jesus principally comprise
the powerless, the marginalized, the weak, and the oppressed—those
outside the circle of power. That means that the follower of Jesus is
expected to take the violence encumbered upon oneself, but at the
same time to be as shrewd as serpents and guileless as doves in dealing
with one's enemies in a non-violent and non-threatening manner and
not go out of one's way to become the recipient of violence.

---

36   See *New American Bible*, footnote 21, 33-46, p. 49.

37   Lev. 24:20: "Limb for limb, eye for eye, tooth for tooth! The same injury
     that a man gives another shall be inflicted on him in return… (W)hoever
     slays a man shall be put to death."
     See also Deut. 19:18b-21, " … if after a thorough investigation the judges
     find that the witness is a false witness and has accused his kinsman falsely,
     you shall do to him as he planned to do to his kinsman. Thus shall you
     purge the evil from your midst. The rest, on hearing of it, shall fear, and
     never again do a thing so evil among you. Do not look on such a man
     with pity. Life for life, eye for eye, tooth for tooth, hand for hand, and
     foot for foot."

Briefly, the Christian scriptures portray a treatment of war and lethal violence quite differently than the Hebrew scriptures. While Jesus accepts the centrality of love of and respect for YHWH as best witnessed and enacted through loving treatment of fellow human beings, i.e., through the exercise of justice particularly for preferential treatment of the oppressed, the economically poor, the marginalized, he demands more of people in his commandment of love that is implemented through reconciliation between conflicting parties and persons and the creation of peace. The beatitudes and the interpretative rendition of the last judgment, particularly that recorded by Matthew, must be considered the heart of Jesus' thinking on how to live as he lived. Although misinterpreted for most of the Christian historical period, Jesus, contrary to contemporary and popular belief, did not condone the use of violence, inclusive of lethal violence and war. Jesus neither is known to have used weapons nor advocated such and the early Apostolic community refrained from holding and using such. The Christian scriptures have been grossly misinterpreted in Jesus' statements regarding the use of weapons and the scripture writers' statements for Jesus at the Last Supper and in the Garden of Gethsemane. Jesus is known to never use physical or lethal violence on any person; any representation to the contrary based on scriptural interpretation is proven incorrect according to the most authoritative scripture scholars. Correct exegesis demonstrates the impatience of Jesus that his disciples fail to understand the true meaning of his teachings with regard to violence. Finally, Christians all too often fail to realize that the model for living in the face of violence is found in Jesus himself. Jesus forbids retaliation, forbids hatred, and, contrary to what is thought common sense, returns only love when confronted or receiving abuse, harassment, evil itself, and even death!

CHAPTER 4

Early Christian Approaches to War & Peace
(from Apostolic Through Late Patristic Period)

Given the teachings and practices of Jesus with regard to war and violence, in contradistinction to the new mandate of love, how then did the early Christian communities interpret and practice Jesus' teachings, either as they were being worked out and written down or as they were being re-interpreted in the first four centuries after Jesus' death? In order to understand Christians' response to war and peace in the apostolic and patristic periods, it behooves one to view Christians' interaction in their societies more generally.

Paul & the Use of Civil Authority
with Respect to Violence

Despite the aforenoted comments in the previous chapter with regard to Jesus' saying on the payment of taxes, Paul in Rom. 13:1-7 presents us with a possible dilemma, and apparently in contrast to Jesus because Paul as a Roman citizen, which Jesus was not, sought to use the benefits of the Roman system for the purpose of evangelization. In Romans, Paul asserts that all authority comes from God, inclusive of that exacted by the Romans, and requires subordination. It behooves the reader to be conscious that Paul is writing about civilian government, not police power or military force that is often used for exacting subordination. Paul was conscious that civilian authority, inclusive of Roman rule, was not an inspiration to do good, but acted to instill fear to avoid evil (Rom. 13:3). Joseph Fitzmyer, SJ provides to us the basis for understanding Paul's interpretation of Christian living which recognizes that Christians are free of the (Mosaic) law, but subject to civil authorities whose rationale was interwoven with worship of other deities.

> Obedience to civil authorities is a form of obedience to God himself,
> for man's relation to God is not limited to a specifically religious

or cultic sphere. The supposition that runs through this paragraph
(13:1-7) is that civil authorities are conducting themselves uprightly
and are seeking the interests of the community. The possibility is
not envisaged either of a tyrannical government or of one failing
to cope with a situation where the just rights of individual citizens
or of a minority group are neglected. Paul insists on merely one
aspect of the question: the duty of subjects to legitimate authority.
He does not discuss the duty of civil authorities here."[1]

The critical criteria and question before us focuses on the issue of
how the Christian is to act when the authority, though legitimate, is
not acting in the interests of the citizens. Even though Paul does not
directly address this and his presupposition is that the authority is
legitimate and in the interests of citizenry, not even a common case
in Paul's time, what should be expected of the Christian in following
the directives or commands of authority, even oppressive, exploitive,
and lethally threatening governments? It must follow that, because
the premise, namely that the authorities are acting uprightly in the
interests of the community, is not met, the Christian is not required
to follow or be subordinate to this type of authority, although it may
be legitimate. It would seem that the Christian in this case would in
conscious judiciously oppose such authority. Paul continues, "Therefore, whoever resists authority opposes what God has appointed, and
those who oppose it will bring judgment upon themselves. For rulers
are not a cause to fear to good conduct, but to evil." (Rom. 13:2.)
Paul implies that the exercise of good is more persuasive than acting
in evil manner, whatever that may mean. The following two verses
may be interpreted to require the Christian to do good, even when
confronted with evil, inclusive of the threat of one's own destruction.
Paul implicitly accepts the use of lethal and penal force exercised by
governments because the state exists for a good purpose, *eis to agathon*,
to force recalcitrant citizens to maintain order and to pay taxes for
the maintenance of order in the community. (Fitzmyer, 1970, 326)
Unfortunately, neither Paul nor other scripture writers directly provide
guidance on how the Christian is to act in the face of legitimate, but
possibly immoral, governments that benefit, not the community's

---

1 Joseph A. Fitzmyer, SJ, "The Letter to the Romans," *The Jerome Biblical
  Commentary*, p. 326.

interests, but special interest groups and that exploit and burden their own citizens and citizens of other nations.[2] Given the image of YHWH as the protector of the oppressed, marginalized, weak, and minority in YHWH aiding the Israelites at the Exodus, an image subscribed by Jesus, one may deduce that neither Jesus nor Paul would approve of subordination to a government that is not acting as YHWH would have acted on behalf of the interests of these people. There remains, though, the premise of Paul that the Roman authorities were acting legitimately, something questionable given the enslavement and occupation of Israel. One may seriously and substantively question whether Roman authorities acted in the interests of the community they governed through fear of the sword and oppressive taxation, even though many, but not all, Christian scriptural commentators mistakenly viewed and portrayed the Roman Empire as providing in the peace and order of the Roman Empire the milieu in which Jesus came. It could be presumed that Paul would caution prudent and judicious enactment of one's conscience in opposing the legitimate authorities. Anyone can easily see what happened to Paul and probably many of the other disciples in declaring liberty and justice for all people but never resorting to physical and lethal violence. We would fail in our interpretation of this writing of Paul if we overlooked the underlying and overpowering focus of Paul's letter to the Romans that, just as Jesus was obedient to his God unto death on the cross, our own conformity to Jesus' death and the imitation of Jesus remain the foundational elements of Paul's vision of the moral life, in contrast to the disobedience of the symbolic Adam.[3] For Paul, this acts as the paradigm of faithfulness and the basic *kerygma* of the Christian message of *euangelion*, the proclamation of the good news of salvation.

Finally, we must note that in Rom. 12:21, echoed in 13:4 and analogously offered in Peter 2:13-17, Paul admonishes the community in Rome, "Do not be conquered by evil but conquer evil with good." Thus, Paul himself neither justifies the use of lethal force nor encourages even civilian authorities to use this force. McSorley poignantly

---

2 Fitzmyer offers no suggestion in his commentary either.

3 Richard B. Hays, *The Moral Vision of the New Testament: A Contemporary Introduction to New Testament Ethics* (San Francisco: Harpers, 1996), p. 31.

interprets this text, "The state's alleged authority to kill and to ask others to kill is condemned by this text. Here the violence of the state, the killing done by the state would be evil. It is to be overcome by good…. This is a pacifist attitude, not the attitude of a militarist…. As long as public authorities order what conscience approves the Christian must submit to it."[4] The author of Revelation in the story of the Apocalypse, where the Lord of Lords, the slaughtered lamb, overcomes "the power of violence as the illusory power of the Beast, which is unmasked by the faithful testimony of the saints."[5]

NON-VIOLENCE OF APOSTOLIC & PATRISTIC PERIOD CHRISTIANS AS A THREAT TO THE STATE

Christians in the apostolic and early Christian era not only maintained an aloof and removed attitude toward the state, but quite possibly presented a threatening posture toward governmental authorities, particularly those of the "pagan" Roman Empire. They certainly raised threatening questions of their allegiance, given their non-recognition of the Caesars and Augustuses as gods. Tertullian wrote that "Nothing is more foreign to us than the State."[6] They adopted an actual lifestyle that contradicted the myopic practices of both the Roman state and the Jewish religion (though not counter to the directions of the prophets) in that they shared their goods and even their homes with foreigners who historically had been viewed with suspicion and ridicule.[7] Paul in his letter to the Colossians (3:11) and Luke in Acts (2:5-13) emphasize the universality of peoples as called to become followers of the one, true God and receptiveness of the Christian community towards all

---

4 McSorley, *New Testament Basis of Peacemaking*, pp. 44-45.

5 Hays, *The Moral Vision of the New Testament*, p. 340.

6 TR Glover, *Tertullian* (LCL), quoted in Gerhard Lohfink, *Jesus and Community* (Philadelphia: Fortress Press, 1984), p. 165.

7 Justin Martyr notes that " … we who hated and killed one another and would not share our hearth with those of a different tribe because of their [different] customs, now, after the coming of Christ, live together with them." Quoted from TB Falls (ed.), *The Fathers of the Church* (Washington, DC: Catholic University Press) by Gerhard Lohfink, *Jesus and Community*, p. 158.

people in opposition to paganism (e.g., worship of the emperor as a god in the Roman empire).

As Stanley Hauerwas states, the Christianity of the apostolic and primitive Christian era posed a threat to the state itself because Christians viewed themselves as belonging and loyal to another ruler, a divine and loving God, that superceded any demands of state and governmental authorities.[8] To be a Christian behooved one to work to realize a new kingdom, the rule of God which recognizes every person a creature of God and necessitates equal treatment and justice on behalf of the oppressed and poor. Even today, for the Christian, the Church and not the nation state or the national community is primary. The Church then becomes a counter-culture, a culture in direct opposition to the status quo of political and religious society. John Dominic Crossan, in his understanding of Paul, asserts that the apostle Paul came to see his mission as creating around the Mediterranean a community that sought to focus on a new society, inclusive of a political society, with values, morals, and deity that directly opposed the existing powers.[9] Paul understood his mission as inaugurating the kingdom of God on earth in opposition to Rome's rule by proclaiming the liberating message of the Gospel that entailed the practice of equality, care of the poor, and realization of a just society under God's rules, not Rome's. Paul and the early Christians just did not offer, but declared an alternative faith and the divinity of Jesus in opposition to Caesar, the ruler of an imperial state. This evangelical message could not be interpreted anything different than as a threat to the political institution of the Roman empire.

According to Hays' interpretation of Paul's eschatology, "The community is engaged in cosmic conflict. As the advance representatives of God's new creation in an unwilling and hostile world, the church should expect to experience the same sort of opposition that Jesus did, the same sort of opposition that Paul himself encounters. The

---

8 Arne Rasmusson, *The Church as Polis: From Political Theology to Theological Politics as Exemplified by Jürgen Moltmann and Stanley Hauerwas*, p. 369.

9 See John Dominic Crossan and Jonathan L. Reed, *In Search of Paul: How Jesus' Apostle Opposed Rome's Empire with God's Kingdom* (San Francisco: Harpers, 2004).

battle is to be fought, however, not "according to the flesh"—not
with weapons of violence—but with proclamation of the truth (cf.
2Cor. 10:3-6)."[10] The seed that Paul brings to the Christian *kerygma*
is rooted in the teaching of Jesus and centers on the commonality of
all persons, diminishing differences of social, gender, status, language,
or ethnic traits. As "sons of God," Paul tell us in Gal. 3:28, we all
belong to a single family and share in the same inheritance; Jews and
Gentiles should not be separately treated in the Christian community.
So too, tolerance and understanding are required for dealing with the
diverse human community.

Yet the Christians paid their taxes or tribute to the emperor, although
they must have done so with some hesitation, appeared loyal to the
state in recognizing authority, and even prayed for the emperor but
not to the emperor or under the *tyche* oath, the enemy in principle as
a declared god. The irony of the synoptics' story about paying tribute
to the emperor was not lost on the early Church (Mt. 22:15-22; Mk.
12:13-17; Lk. 20:20-26). It was clear that Jesus rejected Roman rule
in this story, but did not rebel against it. The fact that the Pharisee
had the coin upon which was imprinted Caesar's image, a god in the
Roman empire, blotted and tainted the House of Israel. Jesus really
advises that people "give to God what belongs to him, which is the
government of the people, unjustly held in Caesar's power."[11] Jesus
then was effectively criticizing the tribute as unjust and intolerable
because of the cult of the emperor, something conveniently overlooked
in contemporary society. Being such, the early Christians posed a clear
and latent threat to the Roman system of government, but also raised
many questions to be answered by any government.[12] Minucius Felix,
the early Christian Apologist, in his *Octavius* (35.6), in which he
expressed the same sentiments, painted a picture of the early Christians
in the first two centuries after Christ as being numerically a very tiny
part of society in opposition "to the entire rest of society *in their faith*

---

10   Hays, *The Moral Vision of the New Testament*, p. 26.

11   Carlos Bravo, SJ, "Jesus of Nazareth, Christ the Liberator," in Jon So-
     brino, SJ and Ignacio Elacuria, SJ (eds.), *Systematic Theology* (New York:
     Paulist Press, 1992), p. 117.

12   *Ibid.*, p. 120. See also critique of Rome's political domination as unjust
     in Mk. 5:9,13; 10;42; 12:16,`7; 13:14; Lk. 13:32 ff.

and in their manner of life."[13] It may be deduced then that the early Christians, while open and receptive to peoples and cultures from anywhere, appeared as threatening to civil authorities, something that changed with the acceptance as the sole state religion in 381 ce. Prior to 381, the patristic Hippolytus "characterized the Roman state as a demonic imitation of the true state, that is the Christian people." (Lohfink, 1984, 165)

Followers of Jesus, Their Relationship to Government, & Military Service Prior to the Fifth Century

Despite such coolness to the state, Christians were encouraged to hold public office and, in fact, witness to many examples of such. Origen in his *Contra Celsum* (8.75) clearly demonstrates in the early third century ce his advocacy that Christians assume public office in their own cities.[14] Although Lohfink emphasizes that early Christians as both an ideal and in actuality acted as a people counter to the rest of society, a contrast society,[15] they were, as demonstrated by Origen, very socially responsible and civilly involved in local government as

---

13 Lohfink, *Jesus and Community*, p. 159.

14 *Ibid.*, p. 167. In fact, in addition to the explanation offered by Origen, they served as judges, local administrators, etc. Origen states therein, "We know of the existence in each city of another sort of country, created by the Logos of God. And we call upon those who are competent to take office, who are sound in doctrine and life, to rule over the churches. We do not accept those who love power." The early Church attempted to become a truly egalitarian society, with none having domination over others. Hippolytus, in his *"Commentary on Daniel"* (4.9) confirms the same and the apologist, Minucius Felix, in his *"Octavius"* (12.5-6) further demonstrates the excessive seriousness of the early Christians relating to the rest of civil society and governmental activities, attested by Lucian of Samosata in his satire, *"The Passing of Peregrinus"* (12-13). Referenced by Lohfink, *Jesus and Community*, pp. 162 and 164-165.

15 This understanding of Christianity as a counter-society has also been advanced by many other theologians such as John Yoder, Stanley Hauerwas, etc. A contrast society, or a counter-culture, would seem to be the meaning intended by the gospel writers when they speak of the followers of Jesus being a leaven for the world, i.e., a leaven of love, the basis of Jesus teaching.

conscientious members of the Church, but refrained from frivolous, immoral and military acts related specifically to the Roman state and any violent exercise of national affairs. They exercised this approach to civil duty precisely because they considered themselves as founding a new state and a new country under the exercise of the Logos of God, that is, a Church community according to the teachings of Jesus, teachings that superceded any civil law.

For more than one century after the death of Jesus, until around 170 AD, the Church undisputedly, univocally, and consistently was pacifist and remained so in Church teaching of the fathers for two more centuries, but with increasing compromise of its non-ordained followers until Constantine and the later cementing of "righteous" violence by Augustine.[16] Primitive Christian writers denounced military

---

"He spoke to them another parable, 'The kingdom of heaven is like yeast that a woman took and mixed with three measures of wheat flour until the whole batch was leavened.'" (Mt. 13:33; see also Lk. 13:20-21.) This Q parable, which Crossan asserts as Jesus' authentic teaching (Crossan, *The Historical Jesus*, p. xviii), has the woman taking an enormous amount of meal for the yeast, which magnifies the flour enough to feed more than 100 persons, a tremendous amount symbolic of the greatness of the kingdom's effect. Interestingly, the term leaven used elsewhere in the scriptures refers to the expansion of corruption.

16   The Constantinian shift in the thinking on war and lethal violence by the Church totally changed the Church. Arne Rasmusson, *The Church as Polis: From Political Theology to Theological Politics as Exemplified by Jürgen Moltmann and Stanley*, p. 222, asserts that this shift caused the Church to no longer act as a minority, contrast society that faith identified the Church and the believer, but to become an invisible Church that was identified "primarily as the hierarchy and sacramental institution, with the consequence that faith and Christian life primarily were understood in inward terms." He further notes, based on the thinking of John Howard Yoder and Stanley Hauerwas especially, that the ethical thinking of the Church shifted significantly. "When the church consists of everyone, and its role is seen as civilizational religion keeping society together, ethical discourse is assumed to be directly applicable to anyone, irrespective of whether these resources (i.e., based on Yoder, resources like personal commitment, regeneration, the guidance of the Holy Spirit, the consolation and encouragement of the brotherhood, training in a discipleship life-style, etc.) are present or not. The consequence is that a

service because of their faithfulness to Jesus and to their baptismal promises. The emperor worship within the Roman army acted only as a secondary motive. To be engaged in military activity was war-calling and entailed blood-shedding. Thus, early Christianity in following the teachings of Jesus renounced military activity.

Scripture scholars and theologians have debated the real reasons why the early and primitive Church eschewed and proscribed military service, though. While many respected scholars, such as Stanley Hauerwas, John Howard Yoder, Jean Bethke Elshtain, Gerhard Lohfink, James W. Douglass, Joseph L. Allen, and Roland H. Bainton, to name but a few, other than the scripture scholars cited above, clearly support the position that the Church was non-violent as a necessity for following the teachings and spirit of Jesus, other theologians contest this. Theologians of the likes of Ernst Troeltsch, Albert Nolan, James Turner Johnson, John Helgeland, etc. have disputed the reasons for non-violence in the early church and have attributed this posture to factors other than theological or different interpretation of Jesus' teachings. Johnson and Helgeland, for example, have charged that early Christians sought to avoid the military because they wished to devote themselves purely for the service of and reflection on Christian ideals, but later, when they came to realize that the eschaton was not immediately upon them, avoided conscription in the Roman legions because of the issue of idolatry.[17] Albert Nolan argues that Jesus was not

---

minimalistic ethics (theologically often legitimated in some form of natural law terms) is accepted, which is complemented with 'evangelical counsels' for a motivated spiritual elite. As civilizational religion providing the empire with a common ethos, Christianity did not require conversion and membership in a counter-culture, but 'became that set of beliefs which explains why the way things are is the way things were meant to be for any right-thinking person, converted or not.'" [Stanley Hauerwas, *Naming the Silences: God, Medicine, and the Problem of Suffering*, (Grand Rapids, Mich.: 1990) p. 55]. With this shift, Hauerwas correctly identifies a different way of Christian thinking about history and eschatology wherein the provident rule of God could be seen in the emperor and the Roman Empire (a la Eusebius).

17 See James Turner Johnson, *The Quest for Peace: Three Moral Traditions in Western Cultural History* (Princeton, NJ: 1987), p. 13 and John Helgeland, "Christians and the Roman Army A.D. 173-337," *Church History*

a pacifist in principle, that evidence is lacking that Jesus thought force should never be used, that Jesus used force and coercion to remove the traders from the temple and his disciples from the wilderness, that the antitheses such as turning the other cheek are merely symbolic contrasts to the thinking employed in the Hebrew scriptures, that the kingdom of God could be established with force, that Jesus' comment to his disciples in the Garden at his arrest was issued as a rational response to avoid bloodshed when faced with overwhelming odds, etc.[18] Given these comments, though, it clearly demonstrates from the exegesis of scriptures noted herein that Nolan has totally misinterpreted the scriptures and, in doing so, has missed the point of Jesus' message, especially when he insinuates that Jesus could have used violence as a temporary measure in lieu of more serious violence.

In reaction to these claims, Hauerwas counters, "There can be no doubt that the fundamental reason the early Christians had an aversion to military service … was that faithfulness to the example of Jesus. They simply did not believe they could be followers of Jesus and at the same time pick up arms against the enemy."[19] Adolf von Harnack reacts similarly when he concludes that "bloodshed was in principle rejected in early Christianity."[20] Bainton also emphasizes that prior

No. 43, 1974 and John Helgeland, Robert J. Daly and J. Patout Burns, *Christians and the Military: The Early Experience* (Philadelphia: Fortress Press, 1985), cited in Arne Rasmusson, *The Church as Polis: From Political Theology to Theological Politics as Exemplified by Jürgen Moltmann and Stanley Hauerwas*, p. 310.

18 Albert Nolan, OP, *Jesus Before Christianity: The Gospel of Liberation* (London: Darton, Longman and Todd Ltd, 1977), pp. 110-111. Nolan employs a scriptural interpretation that supports his approach to liberation theology in South Africa, an approach that other liberation theologians, but not all, have used to support undesired, but necessary, overthrow of oppressive governments and structures. We will examine this further when we review herebelow the thinking of Jürgen Moltmann herebelow and consider the actions employed by Camillo Torres in Colombia.

19 Stanley Hauerwas, "Christianity and War," *The Charlotte Observer*, Feb. 10, 1991, 1C, cited by Rasmusson, *The Church as Polis*, p. 309.

20 Adolf von Harnack, *Militia Christi: The Christian Religion and the Military in the First Three Centuries* (Philadelphia: Fortress Press, 1981) cited

to 170-180 ce there is no record of Christians engaged in military "service" and that Celsus, the non-Christian critic of Christianity, attacked Christianity because the state would be left defenseless due to the failure of Christians to accept military practice and Celsus knew of no Christians in the Roman legions.[21] However, Tertullian in his Apology of 197 ce and in *De Corona Militis* of 211 ce acknowledges that Christian were in the military and argues against their voluntary enlistment, respectively.[22] In the second century, the Church would not readmit to communion persons guilty of bloodshed, something incumbent on military action. One cannot fail to notice that even Bainton is aware that the diminished expectation of Christians in the third century ce toward an approximating eschaton diluted Christian thinking with regard to war and non-violence. (Bainton, 1985, 76) Bainton, nevertheless, maintains that this diminished expectation did not provide a basis for relinquishing non-violence because Christians essentially viewed themselves as pilgrims and strangers and held out their certainty of vindication in a future life—emphasis on a spiritualization of the concept of an eschaton as seen in the thinking of Hippolytus, Lactantius, Clement, Origen, Tertullian, *et al.*[23]

---

by Rasmusson, *The Church as Polis*, p. 309.

21   Roland H. Bainton, *Christian Attitudes Toward War and Peace: A Historical Survey and Critical Re evaluation* (Nashville, Tenn.: Abingdon Press, 1985), p. 68. Bainton quotes Celsus as stating, "If all men were to do the same as you, there would be nothing to prevent the king from being left in utter solitude and desertion and the forces of the empire would fall into the ands of the wildest and most lawless barbarians." (*Contra Celsum*, VIII, 68-69.)

22   Roland H. Bainton, *Christian Attitudes Toward War and Peace*, p. 68. It is not clear why Bainton overlooked the conversion of Roman soldiers in Acts 10, but it is known through Tertullian that many Roman soldiers left the military upon their conversion.

23   Bainton contends that Hippolytus and Lactantius placed the event of the eschaton some three and two centuries, respectively, after themselves; thus, it was not considered by them to be an immediate event.

Fathers of the Church, Military Service, & the Issue of War & Lethal Violence

Despite the protests of aforenoted theologians that Jesus was not a pacifist and that non-violence and opposition to any participation in war were merely political expediency or misguided thinking of primitive Christians awaiting an early eschaton, it behooves us to examine the thinking of leading fathers of the early Church to see if they opined otherwise. Not one recognized leader in the primitive Church of the first three centuries could be found who approved or advised joining or participating in military activity. Participation in military activity or war diametrically contradicted, as it still does, the baptismal commitments, precisely because of the possibility of killing another person, or even being commanded to such.

Justin, the martyr who was killed by Marcus Aurelius in 165 ce, was perhaps the greatest of the early Christian apologists and known for relating the Gospels to Greek philosophy, has stated unequivocally the position of the early Christians with regard to their thinking of war. "We refrain from making war on our enemies ... for Caesar's soldiers possess nothing which they can lose more precious than their life, while our love goes out to the eternal life which God will give us by his might ... We who used to kill one another, do not make war on our enemies. We refuse to tell lies or deceive our inquisitors: we prefer to die acknowledging Christ."[24] Similarly, in *Trypho* ("The Dialogue against Trypho"), he proclaims, "We who were filled with war and mutual slaughter and every wickedness have each of us in all the world changed our weapons of war ... swords into plows and spears into agricultural implements, and cultivate piety, justice, love of mankind ... ."[25] Lest one doubt the strength of this position, he stated more clearly the abhorrence for war such that Christians and catechumens were to avoid engaging in military, be it the Roman legions or other bellicose activity or even attendance at gladiatorial games. He forbade baptism of a catechumen who entered the military.

Iranaeus of Lyons, who seems to have originated in the eastern part of the Roman Empire because of his language and ideas and who was a disciple of Polycarp who was a disciple of the apostle

---

24   1 Apology, XXXIX.

25   "Dialogue with Trypho,"CX..

John, in his *Adversus omnes Haereses* ("Against All Heresies") in the late second century, defended the tradition of remaining faithful to the apostolic witness of peace and non-violence in the face of non-Christian interpretations when he "referred the prophecy of beating swords into plowshares to the Christians who do not know how to fight, but when struck offer the other cheek."[26] Killing, the purpose and profession of the military, was incompatible with Jesus' teaching of love as interpreted in the early Church.

Origen, probably the greatest thinker in the early Church because of his interpretation of the scriptures, greatly influenced eastern Christian thought and held positions just as adamant as those of Justin nearly one century earlier. In *Contra Celsum,* ("Against Celsus" 8, 73), he states:

> We Christians no longer take up sword against nation, nor do we learn to make war any more, having become children of peace for the sake of Jesus who is our leader ... and no one fights better for the king than we do. We do not indeed fight under him although he require it, but we fight on his behalf, forming a special army, an army of piety, by offering our prayers to God.

He expressed similar sentiments in *Contra Celsum* 5, 33 when he exclaimed,

> For we no longer take sword against a nation, nor do we learn any more to make war, having become sons of peace for the sake of Jesus, who is our commander.

Clement of Alexandria, the teacher of Origin, proclaimed, "We are the race given over to peace," and "We have made use of only one instrument, the peaceful word, with which we do honour to God."[27] He further remonstrated in preaching to the non-baptized, "If you enroll as one of God's people, heaven is your country and God your lawgiver. And what are his laws? ... Thou shalt not kill.... Thou shalt

26 *Adversus omnes Haereses*, IV, 34, 4 cited by Bainton, in *Christian Attitudes Toward War and Peace*, p. 73.

27 "Tutor, 1, 12, 98 and 4, 42, cited in McSorley, *New Testament Basis of Peacemaking*, p. 74.

love thy neighbor as thyself. To him that strikes thee on the one cheek, turn also the other."[28]

Tertullian, 160–c. 225, the father of Latin theology, a proponent of the sufficiency of scripture as the source of Christian apologetics, and defender of the Church against Marcion, for example, asked, "If we are enjoined to love our enemies, whom have we to hate? If injured we are forbidden to retaliate. Who then can suffer injury at our hands?"[29] Tertullian, no less than the aforenoted Church fathers, stands against Christian engagement in military activity. Although he acknowledged in his *Apologeticus* of 197 ce that Christians were engaged in both government and the military, he rebuked the voluntary enlistment of Christians in the military in his *De Corona Militis* of 211 ce.[30] Tertullian's position on Christian participation in war and in the military is well demonstrated in the following excerpts.

> Shall it be lawful to make an occupation of the sword, when the Lord proclaims that he who uses the sword shall perish by the sword? And shall the son of peace take part in battle when it does not become him, even to sue at law? … The very act of transferring one's name from the camp of light to the camp of darkness is a transgression. Of course, the case is different, if the faith comes subsequently to any who are already occupied in military service, as with those whom John admitted to baptism, and with the most believing centurions Christ approves and whom Peter instructs: all the same, when faith has been accepted and sealed, either the service must be left at once, as has been done by many or else recourse must be and to all sorts of quibbling, so that nothing may be committed against God… Do leaves make up the laurel of triumph—or do corpses? Is it decorated with ribbons or tombs? Is it besmeared with ointments, or with the tears of wives and mothers—perhaps of some even who are Christians—for Christ is among the barbarians as well?[31]

---

28 "*Protrepticus*," X, cited in Bainton, *Christian Attitudes Toward War and Peace*, p. 77.

29 *Apologeticus*, XXXVII,

30 Bainton, *Christian Attitudes Toward War and Peace*, p. 68.

31 "On the Garland," 11, 2, cited in McSorley, *New Testament Basis of Peacemaking*, p. 78.

How shall a Christian wage war? Nay, how shall he even be a
soldier in peacetime without the sword which the Lord had taken
away?[32]

Cyprian, bishop of Carthage, writing in the mid-third century, in his
Letters and against the Donatists, emphasizes the dual standard and
hypocrisy of distinguishing the killing of people, "If murder is committed privately, it is a crime, but if it happens with state authority,
courage is the name for it."[33] The killing of another person, in whatever
form, from the time of Cain onward, could not be accepted in any
way according to the teachings of Jesus.

At the beginning of the fourth century, Lactantius in *Divinae Institutiones*, VI, 9 criticized Rome's so-called "just wars" which brought
only subjugation of the world known to Rome. He further criticized
killing, whether in military force or through capital punishment,
and wrote:

> It will not be lawful for a just man to serve as a soldier for justice
> itself is his military service, nor to accuse anyone of the capital
> office, because it makes no difference whether thou kill with the
> sword or with the word, since killing itself is forbidden. And so, in
> this commandment of God, no exception at all ought to be made
> to the rule that it is always wrong to kill a man whom God had
> wished to be regarded as a sacrosanct creature.[34]

McSorley reports that church orders from Egypt, in North Africa where
Augustine accepted Christian participation in war, read, "A catechumen
or believer who wishes to become a soldier shall be rejected because it
is far from God." (Statute 29.) Statute 28 is reported to forbid baptism
for catechumens entering military forces. "They shall not receive into
the Church one of the emperor's soldiers. If they have received him,

32 "On Idolatry," 19, cited in McSorley, *New Testament Basis of Peacemaking*, pa.78.

33 "Letters," 1, 6, and "*Ad Donatum*," VI, 10, cited in McSorley, *New
Testament Basis of Peacemaking*, pa.78.

34 "*Divinae Institutiones*,"VI, xx, 15-16, cited in McSorley, New Testament Basis of Peacemaking, p. 79 and in Bainton, *Christian Attitudes
Toward War and Peace*, p. 73.

he shall refuse to kill if commanded to do so. If he does not refrain he shall be rejected."[35]

Although Christians began to participate in the Roman legions from 170 ce, their numbers remained small initially, but began to grow in the latter part of the third century ce. Diocletian and Galerius, as well as other Roman leaders, attempted to purge Christians from their ranks. Their numbers could not have been significant, though, for leaders of neither the Roman legion nor the state would attempt to significantly weaken the strength of their military. Maximillian, a Christian conscript, refused induction into the Roman army of North Africa precisely because his Christian faith did not permit him to be a soldier; he was executed in 295 ce. McSorley relates the inscription that Pope Damasus placed on the graves of two Roman soldiers who abandoned their command with its blood-smeared swords in order to embrace rejoicing the triumphs of Christ.[36] Bainton directs our attention to the refusal of re-admittance to communion by second century Christians for penitents guilty of apostasy, adultery, or bloodshed, for whom military force in which killing was included is meant.[37]

Given the aforenoted statements by the early fathers of the Church, Bainton correctly observes, "Thus all of the outstanding writers of the East and West repudiated participation in warfare for Christians."[38] While the fathers proscribed engagement in military actions that focused on killing in war, they did not forbad police duty, even within the military, inclusive of protecting the emperor. Tertullian and others, for example, expressly recognized soldiers serving in provincial administration, fire fighting, custody of prisoners, protection of transport and the mails, etc. precisely because their duties did not encompass the killing of other individuals or engaging in armed conflict. (Bainton, 1985, 79)

The pacifism of the early Christian community and its leadership, especially, can be divided into three types, observes Bainton. The

---

35 McSorley, *New Testament Basis of Peacemaking*, p. 82. McSorley cites John Ferguson, *Politics of Love: The New Testament and Non-Violent Revolution* (Cambridge, UK: Jas. Clarke Publishers), p. 44.

36 McSorley, *New Testament Basis of Peacemaking*, p. 87.

37 Bainton, *Christian Attitudes Toward War and Peace*, p. 68.

38 Bainton, *Christian Attitudes Toward War and Peace*, p. 73.

first type is represented by Tertullian who claimed that its basis was legalistic and eschatological, namely that the law of Christ prohibited participation in the killing of military action. Therein, the Christian was prepared for whatever the outcome should foreigners invade the Empire. War was to have been considered as under a previous dispensation, necessary for preservation of the Jewish people, or to be understood spiritually. Christian love and Gnostic repugnance of the physical identified the second type. Marcion, in rejecting the violent and vindictive depiction of God in the Hebrew scriptures as shown in the exercise of the ban, the sending of the flood, the smiting of the Egyptians, etc. and the practice of violence therein as witnessed in Moses and Joshua, well represented this approach to pacifism. For Marcion, though, the Gnostic distaste for the physical body and the finality of this world, resulted in a rejection of the terrible baseness of worldly activity. Finally, pragmatic and redemptive pacifism of Christian leaders such as Origen opposed war and violence because it was inferior to a preferred way called for by the counsels of Jesus. Origen offered that Christians could live and actively engaged in society and its social structures without participating in the killing of war, particularly by showing and contributing to a more ideal and disciplined way of living, a higher ethical standard in contrast to that of the state. As such, the Church was both above and separate from the state while engaging society.[39]

What then characterizes the salient thinking and actions of the apostolic and patristic Church prior to Augustine? What were the principle tenets of the non-violent and pacifist leadership in the Church at this time?

- Ecclesial leaders opposed participation in the military primarily because the ultimate intent centered on killing another person, especially in warfare.
- Pacifism and non-violence were advocated not just by insignificant ecclesial leadership, but by the most renown fathers of the Church such as Justin, Cyprian, Clement, Iranaeus, Origin, Tertullian, Lactantius, etc.
- Because of the aforenoted, enlistment in the military contradicted one's baptismal promises. The teaching of Jesus was strictly inter-

---

39   See Bainton, *Christian Attitudes Toward War and Peace*, pp. 81-84.

preted to mean never killing anyone and the early Church, being closest in time, culture, and history to the historical Jesus and his immediate disciples, certainly had a greater appreciation for the basic tenets of Jesus than later Christian baptized.

• With a handful of possible exceptions, no evidence exists that demonstrates that Christian engaged in military activity prior to around 170 ce. Thereafter, numbers began to increase, particularly from the latter part of the third century ce, but are not thought to be significant given the various purges of Christians from the ranks.

• The eastern part of the Roman Empire witnessed the strongest pacifism while at the same time occasioning the earliest involvement of Christians in the military and warfare.

• From the end of the second century ce and thereafter, Christians are known to have been soldiers, acknowledged by ecclesial leaders, but engaged in non-violent activities associated with civil administration and police duties. Many cases exist of Christians refusing enlistment, conscription, and induction into the military and on not too few occasions did baptized soldiers simply abandon their posts because of their unwillingness to participate in the violence of military activity.

• The pacifism of the early Church was not a matter of political expediency of a growing minority, but arose from their understanding of the Jesus' teaching of love; nor did Christians practice pacifism and non-violence because of their early perception of an approximating eschaton.

• The Christian practice of pacifism and non-violence did not exclude active involvement in other civic duties and functions, but in reaction to gradual Christian sanctioning of military warfare and its incumbent violence, many Christians emphasized withdrawal and monastic type of life. If killing was part of state function, Christians neither could participate nor condone such, were willing to accept whatever violence resulted from their refusal to defend themselves, and witnessed this by never revolting even under lethal persecution. They clearly represented a contrast society.

• Depending on region and period, Christians who participated in military activity, especially warfare, were forbidden to be re-received into the Christian community or Eucharist, but at other times and regions were accepted there and buried in the Church, even though they may have been a part of the three principal prohibitions of adultery, idolatry, and blood(shed).

Gradual Change in Christian Practice of Non-Violence in the Late Patristic Period

What then prompted and encouraged change in the mentality of Christians regarding the practice of war and killing other individuals? Was it merely the gradual acceptance of Christianity by the Roman State and gradual appearance of baptized Christians in the leadership of that state that resulted in a change of attitude on both the Christians and the State, resulting in a realization by the political leadership that their bankrupt theological system of religion was not threatened by Christians who had little problem with the political apparatus while not recognizing divinity of Caesars and the Augustus and their gods? Or, was it the co-opting and accommodation by the Christians into accepting the mores and practices of the state as they became the leaders and bearers of political governance? With the gradual termination of persecution of Christians after Diocletian (who followed in the footsteps of Maximinus Thrax and Decius), the ascendancy of Constantine after the Christian persecution by Galerius, with Constantine's acceptance of Christianity, and with the expectation that unity within Christianity was needed for a strong Roman government, Christians appeared not just at municipal and regional leadership but at the highest levels of the military and the Roman state.[40] Constantine entitled himself "Victor," a title used by the "pagans" for their gods and by the Christians for their martyrs, but, as Bainton notes, this designation "was assumed by the Christian emperor on the ground that what the martyrs had commenced with their blood, he had completed with his sword."[41] What twisted irony!

Nearly one century before Constantine, though, Christians in the eastern part of the Roman Empire embraced and entered the military,

---

40   Richard E. Rubenstein, *When Jesus Became God: The Epic Fight over Christ's Divinity in the Last Days of Rome* (New York: Harcourt Brace & Company, 1999), pp. 194 - 202. Clearly, Christians were engaged in the military well before Constantine. Rubenstein relates how in 363 Valentinian, a Pannonian general in the Roman army and a Nicene Christian became the emperor and appointed his brother, Valens, Augustus of the East.

41   Bainton, *Christian Attitudes Toward War and Peace*, p. 86. One should not forget that Constantine was only baptized at his deathbed.

as in Melitene in present day Armenia, and the king of Edessa in Syria, for example, made Christianity the religion of that state. In reaction to the Church of Syria sanctioning military warfare, Christians reacted with ascetical zeal and removed themselves from society to undertake monastic practice. In Mesopotamia, it is reported that a garrison of Christian soldiers threw off their command and withdrew from the military. Despite the acceptance of warfare and Church-sanctioned military actions, Hellenist Christians were the strongest opponents of war and military action.

Certainly, Christians, although espousing peace, were not devoid of violent and atrocious acts, even amongst their leaders in the patristic period. Athanasius, bishop of Alexandria from 328 ce, engaged in hostile and violent activity in the dispute over the divinity and humanity in the nature and person of Jesus, a dispute with Arius and his followers. Athanasius was accused and seemed to have supported violent attacks on the Arians. Christians, unable to unite the empire spiritually and ideally as sought by Constantine, became notorious for their internecine and brutal fighting and mutual hatred arising from theological disputes.[42] Damasus, a violent Nicene creed supporter, was elected bishop of Rome and pontiff under violent circumstances in which more than 160 men and women were killed in a basilica

---

42   Rubenstein, *When Jesus Became God*, p. 194. Rubenstein cites the historian Ammianus with regard to the deadly hatred amongst Christians. Athanasius ordered, according to the Melitians' false accusation, "one of his principal supporters, a bishop in upper Egypt," to burn down the house of Arsenius, the Arian bishop of Hypsele and murder its occupant; Athanasius also, according to the Melitians, beaten an Arian priest, Ischyras and destroyed the property of his church. Although Ischyras later recanted, probably under duress, he later recanted his recantation. (Pp. 121-122.)

While Constantine had hoped that Christianity would facilitate unity within the empire, it proved the opposite and effectively failed to help the empire defend itself from outward attack. (Pa. 194.)

Constantine cannot be considered any sort of respectable model of Christian convert. He not only executed his son Crispus but is rumored to have killed his second wife, Fausta, if she did not commit suicide; moreover, one son, Constans, killed in fratricidal warfare his older brother, Constantine II.

in the struggle with Arian opponents. Such had become the way of Christians—by their acts you shall know them!

The appearance of Constantine poses several dilemmas and problems for understanding the accommodation made by the Church to leadership of the Roman Empire in the changing status of the Church within the Empire. The father of Constantine, Constantius, who was one of the four tetrarchs actually ruling the Empire through military force, was known to have disregarded the imperial decrees in their punitive treatment of Christians and their property. Constantine followed in his father's footsteps both with regard to becoming one of the tetrarchs and in his treatment of Christians, and actually went much further in having Church bishops in his inner circle of counselors. No wonder, after centuries of intermittent and active lethal persecution of Christians, Constantine with his protection of Christians and his manipulation of Christians to their favor was heralded as the Lord's Annointed because he discomfited the attackers of Christians and the Church. According to Eusebius of Caesarea, a Church historian who wrote a laudatory biography of Constantine ("Oration on Constantine") at the end of Constantine's reign along the line of thinking of Melito and the Asian bishops of the second century, Constantine was the tool that God (the Logos) used to bring Christendom from the jaws of persecution and overthrow the "heathen" gods of the emperors of Rome; Eusebius portrayed him as a model ruler and redeemer, one for whom there could now be one faith, one lord, one baptism, one empire, and one emperor.[43] Eusebius' historical treatment of Constantine can lend no better explanation to the Logos working through Constantine for the benefit of Christians than that the petty fighting between pagan deities, that resulted in bloodied borders being redrawn in order to keep militant gods happy, was the result of polytheism, the remedy of which lay in monotheism and world monarchy that Constantine brought with defeat of remaining rival tetrarchs under his unified Roman Empire.[44] With this ideological thinking, the Roman

---

43   Peter Iver Kaufman, *Redeeming Politics* (Princeton, NJ: Princeton University Press, 1990), p. 13.

44   Kaufman, *Redeeming Politics.*, p. 22. Kaufman adds: "though enormously successful in war, Eusebius's Constantine was always more impatient to sign a truce than to conquer or re-conquer territories.... Eusebius

Empire and Christianity were conjoined for happy historical development of pacification of the known Western world, the promotion of
proclaiming the gospel without persecution, the fortuitous realization
of peace as interpreted both by the Roman state and by the Church
in the form of Pax Romana. Nevertheless, despite the very favorable
treatment of Constantine by Eusebius that has swayed Christian
tradition and changed the thinking of Christians on association with
governing through military force, Constantine was a clever general
and politician, though admittedly reported to be more humane in his
military treatment of defeated foes than his peers. With the reign of
Constantine, the state in the Roman Empire began to be viewed no
longer as a persecuting adversary, but more as a ruling and dominant
partner with Christians in governing the church and maintaining
social order under an acceptable god. The influence of Eusebius, upon
(a) the viewing of the Roman emperor as a crusader larger than life,
(b) the relationship between the Church and the state that became
symbiotic after 381, and (c) the zealous acceptance of the leadership
of Constantine as the instrument for bringing the reign of the Logos
over the pagan gods and unification of the empire, induced enormous
change in Christian thinking about the function of and participation
in the role of the state, inclusive of waging inter-group lethal war, and
accommodation towards accepting the status quo.[45]

---

was willing to transfer the emperor's instincts for reconciliation to the
empire's chancery (for edicts and official correspondence owned that it
was unwise to battle superstition with violence)." (Pa. 23.)

45 See Kaufman, *Redeeming Politics*, pp. 13-29, for a more detailed analysis of the influence of Eusebius' thinking upon the Church in his biography of Constantine. He further expounds on the role and influence of
Orosius, a Christian apologist, who explained the invasion of Italy and
the sacking of Rome as another opportunity for God to rescue the empire
and its new religion and conversely the opportunity for the invaders to
be conquered and redeemed by the empire's new religion. " ... God had
ordained the empire as his special instrument for the world's redemption
and conquest." (p. 31) Kaufman underscores the influence of Orosius,
which in the fifth century expanded upon the thinking of Eusebius, with
regards to God's sanctioning the conquests of Augustus by the granting
of a sign—the incarnation of the Logos enrolled in the census of Caesar

Richard Rubenstein concludes that Christian thinking toward war and inter-group lethal physical violence changed as Christians assumed political and military leadership within the Roman Empire.[46] In order to assure unity and provide a spiritual foundation and *raison d'etre* to the Roman Empire in the face of the increasingly perceived decadent pagan religion, Constantine used Christianity to his political advantage. However, with the theological disputes amongst leading Christian bishops (particularly Athanasius, later the Cappadocians and the Arian controversy), religious discord threatened the tool of political unity and rationale, something that Constantine attempted to overcome through his Episcopal advisor, Hosius. Once Christianity became a politically manipulative issue, political and military forces of the Empire used to their benefit one faction or another within Christianity and the same respective Christian sects correspondingly exploited politics and military force for their own advantage. Clearly, with Constantius, Valentinian, Valens, etc., the bishops of the Church were no longer merely elected by their worshiping communities, as in apostolic times, but were selected or readily dismissed under the influence, if not direction, from emperors of either the west or east. Thus, the leadership of the Church was intimately connected with the politics of the state.

Not only the ordinary faithful and baptized were acting differently from the Church of the apostolic period and next two centuries, but the leadership as well. Even Ambrose, bishop of Milan and a theological doctor of the Church, is accused of not just tolerating, but also promoting physical violence. When a mob led by Christian monks burned a Jewish synagogue and a chapel used by heretical Valentin-

Augustus, and later reconfirmed in the actions of Constantine as the admirable deputy of God, like Caesar Augustus.

46   Rubenstein indicates (a) that within little more than one decade Christianity was transformed from a persecuted sect effectively into the religion of the imperial family and (b) that Constantine not only granted special favor and status to Christians, partially in justifiable retribution for their persecution but proclaimed that Christian priests were to have special privileged treatment similar to that afforded the priests of the Roman religion in order to make Christianity the unifying force in the face of a decadent and dying old religion of the Roman state. Rubenstein, *When Jesus Became God*, pp. 45-46.

ians in Mesopotamia, Emperor Theodosius ordered the perpetrating Christians disciplined. Ambrose countered and threatened the emperor with excommunication unless he rescinded his order. Thereupon, Theodosius retracted the order.[47] With Theodosius' imperial ban of Arianism in 380 and his official declaration that Christianity (non-Arian, that is) was the sole religion of the state in 381, waves of religious violence, assassinations, and harassment ensued as Christians attempted to impose the new religion on outsiders. Theodosius II went further when he restricted induction into the Roman military to Christians. By the late fourth century, bishops and clerics (presbyters and deacons) undertook symbiotic rule over both civil and ecclesial functions to the extent that, though unarmed, they often incited and led their militaries in battle until lay participation was sanction while clerical involvement was censured.

EXOGENOUS FACTORS INFLUENCING AUGUSTINE & FIFTH-CENTURY CHRISTIANS ON WAR

By the late fourth and early fifth century, a noteworthy change arose within Christian thinking of bishops and other ecclesial leaders in regards to the treatment of war and institutionalized inter-group lethal physical violence. What prompted a further change in Church thinking toward complicity with, if not outright acceptance of, war and violence? In addition to the social changes occurring within the Church as part of the Roman state, in effect a co-opting and accommodation by the Church toward the state and the increasing consciousness toward governance with inter-group lethal force, the threat of forces from outside the Empire (the Goths, Visigoths, Franks, Vandals, etc. and the threat of non-European Huns),[48] intermittent invasions by the Goths, and the actual sacking of Rome in 410 certainly influenced

---

47   Rubenstein, *When Jesus Became God*, p. 225.

48   Rubenstein notes that Bishop Ambrose of Milan interpreted the absolutely devastating defeat of Emperor Valens of the East (an Arian supporter) and his formidable army at Hadrianapolis by the Visigoths (many of whom were Arian) who were grossly abused by Valens as justification by God that the Arians were heretics and that the western Emperor and Rome, being Nicene supporters, were rewarded for their orthodoxy. (Pa. 218.)

Church leaders such as Augustine.[49] Ambrose, under whom Augustine studied, was pretorian prefect of northern Italy for many years before being forced to become bishop of Milan, had no troubles with accepting military involvement by Christians in war conducted justly and thereby influenced Augustine. Ambrose interpreted just war from not only the standpoint of a civil servant, but also in view of Roman authorities fighting Arian-faith "barbarians" and with the model of Moses undertaking violent wars for the benefit of the chosen people. Ambrose considered pacifism to be a matter for private individuals and clerics who were called to a higher ideal. Ambrose further cemented the practice of Christian non-violence and pacifism to those seeking spiritual pursuits, while accepting the enactment of warfare to those pursuing justice.

Augustine, while accepting Mt. 5:38-48 and denying even self-defense, theologically contorted this text to permit violent and lethal military activity on behalf of an innocent third party, the just war theory that has perverted the meaning of Jesus' teaching. This interpretation, however, runs diametrically counter to the very example set in Jesus' own life. Hays captures this essence, "He (Jesus) does not seek to defend the interests of the poor and oppressed in Palestine by organizing armed resistance against the Romans or against the privileged Jewish collaborators with Roman authority. Rather his activity consists of healing and proclamation. He preaches love and submits to being persecuted and killed."[50]

Paulus Orosius, for example, a Christian apologist driven from Spain to North Africa, where Augustine was working, by the invasions of northern and eastern "barbarians," particularly the Vandals, into the western Roman Empire, re-interpreted the role of Constantine and the newly Christianized empire of Rome and Constantinople. Orosius assisted Augustine in defending Christianity against the onslaught of pagan criticism that the new Christian God was responsible for Rome's demise and Constantine's diminishment of Rome's gods. By then, Christianity had become so intertwined with the Roman state

---

49 Arne Rasmusson, *The Church as Polis: From Political Theology to Theological Politics as Exemplified by Jürgen Moltmann and Stanley Hauerwas*, pp. 232.

50 Hays, *The Moral Vision of the New Testament*, p. 324.

that the defense of the empire against these invasions was interpreted as Christianity's first military activity and synonymous with its first Crusade. Even beginning with Constantine, the Roman emperors frequently interfered and intervened in the governance of the Church through the appointment or dis-appointment of bishops, calling of Church councils, using the Christian God for the benefit of state affairs, etc. Relying on this background, Orosius praised Constantine for his gentleness, his considerate character, and his even-handedness with regard to defeated foes. He further stressed that many of the invading tribes had cast aside their weapons for ploughs and accepted the new Christian religion themselves. The attacks by the invading "barbarians" not just upon the empire but also against Christianity could not be explained simply by religious rationalization about persecution as punishment for sin, analogous to that of the prophets in the Hebrew Bible; thus, Orosius explained them as part of God's redeeming plan to bring new converts into Christian truths. It can be fairly said that the Christian religion became, not just the state religion, but an attribute and justifying ideology of the state itself. The defense of the Roman empire became a defense of Christianity too, a new approach contrary to that of a persecuted minority of the third century.[51]

AUGUSTINE'S DEVELOPMENT OF
JUST WAR RATIONALE IN THE CITY OF GOD

Augustine sought in his *City of God* (Book IV, especially chapter 15 and Book XIX, chapter 13 with regard to his treatment of peace), partially a Christian apologetic validating the role of Christianity as the religion of the state, to defend the actions of the Roman Empire and the defense of Christianity as the only true religion.[52] Augustine

---

51   Kaufman, *Redeeming Politics*, see pp. 29-34.

52   Augustine, "The City of God," translated from *De Civitate Dei* by Marcus Dods in Robert Maynard Hutchins, ed., *Augustine, Great Books of the Western World*, vol. 18 (Chicago: Encyclopaedia Britannica, Inc., 1952), pp. 196-197. Augustine began this work in 413 and completed it serially over the next 13 years. In 426, the Vandals, after conquering Spain, invaded North Africa, where Augustine was bishop of Hippo since 395, in order to fight the forces of the Roman Empire on the side of forces engaged in civil war with the Romans. It is no coincidence that the Van-

demonstrates that the long duration of the Roman Empire was accept-able to Christianity and that, based on the power of the Christian God, earthly kingdoms and empires are founded and maintained. Influenced by both his North African heritage and his Roman citizenship, by his classical upbringing, by the fundamental teaching of the Sermon on the Mount, by the persecution of a Church oppressed by sinful men, by his cohabitational relationship, and by the oversight of his fretting mother, Augustine saw life from many sides, but eventually acquiesced to the interpretation of the teachings of Jesus and that they were to be held as ideals whose realization would not be seen in this world until one is released from this corruptible body (his influence from the Manichees), although one should see to enact the ideals, impossible though it may be. Bainton infers that Augustine attempted to unify these opposing influences in regard to the issue of waging just war and lethal violence by relegating the traditional Christian teaching of love and practice of pacifism, non-resistance and non-violence to the interior disposition and character of a person while rationalizing that killing and warfare are necessary acts of benevolent severity to assure order and justice (the vindication of injustice).[53] He allotted the taking of life to proper authorities, not to their Christian subjects.

---

dals were in the process of defeating the Roman legions of North Africa, who sought refuge, were surrounded and under siege at Hippo, the center of North Africa's Christian community for whom Augustine as ruling bishop had been both civil and ecclesial adjudicator.

53   Bainton, *Christian Attitudes Toward War and Peace*, p. 97, quotes Augus-tine from various Augustinian works: "If it is supposed that God could not enjoin warfare because in after times it was said by the Lord Jesus Christ, 'I say unto you, Resist not evil ... ,' the answer is that what is here required is not a bodily action but an inward disposition.... Moses in putting to death sinners was moved not by cruelty but by love. So also was Paul when he committed the offender to Satan for the destruction of his flesh. (Cf. *Contra Faustum*, XXII, 76 and 79.) Love does not preclude a benevolent severity (*Epistolae*, 138, ii, 14), nor the correct which com-passion itself dictates. No one indeed is fit to inflict punishment save the one who has first overcome hate in his heart. The love of enemies admits of no dispensation (Sermons, I, xx, 63 and 70), but love does not exclude wars of mercy waged by the good (*Epistolae*, 138,88, 15)."

What motivated Augustine in the *City of God* and other works to counter the thinking of the respected fathers of the Church, whom he read and knew well? Augustine was worried about the backlash on Christianity when Rome fell in 410 to Alaric and the Goths. In brief, this fundamental change in Christian thinking, solidified by Augustine, perverted Christianity thereafter, even today, for the following reasons. Once Christians, inclusive of faithful believers and clerical leaders, were no longer only in a position of being ordinary citizens of the state or members of the Roman Empire, whether persecuted or accepted, they and their religion became identified with the state. The state, created by God as a good but not always acting justly, became symbiotic with the religion, as the sole rationale and reason for undergirding the tenets for rule of law and of god and the preservation of the well-being of community and the state; the religion became the state in as much the elite leadership of both the state and the clerical and theological thinking assumed an identity no longer as a persecuted minority but as the basis for fundamental values and belief system for governing the state. This latter perspective was further augmented with the internal and external attacks upon the Roman Empire by dissident practitioners of traditional Roman religion and its followers of those gods and by invading tribes and ethnic groups, respectively. For Augustine, despite the lust, the cruelty, the abominations, the bloodshed, and the robbery committed by Rome in wars on others, Rome and the Roman Empire since Constantine acted differently to make its actions justifiable and should be treated with a changed heart precisely because the leadership was now Christian, its religion Christian, and it sought to protect, not persecute, Christians in the face of invading pagans who did not share the newly adopted faith of Rome and whose customs, ways, and culture were alien to those adopted over several centuries in the Roman Empire.

In summary, the apostolic communities of Jesus' followers and the following century unquestionably adopted a position contrary to armed struggle, war, and lethal violence specifically because they were contrary to the basic teachings of Jesus. They maintained the proscription of military participation because Jesus taught that killing another person physically or even metaphorically was evil; the fact that involvement in the Roman Legion entailed at least indirect acknowledgement that the Caesar or the emperor was god was only a secondary reason preventing military involvement. Beginning around 170 ce, though, some Christians joined the Roman Legions, according to reliable, ancient records, but their numbers were never even a significant minority. Nevertheless, the leading fathers of the Church persisted until Ambrose and Augustine that participation in the profession of the military, namely killing, was sinful and contrary to essential Church teaching. No exception can be found to counter the statements of the fathers of the Church, until Augustine wrote his *City of God*. Both the apostolic and patristic communities took the teachings of Jesus very seriously and never complicated the guidance of Jesus with the demands of the state. With the acceptance of Christianity by Galerius in the Roman Empire in 311 ce, the assumption of uncontested leadership as the emperor by Constantine who clearly favored and used Christianity for the advantage of the empire after 312 ce, and the declaration of Christianity as the sole religion of the state by Theodosius in 381 ce, Christianity gradually became symbiotic with the Roman state. Thus, when the Roman Empire and Rome directly came under siege from non-Christian ethnic groups, with the political and military leaders of the Empire being Christian, warfare became an implicitly accepted method of rationalizing the Empire's defense. Regretfully, even prior to that period, Christians had lost their innocence and had often engaged in lethal attacks on one another in thrashing out their theological differences. Augustine, in his *City of God* written in 411, provided the validating rationale for Christians to embark on a totally new and different approach to conflict resolution that has perverted the essential teachings of Jesus even till today.

CHAPTER 5

THE MORALITY OF WAR & INTER-GROUP LETHAL CONFLICT-RESOLUTION:
RECENT CHRISTIAN PERSPECTIVES REGARDING THE PROBLEM OF JUST WAR RATIONALE

Not only the attacks by the Christianized Roman legions on the invaders of the Roman Empire in the late fourth and early fifth centuries, but also the Crusades against the Moslem occupation of Jerusalem posed a clear contrast to the position on war of the early Church; the conduct of clerical leaders sanctioning lethal violence in the aforenoted situations represented a morally reprehensible precedent in Christian history that has oft been copied to present day society. Joseph Allen has helped to evaluate the role of the Crusades and crusader mentality in the moral perspective of war. Christians historically, according to Allen, in discriminating their moral judgment of war have supported or led their country's wars as crusades of good against satanic-type evil, have lived as pacifists as was elaborated above, or have followed just-war tradition.

With regard to the crusader mentality, Allen notes four key features, that characterize the convictions and logic of crusaders, and indicates four critical problems associated with this approach to war. The crusader mentality has the following characteristics or variations thereof.

1. *Crusaders see a justifiable war as a conflict between forces of good and forces of evil* ...
2. *Crusaders characteristically pursue absolute and unlimited goals* ....
3. *When warfare is seen as the struggle of forces of good against evil for unlimited, absolute goals, the means of war are unrestrained* ....
4. *In the twentieth century a crusade approach tends to promote total war.*[1]

---

1 Joseph L. Allen, *War: A Primer for Christians* (Dallas: Southern Methodist University Press, 2001), pp. 9-12. Italics are Allen's.

Not unlike the Israelites of the Hebrew scriptures fighting for homeland against the Canaanites and Assyrians or the Crusades supported
by Urban II at the end of the eleventh century against the Moslems,
crusaders self-righteously identify themselves and their violent actions
with the forces of good in pursuit of absolute and unlimited goals,
be they political or couched in religious terminology, against forces
of opposing groups equated with evil. As such, the means of war are
unrestrained and its leaders throw all their resources against an enemy
characterized as vile and demonic in order to make war in contemporary times against an entire people, be they anyone defined as terrorists or the unknown "they." This mentality, as defined by Allen,
is not restricted to Christians, but may be utilized by any religion or
denomination and, in fact, by non-religious practitioners. One can
hardly help but notice the close similarity of these characteristics with
both Bush administrations in their two wars with Iraq.

Allen identifies four core problems of the crusader mentality, not just
the issue of its fallacious or mistaken religious interpretation associated
with waging war, but emphasizes its shortcomings in terms of myopic
and simplistic understanding of the world and its non-self-reflective
belief that the crusader's answers to others' problems can resolve perceived threats to one's own peace.

> 1. *Its* (the crusade approach's) *views imply an inadequate understand-
> ing of God* ....
> 2. ... *it is morally simplistic* ...
> 3. *Crusaders' absolute goals seem to presume that a crusade might bring
> about perfect conditions in the world* .... Finally, *a crusade approach
> is indiscriminate about the enemy people.*[2]

With regard to the Code of Canon Law in the Catholic Church, one
would assume that it would treat the issue and participants in lethal
war with some perspicacity and reasoned depth. Unfortunately, the
Code deals only in one brief canon with homicide from the perspective of physical violation of human life, integrity, and freedom, and
with the issue of abortion; it spends more reflection on issues related
to sexual morality than on the issue of violent human interaction as

---

2 Allen, *War*, pp. 13-15. Italics are Allen's.

related to war and lethal violence.[3] While war is usually enacted by secular governments, Christians and Catholics in the twentieth century have been involved in most wars and, therefore, it seems only logical that the Church would attempt to legislate on aspects related to Christians participating in this activity. The silence of the Code in this matter speaks volumes in raising questions about the complicity of the Church in not leading the faithful to moral practices so central to the early Christian communities.

THE MORALITY OF JUST WAR

Augustine labored particularly in the *City of God* to provide the rationale approving the use of lethal violence by the state with Christian soldiers as instruments and Christian leadership directing, and based his reasoning on Rom.13:1-7.[4] He failed to identify the specific causes that could be considered just for waging war. Contrary to views of the early Christians who, under the ideology and religion of the Roman Empire, were led to consider the emperor as a god and, therefore, were left suspicious about serving directly to the state apparatus, Augustine, with Christians now being the leaders of both the political and military systems of the Empire, found this statement of Paul convenient. Further, based on Paul's premise, Augustine reiterated the thinking that the authority of the state and its instruments came from God, a type of divine-right thinking. He also believed that a just war is preferable to an unjust peace and maintained that the use of force is necessary—though always regrettable—in a fallen world in order to

3 John P. Beal, James A. Coriden, Thomas J. Green (eds.), *New Commentary on the Code of Canon Law* (New York: Paulist Press, 2000), pp. 1601-1602.

4 Rom. 13:1-7: "Let every person be subordinate to the higher authorities, for there is no authority except from God, and those that exist have been established by God. Therefore, whoever resists authority opposes what God has appointed, and those who oppose it will bring judgment upon themselves. For rulers are not a cause of ear to good conduct, but to evil.... Then do what is good and you will receive approval from it, for it is a servant of God for your good. But if you do evil, be afraid, for it does not bear the sword without purpose; it is the servant of God to inflict wrath on the evildoer. Therefore, it is necessary to be subject not only because of the wrath but also because of conscience... ."

vanquish evil, but that its ultimate goal must be to restore peace.[5] In his attack on the Manichees, Augustine argues that "properly understood, Jesus' teachings did not in all cases call for literal obedience." Thus, in Mt. 5:39 regarding turning the other cheek, this does not require bodily action, but inward disposition. Augustine argues that one can kill only when ordered by God or by legitimate authority of the state. Anyone who obeys such, does not kill but only acts as an instrument of the legal authority.[6]

John Langan, SJ, has outlined eight key elements of Augustine's just war theory as outlined here below:

1. A punitive conception of war.
2. Assessment of the evil of war in terms of the moral evil of attitudes and desires.
3. A search for authorization to use violence.
4. A dualistic epistemology that gives priority to spiritual goods.
5. An interpretation of evangelical norms in terms of inner attitudes.
6. A passive attitude towards authority and social change.
7. The use of scriptural texts to legitimate participation in war
8. An analogical concept of peace[7]

It behooves the reader to be conscious of the duality that Augustine reinforces in the distinction between physical, exterior acts of lethal violence in contrast to the spiritual, inner peace of one's relationship with God, anything but a holistic approach. Moreover, as noted above with regard to the premise that all legal and civil authority derive from divine authority and in light of the preference for inner, spiritual goods, Augustine naturally and possibly unquestionably accepts the authority and directives of the state while concerning himself with spiritual interests. Finally, given the exegesis and scriptural analysis hereabove, Augustine's conclusions with regard to war and lethal violence can be none other than mistaken because the teachings of Jesus

---

5 Augustine, *City of God*, Book XIX, Chapt. 7, p. 515.

6 See Robert L. Holmes, "A Time for War?," *Christianity Today*, Sept. 21, 2001.

7 John Langan, SJ, "The Elements of St. Augustine's Just War Theory," *Journal of Religious Ethics*, 12.1, Spring 1984.

do not legitimate such. Interestingly, Augustine with candor seems to equate wrong-doing as the cause of war to those actions undertaken by the opposing party, meaning the party other than the state that is Christian and doing good. Thus, Augustine can be interpreted to acquit the Roman Empire in its governance and place blame on the invading Vandals, Goths, etc.[8] "My country, always right!" Augustine justifies war itself from the standpoint that he considers the objective of all wars to be nothing other than peace, that is the type of peace desired by the warring country. "For every man seeks peace by waging war, but no man seeks war by making peace."[9]

NATURAL-LAW BASIS OF JUST WAR THINKING & JESUS' TEACHING ON WAR

If just war theory draws on natural-law tradition, one must ask whether the natural law trumps the teachings of Jesus. The natural law is central to Catholic moral theology and is a kind of reasoning that faith informs, but capable of understanding and formulation by people of any or no faith, that it is based on human experience, and that the Church can apply always, everywhere, and for everyone. "To live according to the law given in nature is to live according to what reason commands…. (T)he 'order of reason,' focused on the human capacity to discover in experience what befits human well-being."[10] According to Thomas Aquinas, though, the natural law is a means of returning to God through participation in "eternal law" by way of

8 Augustine, *City of God*, Book XIX, Chapt. 7, p. 515: "But the imperial city (meaning Rome) has endeavoured to impose on subject nations not only her yoke, but her language, as a bond of peace, so that interpreters, far from being scarce, are numberless. This is true; but how many great wars, how much slaughter and bloodshed, have provided this unity! … hostile nations beyond the empire, against whom wars have been and are waged, yet, supposing there were no such nations, the very extent of the empire itself has produced wars of a more obnoxious description—social and civil wars …."

9 See Augustine, *City of God,*, Chapt. 12, pa.517.

10 Richard M. Gula, SS *Reason Informed by Faith: Foundations of Catholic Morality* (New York: Paulist Press, 1989), p. 222-223.

reasoning.[11] For Aquinas, both natural and human law, which can only pertain to the external and manifest, must flow into the eternal law and divine laws which help direct the interior of men, but the eternal and divine laws can only be known by men imperfectly because of human limitations. The eternal law as the point of reference posits that the ultimate norm of morality becomes what God requires, namely authentic human experience. For Aquinas the initial inclination on which the ultimate norm of natural law is based rests on preserving and protecting human life. While life is precious, whether one recognizes the natural law or not, this inclination and the ultimate norm of morality are in direct contradiction to the teaching of Jesus reviewed above on the Christian scriptures.

We must raise the following questions. Has Jesus' teaching been misinterpreted with regard to non-violence? Is Jesus' teaching exceptional with respect to the natural law? Did Jesus really mean turn the other cheek and give your life up for another? Has the natural law theory overlooked the teaching of Jesus because the theory as applied by Aristotle, Gaius, Cicero, and Aquinas is philosophically based on

---

11 Thomas Aquinas, "Summa Theologica" (I-II, qq. 90-97), in Robert Maynard Hutchins, ed., *Great Books of the Western World* (Chicago: Encyclopaedia Britannica, Inc., 1975), vol. 20, pp. 205-239. Gula, *Reason Informed by Faith*, p. 225, notes, as the basis of the natural law and the related natural inclination which seemingly contradicts the aforenoted teachings of Jesus on non-violence, that "specific norms of natural law (are) based on natural inclinations. The origin of our specific moral obligations lies in these natural inclinations which give content to the fundamental requirements to do good and avoid evil.... The first inclination to the good is common to all created reality. It is the tendency to persevere in being. Preserving and protecting life as a basic value belongs to the natural law on the basis of this inclination." This inclination, Aquinas reasoned, provides the basis for self-defense, contrary to the thinking of Augustine who recognized that lethally violent defense was permitted on behalf of others, but not oneself. (The second inclination, arising from the *jus naturale* developed by Ulpian, deals with the things in humans in common with animals, i.e., largely related to sexual activity and raising of offspring.) The third inclination pertains to the tendency toward truth and cooperating with one another in human existence, inclusive of matters related to justice. (II-II, q. 64; p. 222).

the philosophy of *jus gentium*?[12] If the non-violence spoken by Jesus is Jesus' real intent, it certainly goes against common sense, and, thus, is seemingly irrational, namely counter to reasoning and the inclinations suggested by Aquinas. If such is the case, then the practice of the teaching of Jesus with regard to non-violence really makes the Christian community a counter-culture or contrast society which is both foolish (as raised by Paul) and a threat to the establishment if implemented in political cultures. We need to be conscious, as Russell B. Connors and Patrick T. McCormick have indicated, of the shortcomings of the natural law morality, particularly with respect to detailed application. Everyone can accept the natural law morality of doing good and avoiding evil. "But when it comes to much more detailed questions (questions which engage our 'practical reason', the natural law may not be the same for all, and on such specific questions it may not be able to be recognized or known by all."[13]

Aquinas in Summa Theologica, II of II, Q. 40, Art. 1, lays out his understanding of the issue of war. With regard to the treatment of war and also law, Aquinas relies heavily, if not almost exclusively, on the thinking of Augustine. As such, for Aquinas, it is justifiable to wage war and does not contradict the divine precept, is not contrary to an

---

12   With the influence of Gaius, derived from Aristotle, on the distinction between *jus civile* and *jus gentium,* (civil rights as related within a legally autonomous society and rights, and laws regulating the relationship between autonomous territories, respectively), in contradistinction to Ulpian's development of *jus naturale* related to commonality between human and animal in nature, the centrality of reasoning dominates over base animal nature and its characteristics. It is largely the *jus gentium* and to a lesser extent the jus civile that we deal with herein. For the second inclination based on an Ulpian-style *jus naturale* as it relates to self-defense, see Augustine's *City of God*, Book XIX, Chapter 12.

Marcus Tullius Cicero, in his "On Duties," noted that war was a last resort and that no war could be just unless it sought to recover goods, repel aggression, honor agreements with allies, etc., but prior to initiation, one had to demand satisfactory retribution, warn the other party, and formally declare war.

13   Russell B. Connors, Jr. and Patrick T. McCormick, *Character, Choices & Community: The Three Faces of Christian Ethics* (New York: Paulist Press, 1998), p. 179.

act of virtue, i.e. peace, and is not a sin. Aquinas reasons based on a sermon delivered by Augustine:

> Augustine says ...: "If the Christian Religion forbade war altogether, those who sought salutary advice in the Gospel would rather have been counseled to cast aside their arms, and to give up soldiering altogether. On the contrary, they were told" 'Do violence to no man; ... and be content with your pay' (Luke 3.14). If he commanded them to be content with their pay, he did not forbid soldiering."[14]

One must not overlook the difficulty of Augustine in accepting war and violence. While soldiering is not forbidden or discouraged directly, the crux for Augustine lies in the act of justifying killing. Aquinas continues his argument, based on Augustine's acceptance of just war, that three conditions precedent must be met for war to be necessary.

> First, the authority of the sovereign by whose command the war is to be waged.... Secondly, a just cause is required, namely that those who are attacked should be attacked because they deserve it on account of some fault. Therefore Augustine says (Q. X, *super Jos.*): 'A just war is usually described as one that avenges wrongs, when a nation or state has to be punished, for refusing to make amends for the wrongs inflicted by its subjects, or to restore what it has seized unjustly.' ... Thirdly, it is necessary that the belligerents should have a right intention, so that they intend the advancement of good, or the avoidance of evil. Hence Augustine says (*De Verb. Dom.*): 'True religion does not look upon as sinful those wars that are waged not for motives of aggrandizement, or cruelty, but with the object of securing peace, of punishing evil-doers, and of uplifting the good.' For it may happen that the war is declared by the legitimate authority, and for a just cause, and yet be rendered unlawful through a wicked intention.[15]

Aquinas then rationalizes the execution of killing in soldiering because the soldier is merely following the commands of authority, whose authority Aquinas infers has been conferred by God for the orderly administration of society, and because, as such, the soldier is acting

---

14 Augustine, "*Epistolum ad Marcel,*" CXXXVIII, chapter 2 as referenced in Aquinas, *Summa Theologica*, vol. 2, p. 578.

15 Aquinas, *Summa Theologica*, vol. 2, p. 578.

as the instrument and, therefore, is not liable for the act (of killing that the sovereign authority of the state commands). One cannot overlook the premise and logical assumption held by Aquinas that the authority of the sovereign or the state comes from God, and not the people, but this will be considered elsewhere. Again, following Augustine, Aquinas analyzes that we be ready to obey these precepts and "refrain from resistance or self-defense. Nevertheless, it is necessary sometimes for a man to act otherwise for the common good, or for the good of those with whom he is fighting." (Aquinas, 1975, 579) Aquinas thereby provides the psychological and spiritual numbing to the soldier who is ordered to kill and punish others and de facto would seemingly remove responsibility and accountability for individual acts from the instrument. Relying on Augustine, he further validates that war is not contrary to virtue by noting that war should be waged to bring about peace. "Be peaceful, therefore, in warring, so that you may vanquish those whom you war against, and bring them to the prosperity of peace." (Aquinas, 1975, 578) Aquinas fails to explain how the instigation of war in order to induce peace does not result in subsequent wars to rectify the subjection and exploitation that ensue upon the vanquished state or nation by the victor, human nature acting humanly and capriciously as it may.

This aforenoted argument justifying the use of violence and lethal force would seem to be undercut by Aquinas' own treatment of the natural law which, he deduces, in I of II, Q. 90-97, must comply with the law of the spirit, i.e., the law of Christ which means the teachings of Jesus. In I of II, Q. 93, art. 3, Aquinas clearly states that all law is derived from eternal law; eternal law expressed in the teaching of Jesus, namely the act of love, would oppose violence and lethal force as explained in the aforenoted exegesis of the Christian scriptures.[16] In this section of the Summa Theologica (I of II, Q. 90-97), Aquinas briefly surveys the issue of law, inclusive of natural law which becomes

---

16 *Ibid.*, p. 217. Aquinas again quotes Augustine who allows for contradicting himself: "in temporal law there is nothing just and lawful by what man has drawn from the eternal law." Thus, as a corollary, because the eternal law, that is the law of the spirit expressed in the teachings of Jesus as written in the scriptures, does not allow for the exercise of violence and lethal force, any such act is neither just nor lawful because it cannot be drawn from the eternal law.

the foundation for the rationale of law, because it is based and depends on reasoning, and is the core of human nature—namely, do good and avoid evil. Aquinas clearly recognizes that the natural law does not have the authority of the law of the Christ and the Spirit, which as shown above are absolutely non-violent and peaceful. In fact, the natural law should be considered more of a philosophical approach to understanding life and its relationship to ethics, but it differs from a morality based on the teachings of Jesus. As such, the theory of the just war is not, nor can it be, based on the law of Jesus.

In consideration of the natural law's treatment of lethal violence and war, one cannot help to observe other deficiencies in this argumentation. For example, when Aquinas uses the *jus naturale*, the physicalogical emphasis of the natural law, to judge sexual acts, things like masturbation and contraception are considered more serious evils than rape and incest because in the former types the natural act of procreation is thwarted. This, however, must be judged nothing more than perverted moral judgment because in the latter the law of love and the spirit are grossly violated, not to mention the bestial attack on the dignity and rights of another person and the unconscionable abuse on a family member, particularly a child. Analogous to this type of distortion of ethical application, the natural law also distorts the fundamental teaching of Jesus, supposedly on which both Augustine and Aquinas build their philosophical-based theology.

"There is no foundation whatever in the Gospel of Matthew for the notion that violence in defense of a third party is justifiable. In fact, Matthew 26:51-52 serves as an explicit refutation of this idea," claims Richard Hays. (Hays, 1996, 324) Killing another human in any manner can be nothing other than incompatible with following Jesus.

With regard to just war and the execution of lethal violence as permitted in the case of self-defense, Mt. 5:39 negates such as an un-Christian practice. "The larger paradigm of Jesus' own conduct in Matthew's Gospel indicates a deliberate renunciation of violence as an instrument of God's will." (Hays, 1996, 323)

MORAL BASIS IN THE CHRISTIAN SCRIPTURES FOR
NON-VIOLENCE AS OPPOSED TO VIOLENCE

It behooves us to analyze further the gospel basis for a morality of non-violence and opposition to lethal conflict-resolution. Based on the aforenoted review of the Christian scriptures, Christian morality related to war, non-violence, opposition to lethal conflict-resolution rely on the seed planted in Matthew 5:38-48. The Sermon on the Mount begins with the fundamental teaching of the beatitudes—blessing the poor, the mourners, the meek, the starving and famished, the merciful, the pure, the peacemakers, the persecuted (because of their support for righteousness and justice), and the reviled. Thereafter, the six antitheses contrast the teachings of the Hebrew scriptures with the core teachings of Jesus.[17] As noted above, three of the six antitheses, i.e., the second, fifth, and sixth, relate to anger at another human to the point of killing, retaliation for physical harm and oppression, and loving one's enemies. Who are one's enemies that this scripture infers? Are they a person's direct contacts in work, family, neighborhood, or are they foreign or military forces? While enemy (*echthroi*) in verse 5:44 is used for those who persecute the followers of Jesus for their righteousness, it is used as a generic term and in biblical Greek (in

---

17   Luke 6:20-26 in the Sermon on the Plain has Jesus identifying four beatitudes with four woes against the rich, the well fed, the light-hearted, and esteemed. Paul in Rom. 12:14, 16, 17-21 exhorts the Romans to follow the beatitudes that he outlines in line with those of gospel writers, "Bless those who persecute [you]; bless and do not curse them ... Do not repay anyone evil for evil... If your enemy is hungry, feed him; if he is thirsty, give him something to drink... Do not be conquered by evil, but conquer evil with good." In the spirit of the Hebrew scriptures, though, Paul allots vengeance and wrath to be executed by God in eschatological vindication of God's people, not the follower of Jesus who is never encouraged to use violence.

   Hays, *The Moral Vision of the New Testament*, p. 327, indicates that, although Lev. 19:18 directs love one neighbor, there is no clear Hebrew scriptural quotation that characterizes hate of one's enemies, but Ps. 139:21-22 identifies the psalmist as one who hates those who hate the Lord and hates them perfectly. The conventional attitude of loving one's friends (or community, inclusive of community of believers for the Israelites) and hating one's enemies, as interpreted of the Torah.

both Deut. 20:1 and Mt. 5:38) refers to national or military opponents who threaten lethal violence, may be outsiders (foreigners), and
may be one who engages in persecution and oppression; the term is
not restricted for reference to personal, daily antagonists, but is all
encompassing. (Hays, 1996, 328)

The non-violence of Jesus is best demonstrated in Lk. 9:51-56 where
Jesus rebukes the disciples James and John who wish to call down fire
from heaven upon the Samaritans, the despised neighbors of Judah
and Israel and hated by the Jews, because they refused to welcome
Jesus and his disciples on their way to Jerusalem. Earlier in the same
chapter, Lk. 9:23-25, the Lukan Jesus establishes the criteria for discipleship, as a condition that requires one to deny oneself and take up
the cross daily in following Jesus to the benefit that whoever loses one's
life for Jesus' sake will save it. The Markan Jesus also teaches that the
disciple as servant can be expected to suffer the injustices of worldly
and pseudo-religious authorities (Mk. 13:9-13). Paul too suggests an
image of God, different from that of the Hebrew scriptures, in that
God does not treat enemies by killing them, but by sending his son to
die for them. Hays succinctly notes that "This has profound implications for the subsequent behavior of those who are reconciled to God
through Jesus' death: to be 'saved by his life' means to enter into a life
that recapitulates the pattern of Christ's self-giving... Those whose
lives are reshaped in Christ must deal with enemies in the same way
that God in Christ dealt with enemies." (Hays, 1996, 330) Vindication in the face of persecution and suffering, maybe even death, comes
with the resurrection, the only rationale validating the non-violence
of Jesus' followers. "In the resurrection of Jesus the power of God has
triumphed over the power of violence and prefigured the redemption
of all creation." (Hays, 1996, 338)

To what extent are the followers of Jesus called, if not required by
the mandate of love, to effect and practice the guiding teaching of Mt.
5:38-48? Hays has listed several possibilities of applicability to Jesus'
followers. While Mt. 5:48 directs the followers to "be perfect as your
heavenly father is perfect," does this apply to all Christians? Is it not
a challenge only to those called to higher virtue, a super-sanctified
group of followers, a special class within the Church? Was this directive only applicable to the apostolic church when Jesus' followers were

trying to understand the meaning of Jesus' teaching and they were a distinct religious minority within Judaism and the Roman Empire? Was the applicability of this directive merely relevant during the time that the apostolic church thought that the *parousia* was imminent? Is this directive only to be interpreted as an ideal to strive for, but not necessarily to be implemented by all followers? Is this instruction meant only for Jesus' disciples but not for the rest of the Church?

In brief, the instructions of Jesus in Matthew 5 are directed to all of Jesus' followers, not just disciples, are applicable to all periods, require all followers to apply such, are not to be considered an unrealizable ideal but something actually possible (which the primitive Church certainly realized) as Jesus himself suffered it in his death, allow for no conditions of exclusion if one is following the instruction, and demand perfection despite the failure that all humans experience.[18] In implementing the instruction, Jesus' followers are to be the salt and light for the world and show a new order, a counter-culture that makes all things anew and is characterized by higher righteousness free of anger and violence, meekness, mercy, purity, devoted to peace-

---

18 Mt. 7:21-27 leaves no doubt about the question of perfection, as instructed by Jesus for all of his followers. The Matthean Jesus describes the true disciple:

"Not everyone who says to me, 'Lord, Lord,' will enter the kingdom of heaven, but only the one who does the will of my Father in heaven. Many will say to me on that day, 'Lord, Lord, did we not prophesy in your name? Did we not drive out demons in your name? Did we not do mighty deeds in your name? Then I will declare to them solemnly, 'I never knew you. Depart from me, you evildoers.'

"Everyone who listens to these words of mine and acts on them will be like a wise man who built his house on rock. The rain fell, the floods came, and the winds blew and buffeted the house. Bit it did not collapse; it had been set solidly on rock. And everyone who listens to these words of mine but does not act on them will be like a fool who built his house on sand. The rain fell, the floods came, and the winds blew and buffeted the house. And it collapsed and was completely ruined."

When Jesus finished these words, the crowds were astonished at his teaching, for he taught them as one having authority, and not as the scribes.

making, and willingness to suffer persecution. "The Sermon stands in Matthew's narrative scheme as Jesus' programmatic disclosure of the kingdom of God and of the life to which the community of disciples is called…. The community of Jesus' followers is to be 'a city built on a hill,' a model *polis* that demonstrates the counterintuitive peaceful politics of God's new order." (Hays, 1996, 321) Thus, while baptized persons may engage in military activities, they can be viewed as nothing other than an anomaly in a church that is called to suffer in the face of persecution and grave injustice and exercise reconciliation, reconciliation that diametrically differs from activities that may result in lethal violence. When the community of Jesus' believers exercise non-violence, they can be expected to be persecuted, scorned, charged with being ineffective and irrelevant. (Hays, 1996, 338)

MORALITY OF WAR: POSITION OF KARL BARTH & THE DILEMMA OF REINHOLD NIEBUHR

Karl Barth, in poignant contrast to Reinhold Niebuhr, indisputably denies that war can be legitimate or necessary for the follower of Jesus. "All affirmative answers to this question (whether war can be advocated by Christians) are wrong from the very outset, and in Christian ethics constitute a flat betrayal of the Gospel, if they ignore the whole risk and venture of this. Nevertheless…. (A)ll affirmative answers to this question are wrong if they do not start with the assumption that the inflexible negative of pacifism has almost infinite arguments in its favour and is almost overpoweringly strong."[19] Barth, however, allows for the exercise of war in extreme circumstances and emergencies in which the conduct of a state or a nation must opt for war when its very existence or autonomy is threatened or attacked and its very independence is at stake, but not for defense of its viable prosperity. (Barth, 1961, 461)

What if a lethally violent means were used to right an evil or overthrow an evil and tyrannical leadership or government to establish a more just and fair social system, would this justify the use of such violence? Reinhold Niebuhr opines that no ethical grounds can be ruled out in this case, even with regard to violence, killing, and

19   Karl Barth, *Church Dogmatics*, Vol. III/4, translated by A.T. Mackay et al., (New York: Charles Scribner's Sons, 1961), p. 455.

revolution.[20] Jürgen Moltmann concurs and offers the case for such in his deemed necessity to assassinate Adolf Hitler, as in the plot that Dietrich Bonhoeffer was implicated.[21]

THE CATHOLIC CHURCH'S
JUST WAR CONDITIONALITY & ITS FAILURE

The classic just war theory, *jus ad bellum*, as supported by clerical authorities and the teaching authority of the Church (particularly that of the US bishops) since the fifth century has developed seven conditions precedent to engage in war "justly." These conditions comprise: just cause, authorization by legitimate and competent authority, comparative justice, right intention, last resort, reasonable probability of success, and proportionality.[22] Conditions for engagement in just war, *jus in bello*, demand immunity for non-combatants and proportionate means and results for waging war. We shall analyze and evaluate these criteria, indicate their shortcomings and omissions, and consider their appropriateness with regard to Christian morality hereafter.

From the standpoint of Christian scriptures, Hays' consideration cannot be overlooked: "The classic just war criteria … are … neither derived nor derivable from the New Testament; they are formulated through a process of reasoning that draws upon natural-law traditions far more heavily than upon biblical warrants…. (I)t (just war theory) cannot stand the normative test of New Testament ethics…. The New Testament offers no basis for ever declaring Christian participation in war 'just.'" (Hays, 1996, 341) That the just war represents the historic majority and traditional position within Christian theology, then, must be rejected or corrected. In a country that is dependent so much on war for advancement of economic and political interests and with church leaders so complicit either in sanctioning US bellicosity or remaining immorally silent, correction within remains more than

---

20   Reinhold Niebuhr, *Moral Man and Immoral Society* (New York: Charles Scribner's Sons, 1932), pp. 179-180.

21   See Arne Rasmusson, *The Church as Polis*, p. 193.

22   US Catholic Bishops, "The Challenge of Peace: God's Promise and Our Response," 1983 in David J. O'Brien and Thomas A. Shannon, eds., *Catholic Social Thought: The Documentary Heritage* (Maryknoll, NY: Orbis Books, 1998), pp. 512-514.

a daunting task. Despite the historic majority position of just war theory, there remain extremely serious doubts about its validity and appropriateness in contemporary society. Cardinal Joseph Ratzinger declared in February 2003 that "Today we should be asking ourselves if it is still licit to admit the very existence of 'Just war.'"[23]

Despite the aforenoted critique of just war theory and the unacceptability of just war in the understanding and practice of Christian morality according to the teachings of Jesus, it behooves us to consider the seven conditions stipulated by the Church for execution of "just" war. First, war may be permissible with just cause, that is, there is real and certain danger in order to protect innocent life, human existence, and basic human rights. One must ask, what about the innocent lives of those who are maimed and killed by the combating parties because of the supposed righteousness of the just cause warriors. In that case, one state is protecting its own innocent life while killing innocent life of its combatant. Just cause then is in the eyes of the beholder and disregards innocent life and the basic rights of the adversary.

Second, war can be declared by competent authority. In the Catholic tradition, this is joined to the common good and social order. Thus, in supposedly constitutional democracies, one may question whether war is declared by competent authority if in fact the legally authorized organ for this power does not declare war but another authority does. If war is not declared, but military force and lethal violence are exercised under directive, then it is difficult to acknowledge that competent authority has been exercised even though the hostilities have been ordered. Further, in the multilateral world that exists today, one may question the prudence of competent authority that engages in war independently. Any competent authority recognizing its just cause should be able to state its case persuasively in a forum with other national leaders and representatives and, if such cause is just, others should logically accede to such. This is a terribly simplistic view of good and evil, though. Any prudent and judicious authority must realize that it itself is as much guilty and responsible for the development of so-called just-cause war as the accused party. One may question too

23   Mark & Louis Zwick, "Pope John Paul II Calls War a Defeat for Humanity: Neo-Conservatives' Iraq Just War Theories Rejected," *Houston Catholic Worker*, Vol. XXIII No. 4, July 2003.

to what extent the competent authority has engaged the adversary on equal footing and in neutral locus to review the resolution of the conflict and discord.

The US Catholic bishops do not provide a clear definition of competent authority. Competent cannot simply mean holding power, that is the military force to exercise, and having popular or substantive support. The Catholic Church does not lend clear direction either with regard to competent authority because they also correctly allow for problems of conscience that oppose the rationale applied by the competent authority and, thus, rightfully, refuse to accept the war.[24] This simply does not pertain to the freedom of individual conscience, but also acknowledges implicitly and accepts that duly elected representatives of a ruling authority may not be acting wisely or competently, particularly with regard to moral thinking and religious fundamentals. Finally, one cannot fail to overlook that competent authority is a two-way street. Both sides are necessarily adversarial; both have presumably competent authority. The crux of the question hinges on the determination of what constitutes competency. Competency would also have to include the murky evaluation of moral righteousness, a multi-faceted judgment.

What happens in the case of revolution and counter-revolution with regard to competent authority? It would seem that competent authority would pertain only to the government in power and would exclude non-governmental popular or sectarian authority. The US Conference of Catholic Bishops, however, includes anti-government groups, non-constitutional or non-elected groups inclusive, as competent authority because "an oppressive government may lose its claim to legitimacy." (US Catholic Bishops, 1998, 512) The fact that groups opposing the government are armed and capable of overthrowing the government, inclusive of oppressive governments, though, does not constitute sufficient reason for competent authority. The reverse, though, may not be said in the logic applied in religious history for a ruling government, despite the fact that the US Catholic bishops equate mere armed revolutionary force lacking popular support with a ruling government's systematic oppression and curtailment of human rights

24 US Catholic Bishops, "The Challenge of Peace: God's Promise and Our Response," p. 512.

"carried out under the doctrine of 'national security.'"(US Catholic Bishops, 1998, 512)

Thirdly, comparative justice entails determining which side is sufficiently right to warrant the act of killing another human or destroying the means of livelihood of an adversary. This condition emphasizes the presumption against war, which precedes just-war thinking. The Catholic bishops make an astute observation in this regard: "In a world of sovereign states recognizing neither a common moral authority nor a central political authority, comparative justice stresses that no state should act on the basis that it has "absolute justice" on its side.[25] The bishops wisely caution that every party in a conflict should be conscious of the limits of its just cause.[26] The purpose of this guidance is to restrict the means in pursuit of the cause and to relativize absolute claims, to restrain the use of force.

Fourthly, right intention is required, as was seen in Augustine's and Aquinas' conditionality. While related to just cause, right intention seeks to assure that the intent of the party exercising lethal force is pure, not simply that the cause is acceptable. Thus, for a recent example, people with moral conscience have questioned the intent of the US-led invasion and occupation of Iraq in 2003. Although the reasons for this invasion continued to change as they were refuted and disproved, the strategic interests of the US itself was highlighted as the actual intent—that is, oil, Israel, and logistics for control of Mid-eastern oil necessary for the running of industrial economies. The bishops

---

25 One is reminded of the statement of Abraham Lincoln who noted that he prayed that he was on God's side, in response to a comment that we should pray that God is on our side (the Israelites' position in the Hebrew scriptures).

26 The Japanese mentality toward responsibility and accountability with regard to mistakes, compromising acts, and the exercise of offensive acts, which in the Christian culture would include the concept of evil, acknowledges the reality of the world where there is no black and white, but one in which all parties are absolutely necessarily accountable for such actions. The act of an aggressor is partially attributed to the imprudent actions of the recipient that induced said aggression. Japanese courts, for example, in cases of bankruptcy or insolvency, force even the creditors, suppliers, etc. holding senior liens or senior debt positions to forfeit some of their credit as loss, though admittedly less than junior creditors.

again caution that right intention must be the pursuit of peace and reconciliation, inclusive of avoiding unnecessarily destructive acts and imposition of unreasonable conditions. (US Catholic Bishops, 1998, 513) The best of intentions, though, cannot justify poor planning and analysis that make a bad situation worse.

Fifthly, the use of lethal violence must really be the last resort, with all peaceful means exhausted. The Catholic Church emphasizes that "all other means of putting an end to it (i.e., legitimate defense by military force) must have been shown to be impractical or ineffective."[27] Despite this, one cannot fail to question what do reasonable means mean in light of the Christian scriptures directing a person to forgive, not seven times, but seventy-seven times (Mt. 18:22), meaning limitlessly. Just as the offended follower of Jesus is to forgive the offender limitlessly, so too the aggrieved party analogously should limitlessly search for means to avoid lethal conflict. The US Catholic bishops advocate that the role of the United Nations be used to exhaust all means of avoiding lethal conflict.

To engage in lethal conflict requires that there must be a high probability of success which thwarts irrational, ineffective use of force or "hopeless resistance" when the outcome would be either disproportionate to the force used or futile. (US Catholic Bishops, 1998, 513) How does one gauge success, though? The bishops, unfortunately, gauge success at the sacrifice of human life, to be risked even in the deemed necessity to witness certain values, (for example, those deemed primary by the state or warring group). Is success merely the final result of vanquishing the adversary and winning the conflict? Probably not, based on the aforenoted case. Success can only be judged according to natural law theory on whether peace is achieved. Peace, however, cannot mean subjection by the vanquished to the conqueror, because, given innumerable historical precedents, this merely results in an unending spiral where violence begets violence, if not now, then later. Viewed from a long-term historical perspective, it is difficult to find many cases where war actually led to long-term peace. Does success mean the economic and political advantages that accrue to the conqueror? Given the politicization of the previously declared

27 *Catechism of the Catholic Church* (New York: Doubleday, 1995), p. 615.

religious morality of just war thinking, though, contemporary politicians and business leaders are wont to validate the opportunism of
war using a politically modified morality, but probably couched in
religious terminology. It is difficult to imagine, whether in Christian
morality or in pure economic and political valuation, that success is
viewed in the eyes of and effects on the adversary. Success must be
considered subjectively. Objective evaluation of success and its tenets
will certainly be denied unless they prove beneficial to conqueror. This
results in hypocritical duplicity.

Lastly, "proportionality means that the damage to be inflicted and the
costs incurred by war must be proportionate to the good expected by
taking up arms." (US Catholic Bishops, 1998, 514) While this criteria
cannot be judged on the merits of financial values, although they must
be influential even morally as a comparative basis, it remains elusive
because of the difficulty attached to valuing what is the good and good
for whom. One can seriously question, for example, whether the massive destruction inflicted on the people and the infrastructure of Iraq
during the second US-led invasion of 2003, amounting to hundreds
of billion of dollars of destruction, loss of more than 100,000 civilian lives not to mention loss of life to combatants,[28] and the political
vacuum forced on the vanquished, (all at a cost to the US taxpayer for
US-related operations that exceeded US$180 billion by 2005), meets
the test of proportionality.[29] Non-material good remains nebulous
and difficult to value on a comparative basis from the standpoint of
proportionality. The Catholic bishops have demonstrated that this
criteria is to be applied dynamically, i.e., on a continuing basis even
during *jus in bello*. In the case of Vietnam, the bishops after continual

28   While this number of Iraqi dead was statistically extrapolated by Johns
     Hopkins University and Colombia University based on surveys conduct-
     ed in Iraq in 2004, by 2006 a new study undertaken by Johns Hopkins
     with an Iraqi university, Al Mastansiria, in Bagdad indicated that this
     number may have exceeded 655,000 persons dead over an above the nor-
     mal death rate for the population of that country.

29   The survey study conducted by Johns Hopkins University's School of
     Public Health and its peer at Colombia University in conjunction with
     an Iraqi university projected more than 100,000 deaths had statistically
     occurred during the previous 12 months, exclusive of the fighting in Fa-
     luja.

application and consideration judged that destruction being wrought on that country in terms of human life and property damage as well as severing any semblance of national unity no longer warranted use of the just war theory, even though it was fallaciously misapplied initially.[30] One must ask whether proportionality pertains more to the cost-benefit assessment of damage inflicted on an adversary or whether the greater concern is the financial and social cost to the state waging the war. It would seem that the bishops only begin to assess the inapplicableness of proportionality when the US domestic social fabric was rent, particularly in the case of Vietnam.

The Church applies two conditions to *jus in bello*—non-combatant immunity (i.e., discrimination) and proportionate means. The Catholic bishops caution that the easy propensity to escalate hostilities in contemporary warfare, inclusive of nuclear, bio-chemical, conventional, or guerrilla warfare, make it geometrically complicated to determine appropriate military response. The issue of non-combatant casualties which in the 20th and 21st century has risen to nearly 75 percent of all casualties, physical injury and fatality, makes the morality of war and lethal combat intensely questionable. While the bishops in their statement of 1988 were concerned about the effects of nuclear holocaust and bio-chemical warfare, no attention was paid to the ancillary effects of radiated shells and the like that have left inexplicable illnesses on the soldiers engaged in the war theater as well as the residents of areas where such are used. Further, although the bishops roundly condemn total war because of the destructive effects on much of industrialized society, they are silent on the issue of proportionality of means and non-combatant discrimination in limited, conventional, regional wars. They appear complicit on the issue of so-called collateral damage. As long as civilians are not primary or direct targets, the means appear proportionate by the bishops. As noted above, this is not only questionable, it is immoral given the large numbers of non-combatants increasingly killed in urban and guerilla wars in the twentieth century. Not only the recent and on-going 2003 war in Iraq, but the Israeli attacks on Palestinian targets and suicide bombings leave the

---

30 The incident of the Tonkin Gulf that the Johnson administration and the Pentagon generals manipulated, as well as the bogus political logic of the domino theory, undercut any validation of just war theory.

majority of those effected by evil means comprised of non-combatants. Because the end cannot justify the means, in consistency these attacks must be considered immoral even according to *jus in bello* rationale. Further, while both combatants and non-combatants alike may not be directly killed or maimed in hostile and lethal conflict, if the infrastructure is destroyed or goods necessary for sustainable living are effectively embargoed as a part of war-like activity, this differs little from genocidal warfare or the concern expressed by the Church and the US bishops with respect to catastrophic destruction of cities and population. One is reminded of the case of the US destruction of the Iraqi waterworks and the subsequent embargo on chlorine and medical supplies that prevented restoration of these facilities. The US Army Corp of Engineers had issued a report prior to the destruction of these facilities and indicated that as a result of such planned destruction one could expect at least one-half million children easily to die. The US proceeded to destroy the waterworks and executed the aforenoted embargo on Iraqi imports. A 1998 UNESCO report confirmed that at least 500,000 children did die because of these actions. No person with moral character could accept this application of just war theory because it is a clear example violating the principle of discrimination and civilian immunity. "The principle prohibits directly intended attacks on non-combatants and non-military targets."[31] The entire population is dependent upon clean water and treated sewage. To include all civilians with combatants in punitive war effort cannot be judged anything but immoral. The use of the term "collateral damage" demonstrates crass and despicable callousness with regard to the immunity of non-combatants and is obviously devised to sanitize the evil of war in order to retain the support of the general public.

The whole just war theory is steeped in self-justifying rationale for engaging in lethal conflict on behalf of nationalistic or myopic ends. The theory has been abused, not only by Augustine from its initia-

---

31 US Catholic Bishops, "The Challenge of Peace," p. 516. It is discouraging to note that Gen. Colin Powell, when questioned about this activity in 1992 responded that he was not concerned about that but about the safety of his soldiers. Madeline Albright, then US Ambassador to the UN in the mid-1990s, responded likewise with regard to this incident by stating that, while unfortunate such was part of the casualties of war.

tion, but has been frequently used by so-called Christian states to validate their own interests. It lacks the discipline and clarity required for neutral, balanced thinking. Vietnam presents a recent example of the gross misuse of this theory. The Church fell lock step into the pitfall of this easily abusive thinking. With the fall of the French, representing a Catholic state, at Dienbienphu in Vietnam, the US Catholic bishops, in support of the minority and powerful Catholic establishment in South Vietnamese society, proceeded to validate the rising US militarist involvement in Vietnam. The Church, with its short history of dealing with Communist countries in Eastern Europe after 1947, aroused support for the Catholics of Vietnam. The Church in Vietnam, had acted as an extension of French colonialism and quasi-*functionaires* and benefited from French protection such that a disproportionate number of Catholics occupied the wealthier classes and likewise the political leadership. With the US assumption of direction and control through a new client state in place of the French in Vietnam, US Catholic Church leaders fell into the trap of the spurious "domino theory" in fear of Communist influence, despite the fact that an arbitrary and unnatural arrangement for division of Vietnam by colonial and Western powers could not deter a civil war in the southern part of Vietnam. The Church speciously continued to justify and support the dispatchment of increasing numbers of US troops to fight in a civil war that not only the soldiers from the US hinterland, but also the leadership, was incapable of understanding and of appreciating the complexities of the Vietnamese historical conflict. It was only due to the division within the US in the early 1970s, that church leaders, afraid of losing their grip on leadership, began to change their thinking and claimed that proportionality no longer validated the just war theory. The real issue with the just war theory remains the facileness that the theory can and has been used to justify nationalistic causes.

OTHER CONTEMPORARY OFFICIAL CHURCH POSITIONS ON WAR
The Dutch catechism, while apparently acknowledging the theory and use of the just war, advises that a reversal of present armament trends is not just desired, but that universal disarmament with universal inspection be the standard.

Then there is the monstrous factor of 'war.' The principle of self-defense is not the last word. Our faith must be dominated by the thought of peace. The Christian conscience must always try harder and harder to draw stricter limits to the permissibility of war. Christians must try to implement such statements as those of Pope John (XXIII) in *Pacem in terris*: 'Hence justice, common sense and a sense of human dignity demand urgently that the competition in armaments should cease; that the offensive weapons at the disposal of each country should be everywhere and simultaneously reduced, that atomic weapons should be forbidden and that finally all countries should agree to simultaneous disarmament with mutual and effective inspection' (part 3).

... We must obviously strive with all our might to prepare for the moment when all peoples will agree to forbid war of any type whatever. But the necessary condition for this is the setting up of an international authority recognized by all which will dispose of effective powers to guarantee security, justice and respect of the rights of all.[32]

The Catechism of the Catholic Church, having a more recent Catholic approach to war and peace, adopts a slightly different approach with a different perspective. The Catechism acknowledges two of the antitheses of Matthew's sermon on the Mount, against anger and hatred of one's enemies, but caveats that "respect for and development of human life require peace."[33] Contrarily, without peace there can be no respect for or development of human life. Such cannot be the case absolutely, but certainly may exist in many situations. The Catechism then relies on the definition of peace according to Augustine, who bases his approach on the natural law.

> The peace of the body then consists in the duly proportioned arrangement of its parts. The peace of the irrational soul is the harmonious repose of the appetites, and that of the rational soul the harmony of knowledge and action. The peace of body and soul is the world-ordered and harmonious life and health of the living creature. Peace between man and God is the well-ordered

---

32 *A New Catechism: Catholic Faith for Adults*, translated by Kevin Smyth from "*De Nieuwe Katechismus*," (New York: Herder, 1969), pa.424-425.

33 *Catechism of the Catholic Church* (New York: Doubleday, 1995), p. 614.

obedience of faith to eternal law. Peace between man and man is
well-ordered concord. Domestic peace is the well-ordered concord
between those of the family who rule and those who obey. Civil
peace is the similar concord among the citizens.... The peace of all
things is the tranquility of order. Order is the distribution which
allots things equal and unequal, each to its own place. And hence,
though the miserable, in so far as they are such, do certainly not
enjoy peace, but are severed from that tranquility of order in which
there is no disturbance, nevertheless, inasmuch as they are deserv-
edly and justly miserable, they are by their very misery connected
with order. They are not, indeed, conjoined with the blessed, but
they are disjoined from them by the lawful order.... They would,
however, be more wretched if they had not that peace which arises
from being in harmony with the natural order of things."[34]

As such, Augustine accepts inequality and would seem to require
preservation of the status quo to preserve that peace. This contradicts
Paul VI's advice that "if you want peace, work for justice." Justice, as
seen in both the Hebrew scriptures and Church teaching advocates
fair distribution of the world's resources necessary for survival and fair
and equitable treatment without discrimination, something which
Augustine accepts as a given of the natural order. The Catechism does
not seem to accept this aspect of Augustine's definition because, in
line with Paul VI's aforenoted statement, it acknowledges that "Peace
cannot be attained on earth without safeguarding the goods, of persons,
free communication among men, respect for the dignity of persons
and peoples, and the assiduous practice of fraternity."[35]
Augustine considers the basis for peace between men, within the
family, amongst the citizenry to be a "concord." By its usual definition, concord is a state of agreement, i.e., harmony, but it often is
used to mean an agreement by stipulation, compact, or covenant. In
the former, for an agreement to exist, the parties to such must join
together, have commonality of purpose, objective, a closure of the
circle of participants, etc. In the latter, there must be some form of
compact, contract, or covenant between the parties, inclusive of social
custom and family law, conclude a written and binding social contract,
be it marital, civil, bilateral or multi-lateral international. Peace, for

34 Augustine, "City of God," Book XIX, Chapter 13, p. 519.
35 *Catechism of the Catholic Church*, p. 614.

Augustine, would infer a non-dynamic, almost paralysis of order in which every party should remain where and as they are—preservation of the status quo.

Based on the aforenoted rationale and recognizing the fundamental of a commandment, the Catechism, nevertheless, accepts that, because there is no respected social order internationally that holds attributes of competence and power, i.e., military might or the ability to bring violence against another party to enforce directives or decisions, governments may rely on their "right of lawful self-defense," after all efforts to bring about peace have failed based on enactment of four conditions precedent. The conditions of the Catechism differ from those reviewed above and issued by the US Catholic bishops.

Condition/Criteria	US Catholic Bishops, 1988	Catechism of the Catholic Church
Just cause	Yes	No
Competent authority	Yes	Partial
Comparative justice	Yes	No
Right intention	Yes	No
Last resort	Yes	Yes
Probability of success	Yes	Yes
Proportionality	Yes	Yes
Gravity of damage by aggressor	No	Yes
Discrimination	Yes	Yes

The Catechism presents the least convincing case. Proportionality in the Catechism, for example, allows for the use of arms producing evils and causing disorders, e.g., with respect to the deaths of the poor, innocent, etc., just as long as they are not graver than the evil to be eliminated.[36] The US Catholic bishops, on the other hand, require that "the damage to be inflicted and the costs incurred by war must be proportionate to the good expected by taking up arms."[37] Thus, the US bishops require that the good to be achieved must at least be equal to or greater than the damage inflicted, while the Catechism fails to even mention the good to be achieved and allows for damage and evil to the extent of the evil intended to be eradicated. While the Catechism claims to be rigorous in application of conditions precedent or inherent, it remains a far cry from those employed by the US bishops. As noted

---

36   *Ibid.*, p. 615.

37   US Catholic bishops, "The Challenge of Peace," p. 514.

in the above table, the Catechism does not even mention four criteria imposed by the US bishops, which are definitely more restrictive and more morally conscientious of both the teachings of Jesus and the abominable horrors of war. One should not overlook the position of the Catechism that restricts the moral legitimacy of claiming just war to "the prudential judgment of those who have responsibility for the common good,"[38] unlike the position of the US bishops who allow for more judicious responsibility to be on the populace or voters, inclusive of individual Christians with their independent conscience. Nevertheless, the aforenoted evaluation cannot negate the position of the teachings of Jesus with respect to lethal violence, inclusive of war, which is diametrically opposed to the just-war positions of both the Catechism and the US bishops. Finally, one must acknowledge that the US bishops appear to be conscious of this discrepancy because they immediately deal with pacifism and non-violence after discussing just war,[39] cite the Pastoral Constitution of the Church from Vatican II (paragraph 79), and emphasize this type of witness not only from Christians like Martin Luther King and Dorothy Day, but also the precedent set by their predecessor, Mohandhas Gandhi. It remains insufficient to emphasize conscientious objection to war, inclusive of the right to selective conscientious objection.[40]

Augustine, relying on the understanding of war in the Hebrew scriptures, provides the basis for a state of war to coexist with peace. That is, war may be viewed as a means to peace, to preservation or restoration of the status quo. While the Catechism allots that, "Peace is not merely the absence of war, and it is not limited to maintaining a balance of powers between adversaries,"[41] it implicitly allows by

---

38   *Catechism of the Catholic Church*, p. 615.

39   US Catholic bishops, "The Challenge of Peace," p. 517-518.

40   While the Vatican II writers of the "Pastoral Constitution on the Church" (*Gaudium et spes*) [*The Documents of Vatican II* (New York: American Press, 1966), pp. 290-297] and the Catechism heavily reference the same Constitution with regard to their dual positions on war, they manifestly fail to wholeheartedly accept the gospel mandate of love and non-violence demanded by Jesus, though, as a fundamental requirement for Christians called to live like Jesus.

41   *Catechism of the Catholic Church*, p. 614.

default for the coexistence of war with peace, but effectively recognizes that with or without détente any balance of power or actual standoff lacking direct confrontation cannot be considered peace either.

The "Pastoral Constitution on the Church" (*Gaudium et spes*), on which the Catechism heavily depends, commences its analysis of war and lethal violence at the point that the Catechism ends, namely, in line with the thinking expressed later by Paul VI, peace is derived from the appropriate exercise of justice which brings true, not idealistic, harmony to society.[42] The same Pastoral Constitution, however, ends its discussion of the bellicosity of men today and the increasing horror of weapons and the difficult complexity of political relations by opining that it is appropriate to ban war and secure the means to assure execution of such through enactment of an international organ supported by conflicting states.[43] While *Gaudium et Spes* focuses its comments on war, particularly nuclear war and all-out (unconditional and unlimited) war, and popes since John XXIII have not just advocated an end to nuclear weapons, but have condemned their use, precisely because of the issue of discrimination in *jus in bello*, namely that large numbers of non-combatants would be killed indiscriminately as occurred in World War II in fire bombings and nuclear blasts, the same moral conclusion must be drawn to present day warfare. Given that more than 75 percent of the people killed in wars in the twentieth century are civilian non-combatants, war itself, whether declared justifying or not, cannot meet the conditions of just war.[44]

---

42   "Pastoral Constitution on the Church", No. 78, p. 290

43   The same Constitution recognizes the fundamental flaw that prevents such enactment lies in the distrust between states which counter their fears with weapons. The Constitution fails to address sufficiently the issues of failure to communicate and exploitation as a critical aspect which underpins injustice that is propelled into reaction against unchecked and domineering structures. "Pastoral Constitution on the Church," No. 82, p. 296. See also *Catechism*, No. 2317, p. 617.

44   Again, given the case of more than 100,000 Iraqis dead by 2004, exclusive of the US attack on Falluja, have been killed in the US invasion and occupation of Iraq, there is no way that this can be considered eligible to meet just war criteria, as spurious as the theory may be in relevance to the teachings of Jesus.

The dropping of atomic bombs on Hiroshima and Nagasaki on August 6 and 9, 1945, respectively, killed well over 200,000 in each city, if not immediately, then with slow agonizing death from atomic-bomb sickness due to the radiation. Robert McNamara, then military analyst for General Curtis Lemay who directed these attacks with atomic weapons, acknowledges in "Fog of War," that not only himself but Lemay too realized the immorality of these acts.[45] McNamara does not stop at identifying the use of these weapons of mass destruction, but implicates the fire bombings in Japan of Tokyo, Osaka, Nagoya, Yokohama, etc. also as being immoral because of the massive numbers of civilians killed and injured and the expansive property damage.[46] Father George Zabelka, chaplain of the Hiroshima and Nagasaki bomb squadrons admits his own complicity in these immoral acts and judges the church acquiescent.

> To fail to speak to the utter moral corruption of the mass destruction of civilians was to fail as a Christian and as a priest as I see it.... I was there, and I'll tell you that the operational moral atmosphere in the church in relation to mass bombing of enemy civilians was totally indifferent, silent, and corrupt at best—at worst it was religiously supportive of these activities by blessing those who did them.... Catholics dropped the A-bomb on top of the largest and first Catholic city in Japan (i.e., Nagasaki). One would have thought that I, as a Catholic priest, would have spoken out against the atomic bombing of nuns. (Three orders of Catholic sisters were destroyed in Nagasaki that day.) One would have thought that I would have suggested that as a minimal standard of Catholic morality, Catholics shouldn't bomb Catholic children. I didn't. I, like the Catholic pilot of the Nagasaki plane, "The Great Artiste," was heir to a Christianity that had for seventeen hundred years engaged in revenge, murder, torture, the pursuit of power, and prerogative violence, all in the name of our Lord.

---

45   "Fog of War," a 2003 film focused on the eleven most important things learned by Robert McNamara during his years of military and government employment.

46   The same could be said for the fire bombings of Hamburg, etc. in Germany which actually produced the exact opposite effect intended, namely, instead of arousing people's ire at the Nazi regime's leadership, they became increasingly dependent on it for their own survival.

I walked through the ruins of Nagasaki right after the war and visited the place where once stood the Urakami Cathedral. I picked up a piece of censer from the rubble. When I look at it today I pray God forgives us for how we have distorted Christ's teaching and destroyed his world by distortion of that teaching. I was the Catholic chaplain who was there when this grotesque process that began with Constantine reached its lowest point—so far."[47]

Some Real World Issues Related to Just War & the Politicization of Just War

The religious morality dealing with the problems of war, inclusive of the spurious idea to justify war, have in the twentieth century shifted to a politicization of morality. It behooves us to review and evaluate on its own merits and demerits the morality of war, inclusive of justifying war, from this standpoint, rather than from the perspective of religious morals, particularly given the global, multi-religious (and non-religious) world of the twenty-first century. Michael Walzer's most recent edition of his earlier work, *Just and Unjust Wars*,[48] amply demonstrates both the complexities of problems of war and the shift from religiously interpreted and religiously based understanding of war to one that becomes political or politicized, secular morality. Walzer attempts his best to stay above the fray of politicizing and secularizing the morality of war, to remain on a philosophical plane tempered by the detailed reality of specific situations of war, but in the end seems to succumb to the politicization of morality. As a premise, one should be conscious that Walzer assumes that war may be justified, although he characterizes war as criminal because it entails brutality and killing, as Clausewitz enticed his readers to deduce; his intent focuses on the discrimination between just wars and unjust wars.

Walzer stresses from the start of his work that particularly in the post-World War II era there is increasing justification for unilateral intervention (that he terms "duty") on behalf of the aid of certain

47 George Zabelka, "I Was Told It Was Necessary," *Sojourner*, Sept. 8, 1980, pa.14, cited by Richard B. Hays, *The Moral Vision of the New Testament: A Contemporary Introduction to New Testament Ethics*, pp. 318-319.

48 Michael Walzer, *Just and Unjust Wars: A Moral Argument with Historical Illustrations* (New York: Basic Books, 2000).

groups and peoples. While major powers evoke memories of colonist practices in this regard, small and minor state actors have yielded positive results in unilateral intervention (e.g., Vietnam against Pol Pot's Kampuchea or Tanzania against Idi Amin's Uganda), but admittedly are neither altruistic nor lacking in ulterior motives. For major powers, unilateral intervention is almost always questionable because of the inconsistency of the application of this practice. For example, what justifies and motivates the US intervention against Hussein's Iraq when the US failed to intervene against the government-led death squads in its own hemisphere—Chile under Pinochet, Argentina and Brazil in the late 1970s and early 1980s, Guatemalan and Salvadoran ethnic cleansing of native Americans and eradication of government critics, etc. Was the US interest in these countries sufficient to turn the other way because of US backing of oppressive regimes for the benefit of US-based multinationals, the tolerance of violence as long as the US is not greatly effective, but only employ military engagement out of the boogie fear of Communist control in the US' backyard? With the nationalization of US-based multinational interests in Iraq and the discriminating Iraqi treatment unfavorable to US firms, the US would seem more motivated to use persuasive morally justifying arguments to support US intervention. Walzer argues for justifying unilateral intervention by any state at any time when heinous crimes are committed against foreign peoples and groups, but the glaring inconsistency of the application of this policy undermines the feigned veracity supporting it.[49]

---

49   Walzer, *Just and Unjust Wars*, pp. 86-108. The issue of inconsistency of application is most troubling. What deterred Western post-colonial powers or even African neighbors from intervening in the horrible genocide in Rwanda? Did the US inept attempt to assassinate Al Qaeda leaders in the Sudan undermine its confidence and discourage the Clinton administration's courage to send troops to Rwanda, despite popular disinterest? Why did the US fail to intervene in Kampuchea in 1975, even though it was able to muster over one-million troops in Vietnam for nearly one decade? Why did western European powers sit on their hands for so long when the mutual genocide in a partitioned Yugoslavia was occurring? We need not mention the failure of either major powers or neighboring states to intervene on behalf of oppressed groups or peoples in the case of Kosovo, Chechnya, East Timor, Tibet, Sudan, Nigeria, Somalia, etc., par-

The problem of application of a double standard, which Walzer aptly notes as the most important form of moral criticism, undercuts not only the justifying logic but the persuasiveness of unilateral intervention or policy application. For example, when states decry the infringement on human rights, (the basis of morality, inclusive of life and liberty, according to Walzer), yet they themselves fail to apply these rights, their double standard undermines the apparent legitimacy of their claims. When the US, for example, removes itself from judicial application of war crimes under the World Court in order to avoid having its leaders and troops be subject to internationally agreed conventions of war, or when the same government shrewdly imprisons accused or suspected defendants outside US territories in order to avoid US Constitutional liabilities that would be incurred in order to undertake intentional abuse of prisoners' human rights, the double standard calls into question the actual validity of moral pretense. A greater problem focuses on the issue of whether indisputable, clarion rationale justifying one side over another actually exists. It seems poignantly naïve to believe that in today's world, the actions of one side are justified while the opponents are not. We are reminded of the Japanese rationale and practice that all sides in a dispute bear responsibility for any wrong occurring. No black and white world exists. How then does one function morally in such a world?

Walzer assumes from the start that just-war theory and its practice are necessary in democratic societies, although he acknowledges that just war may be practiced by non-democratic societies and tyrants as well. His premise is that we live in a world of power politics, where the elimination or neutralization of both risk and threat is deemed natural.[50] But what does military intervention in the affairs of another state and war upon another entail? To attempt even morally acceptable

---

ticularly when either organized or tolerated genocide occurs. One could easily and sufficiently argue that the national interests were not conducive enough to warrant intervention and the political and economic benefits lacked sufficient incentive vis-à-vis the political and economic costs to be incurred.

50 *Ibid.*, p. 11 Walzer astutely advises, though, that "It is generally true, but especially so in time of violent conflict, that we can understand what other people are saying only if we see through their 'fair pretenses' and

action, certain criteria should have to be met. Walzer, while desiring a morally conscious state and leadership based on philosophical and religious moral guides, recognizes a world driven by power, where the powerful conquer when they can in order to deter invitation of attack and the weak posture or fight to receive the best possible terms of subjection. The moral person, however, whether religious or not and inclusive of the state as person, should first have to gather information on the situation, information that approximates neutrality of perspective just as science requires. If the information discriminates one side or another, any analysis and actions based on this analysis will be skewered and the situation may be worsened because of the dishonesty involved therein. Neutrally gathering information in the real world is nearly impossible. The delineating of acquired information should be arranged chronologically and accurately in order to best observe true cause and effect; it should be categorized in various ways to observe as many sides of arguments in a multi-faceted world. Based on analytical results that are tried and tested by truly unrelated third parties, the moral person must undertake a judgment of some degree about the situation and act judiciously and prudently on that judgment. None of this can facilely be undertaken in either open or closed societies. The mere practicalities and necessary intimacy of relationship required to undertake sound moral judgment and responsible involvement in intervention, for whatever altruistic reason or protection of human rights of third parties, thwart responsible execution of war. To engage in an evaluation of the morality of war, as seen in the aforenoted requirements for a moral person considering intervention, one must be prepared to embark on a thorny, confusing, multi-faceted discussion of what is moral and what are the actual facts.[51]

---

translate moral talk into the harder currency of interest talk." We have noted this in two paragraphs previous.

51 Walzer, *Just and Unjust Wars*, p. 12. Walzer again is cognizant of the difficulties in determining moral justification. He observes correctly, "There are sharp disparities in the weight we attach even to values we share, as there are in the actions we are ready to condone when these values are threatened. There are conflicting commitments and obligations that force us into violent antagonism even when we see the point of one another's positions. All this is real enough and common enough: it makes moral-

If we accept the line of reasoning of Walzer that just war, inclusive of unilateral intervention, is undertaken for the benefit of oppressed peoples, we can see the moral persuasion of arguments advocated by Jürgen Moltmann, Dietrich Bonhoeffer, Camillo Torres, etc. The Christian aspect of their moral argument shall be explored in the following two chapters. We shall confine our investigation here to analyzing the politicized morality of war as presented by Walzer, a morality that he deduces to have arisen from the "moral law." (Walzer, 2000, xix)

Although Walzer infers that war may be initiated as a criminal act, he does not consider war always to be hell, the occurrence of absolute war in which the parties to the conflict exercise no limits as to the use of force, brutality, and destruction or the conscription or induced enlistment of poorer masses forced to fight to sustain themselves. (Walzer, 2000, 23-28) Even though limitless war may not be occurring, it is difficult to imagine it as a contest acceptable to improving the character, integrity, and respect for fellow humans. War is not just force, it is chaos, the breakdown of order (or the Augustinian contrast of the loss of the tranquility of order), harmony, and the established means of non-lethal interaction, as Akira Kurosawa, the famed Japanese film director and producer, depicted in his film, Ran ( ), on the civil wars of Japan. All wars involve to some degree consent of soldiers, the general populace, and political and religious leaders and, to the extent that consent is withheld or objection muffled; war becomes tyrannical, no matter how restrictive its leaders confine it. With or without coercion, war remains nothing other than hell and ugliness of the despicable aspects of human character.[52]

How do people like Walzer interpret justification for engagement in warfare? Aggression, i.e., the coercion of people to risk their lives and property for the sake of their rights, is the crime that purportedly justifies war, he claims, whether lethal defense of these rights is employed or resistance is forgone. The rights in the case of a state are

---

ity into a world of good-faith quarrels as well as a world of ideology and verbal manipulations."

52 Walzer correctly views soldiering in industrialized societies and developing countries, whether enlisted voluntarily or conscripted, to be of a type of mercenary and professional fighter.

defined as territorial integrity and political sovereignty, the exercise of the ability to make autonomous decisions pertaining to the existence and well-being of the citizens and residents—life and liberty of the resident individuals and their community. In the legalist paradigm proposed by Walzer, aggression is a criminal act; both violent response as self-defense in the face of imminent (threat) or effected aggression and "a war of law enforcement by the victim and any other member of international society, are deemed justified.... Nothing but aggression can justify war." (Walzer, 2000, 62) With this paradigm, resistance, states Walzer, is not only justified, it is heroic, even in the face of overwhelming odds of failure, but exercise of such may be so costly that appeasement, i.e., "giving in to aggressors" to avoid war and therein yielding to coercion and injustice, possibly, may be preferable even though the antagonized state relinquishes the values of its citizenry. (Walzer, 2000, 67-68) He concludes that appeasement, while not necessarily idealistic, may be unfortunately realistic (cf. the Munich principle which concedes the loss of rights for sake of survival of citizens), but he seems to argue for resistance in order to deter future aggression precisely because he emphasizes that defense of one's rights is the only justifiable reason for resistance and fighting in the face of aggression.[53]

With the premise that just war is acceptable, Walzer explores the problems regarding preemptive military strikes and preventive war. He emphasizes that pre-emptive military strikes can only occur morally when the threat is imminent.[54] When is a threat really imminent? What constitutes a threat? Walzer acknowledges that this evaluation

53 Walzer rules out "preventive wars, commercial wars, wars of expansion and conquest, religious crusades, revolutionary wars, military interventions." *Just and Unjust Wars*, p. 72. In defense of individual and state rights, though, he does not rule out pre-emptive war in order to defend oneself against violence that is imminent but not yet actual. Inclusive also in pre-emptive war are wars undertaken in order to preserve a balance of power and deter it from tipping in favor of an opponent.

54 Walzer, *Just and Unjust Wars*, p. 74-85. "Both individuals and states can rightfully defend themselves against violence that is imminent but not actual; they can fire the first shots if they know themselves about to be attacked. This is a right recognized in domestic law and also in the legalist paradigm for international society."

and judgment remain complicated and thorny. The purpose of threatening acts is intimately linked to the intent of the one threatening, but also is intertwined with the right of response, or the manipulation of opinion to support a desired response.[55] Walzer then posits his conditions for distinguishing between legitimate and illegitimate first strikes "a manifest intent to injure, a degree of active preparation that makes that intent a positive danger, and a general situation in which waiting, or doing anything other than fighting, greatly magnifies the risk.... Instead of previous signs of rapacity and ambition, current and particular signs are required; instead of an 'augmentation of power,' actual preparation for war; instead of the refusal of future securities, the intensification of present dangers." (Walzer, 2000, 81) Leaders engaging either in preemptive military strikes or embarking on war for preventive purposes, usually to assure to themselves that a balance of power will not be tipped against their state or their political standing, often use lies, misrepresentations, distortion of the truth, or misleading statements to substantiate their decision to embark on war, claims Walzer.[56] This deceptive practice cannot be viewed as either an anomaly or an aberration in the policy-implementations employed by national leaders; it is common practice and spurious reasons and obfuscating logic are generally used to validate hidden agenda of government leaders. As to preventive war, Walzer observes, that in

55 *Ibid.*, pp. 80-81. While injury and provocation are identified with scholastical justification for war, troop movements, military alliances, mobilizations, blockades, military incursions, border skirmishes, monopolization of natural resources (their exploitation, manufacture, delivery, etc.) when needed for national economic survival may also be included in considering the intent of perceived hostile actions, but they remain subject to interpretation and may or may not count as threat or provocation in acts that harm a nation.

56 One cannot fail to observe that the Bush administration in the US in 2001 through 2003 proffered all sorts of reasons for invading Iraq—imminent threat of attack with weapons of mass destruction, the continued development and manufacture of weapons of mass destruction in Iraq, the coalition of the Iraqi leadership with armed and militant international terrorist groups, the support of Al-Qaeda in attacking the US, etc. All of these spurious reasons turned out to be nothing more than excuses to inflame national support for attacking Iraq.

the case of eighteenth and nineteenth century Europe, the arguments supporting preventive wars was based on a utilitarian rationale, but left open tremendous future threats, misapplications, and a perpetuating cycle of violence.[57] Ultimately, according to Walzer, preventive wars or preemptive military strikes are morally permissible when war is perceived to be threatened and "whenever the failure to do so would seriously risk their (i.e., states') territorial integrity or political independence." (Walzer, 2000, 85)

The aforenoted discussion of just war, preemptive strike, and preventive war certainly follows the basic tenets submitted by Augustine and the Scholastics and notes the dangers inherent in the politicization of just war theory. Let us now turn to another contemporary problem related to this theory, the issue of intervention. Given the innumerable historical precedents for intervention and the spurious and moral rationalization and justification for intervention witnessed in Western colonialism, the non-aligned nations after World War II frequently, especially in the 1960s and 1970s, met mutually to support their domestic development and to provide mutual force among non-aligned states in the face of potential resurgence of colonial powers and the vested interests of the super powers (US and USSR) that threatened

---

57 Walzer, *Just and Unjust Wars*, pp. 76 and 77. Walzer notes, "The argument is utilitarian in form; it can be summed up in two propositions: (1) that the balance of power actually does preserve the liberties of Europe (perhaps also the happiness of Europeans) and is therefore worth defending even at some cost, and (2) that to fight early, before the balance tips in any decisive way, greatly reduces the cost of the defense, while waiting doesn't mean avoiding war (unless one also gives up liberty) but only fighting on a larger scale and at worse odds. The argument is plausible enough, but it is possible to imagine a second-level utilitarian response: (3) that the acceptance of propositions (1) and (2) is dangerous (not useful) and certain to lead to 'innumerable and fruitless wars' whenever shifts in power relations occur; but incrementals and losses of power are a constant feature of international politics, and perfect equilibrium, like perfect security, is a utopian dream; therefore it is best to fall back upon the legalist paradigm or some similar rule and wait until the overgrowth of power is put to some overbearing use.... (T)here probably is no practical way of making out that position —deciding when to fight and when not—on utilitarian principles."

the interests of smaller, weaker, and poorer non-aligned developing countries. The non-aligned nations promoted a principle of mutual respect and non-intervention in the affairs of other states, something that the French and the US had ignored in the ensuing development of politics in Vietnam, not to mention precedents established with regard to Korea, Cuba, Germany, Czechoslovakia, Dominican Republic, Haiti, Afghanistan, etc. Walzer, as noted above, defends and advocates intervention, although it contradicts his principle and basic premise that the rights of territorial integrity and political independence are paramount in international relations.

Following the principle of non-intervention with regard to territorial integrity, political self-determination, is not always deemed necessary, in fact, should be disregarded, claims Walzer, because coercive action should be suffered only at one's own hands—namely, from one's own nation state, not from another. John Stuart Mill makes the case that states are self-determining communities although their internal politics may lack freedom and transparency or their citizens may not have the freedom to determine their leadership or vote on their national and international policy. A state lacks the freedom of self-determination when its institutions of government are established by the intervention of another state. Freedom cannot be bestowed; it is attained only when the members of a political community seek and attain freedom for themselves—self help. War and the armies of another state make it difficult, if not impossible, to produce freedom, although they may inspire it. Walzer argues against the premises presented by Mill because they are too constrictive and make it increasingly difficult, if not impossible, to accept just war.[58] He then states three cases that

---

58   Walzer, *Just and Unjust Wars*, pp. 87-89. Walzer acknowledges correctly that "foreign intervention, if it is a brief affair, cannot shift the domestic balance of power in any decisive way toward the forces of freedom, while if it is prolonged or intermittently resumed, it will itself pose the greatest possible threat to the success of those forces." The reasons have nothing or little to attribute to the issue of just war, but relate more to the practicality of power politics and the perceptions of colonized peoples. His assumption that conquest, as opposed to colonization or its perception thereof, works differently and may be successful in both providing incentive for domestic freedoms to promote domestic self-determination, as in the cases of US conquest of Nazi Germany and imperial Japan in

would justify suspension of the principle of sovereign territoriality and permit coercive border crossings or military intervention;

1. When a particular set of boundaries clearly contains two or more political communities, one of which is already engaged in a large-scale military struggle for independence; that is, when what is at issue is secession or 'national liberation;'

2. When the boundaries have already been crossed by the armies of a foreign power, even if the crossing has been called for by one of the parties in a civil war, that is when what is at issue is counter-intervention; and

3. when the violation of human rights within a set of boundaries is so terrible that it makes talk of community or self-determination or 'arduous struggle' seem cynical and irrelevant, that is in cases of enslavement or massacre. (Walzer, 2000, 90)

We cannot easily dismiss Walzer's criteria for unilaterally suspending the ban on incursion or coercive border crossings in the aforenoted three cases. They raise serious questions that confront the justification for war as discussed above. They provide the basis for justifying war for reasons other than self-defense or against aggression, according to Walzer's premises. In effect, Walzer attempts to provide validation for just war rationale to be used in support of other parties engaged in wars of independence in which certain social groups seek their own restrictive self-determination, an iteration of which can be identified as parties to a civil war (the case of secession), and when one or more groups of a society are denied what are considered their

World War II, may be true and applicable in the world of *realpolitik*, but still avoids the issue of justification, other than that the end justifies the means. Walzer intends to justify without logical, deductive proof that intervention may necessitate and validate war—i.e., just war.

In fact, Walzer attempts to find justification for war through intervention based on the premises that territorial boundaries are often arbitrarily or accidentally established and that the relations between political communities within those boundaries remain ambiguous or that the lack of clarity of when self-determination is actually being practiced. This is paramount to tautology. Walzer, thus, claims that the law, (which law he never states) has no authoritative verdict to governing permissible intervention.

human rights to the extent that they would be enslaved or massacred if another external power did not intervene on their behalf. These criteria implicitly follow the thinking of Augustine and a further extrapolation of the application of Aquinas' thinking. As per Mill, their premise rests on the necessary respect for upholding communal autonomy and the burden of proof, according Walzer, rests on the intervening state. Without disregarding the issue of politicization of the morality of the war, particularly in the favor of the party seeking to validate its own interest, (and who can claim political altruism in international politics), the moral validity of intervention remains no less questionable.[59] The duplicity and inconsistency of application of policies justifying intervention belie the justification of intervention in most wars and the actual purpose providing moral backing for just war rationale—i.e., the true politicization of just war thinking to meet state interests.

Beyond the observations noted hereabove, let us then consider the reasons acceptable and justifying engagement in lethal, military activity, i.e., those presented by Walzer for *jus ad bellum*—defense of territorial integrity, protection of self-determination, and its deducible protection of communal liberty. The rationale for such determines the objective of waging war, as irrational as the end actually is, as defined by Walzer. "'The object in war is a better state of peace.' And *better*, within the confines of the argument for justice, means more secure than the *status quo ante bellum*, less vulnerable to territorial expansion,

---

59   It is not small task for the intervening states to make their case to demonstrate that their reasons for intervention are necessitated by more than moral support of other parties. If we take the case of the US intervention in Iraq in 2003 and thereafter, or US intervention in Vietnam from 1963 onward, it becomes increasingly difficult, if not down right dubious, that the intervention is for the benefit of the respectively intervened country. In the former, clearly OIL (Oil, Israel, and Logistics for control of the extraction and shipment of Mideastern oil), and in the latter, oil in the sea off Vietnam amongst other natural resources (tin, rubber, etc.) and the adverse influence on neighboring governments who might have enacted policies contrary to US political, military, and economic interests (e.g., blockage of the Malacca Straits, etc.), were the principal reasons for intervention, not support of the rights of possibly persecuted minorities who sided against the interventionists.

safer for ordinary men and women and for their domestic self-deter-mination." (Walzer, 2000, 121-122) While the state traditionally and customarily exercises authority within its territorial boundaries at a minimum, although it may attempt to influence and exert its authority beyond those boundaries, the physical and geographic borders of the state have historically been established through conflict, disagreement, exploitation and expropriation, and various disputable property claims by one or more parties. Boundaries remain disputable for not just years, but for centuries; their demarcation and appropriateness are nebulous and depend on the power of the rulers or the state. The boundaries between North and South Korea, between North and South Vietnam, between East and West Germany, or between China and Taiwan, the autonomous region off the Chinese coast whose present government has changed its initial objectives of governance, are purely arbitrary and provide no sensible reason for separating the same ethnic groups and nations;[60] they remain a cause for dispute and discord, inviting conflict as they did until they were or are removed. No one needs to recall the dispute over territorial boundaries and land rights in Pal-estine and the present state of Israel. Given this precariousness with regard to the correctness of boundaries as the point of demarcation for domestic rule, are boundaries and territorial integrity satisfactory reasons for engaging in lethal conflict? Further, in view of the afore-noted discussion regarding the justification for intervention in the case of revolutionary, civil, or secessionist wars, the primary importance attached to territorial integrity seems significantly diminished because of the facileness of disregarding boundaries in order to support self-determination of state sub-groups.

The second reason supporting *jus ad bellum* concerns the right of autonomous determination and self-determination, particularly with regard to communal liberty. Wars initiated in order to protect the right of self-determination, whether the domestic rule of law be

60   Walzer, *Just and Unjust Wars*, p. 123, notes correctly that, "The theory of ends in war is shaped by the same rights that justify the fighting in the first place—most importantly, by the right of nations, even of enemy nations, to continued national existence and, except in extreme circum-stances, to the political prerogatives of nationality." If such would be the case, then the aforenoted divided nations have every right to wage war to reunite in order to restore their prerogatives of nationality.

in monarchical, single sovereign, single party, dictatorial, or some form of democratic or representative government, seem rationally laudable and acceptable as means for a society of whatever type to govern themselves as they deem fit, or allow their rulers to deem fit. Aggression against domestic rule would be cause for protecting the right of self-determination. One must question whether the results of war result in the successful protection of these rights. Further, what is the cost in the protection of these rights, and is the domestic population better off or worse off *en toto* through waging defensive lethal war in order to protect the self-determination, of whatever type? What is the level of pain, suffering, brutality, destruction, etc. acceptable to a society in defense of its right to self-determination? In as much as international society is increasingly inter-dependent and domestic policy is intertwined with foreign policy, and vice-versa, particularly in consideration of the globalization of economic and business interests, do self-determination and communal liberties as demarcated by statal governments mean as much or have as much weight in effecting the lives of domestic citizens? Labor policies and management of capital exercised by global corporations bear far greater influence on the lives, happiness, security, and well-being of citizens in both developed and developing countries. If self-determination has any meaning in the twenty-first century, the focus should probably shift from governmental control to valuing the loss of self-determination in a global economy and seeking either to compensate for such, as governments are capable, or to requiring redress from these corporations and restricting their ability to wreak havoc on local communities.

With regard to cases that Walzer identifies as acceptable for intervention according to application of just war rationale, the following observations are in order. Although Walzer places the onus of justification on the invader, practical considerations demand realizable answers and solutions. Intervention in any society, because of wars of liberation or revolution, secession, civil strife, counter-intervention to support one party or another in civil strife, or in protection of domestic groups which are in danger of massacre or enslavement, necessitates the ability and commitment of the intervening state to actually improve conditions in that society. It is difficult to imagine that conditions can be improved if the invading or intervening forces lack the skills, (language, technical, judicial, etc.), have insufficient resources, be deficient in understanding the historical, religious, cultural, ethnic issues, or fail to have long-term vested interests that behoove their continued presence without becoming a colonizer. Possessing these deficient characteristics makes the intervention nothing more than a gross, lethal nuisance that can only exasperate domestic forces seeking support; in brief, as per Mao Tse-tung, politics out of the barrel of a gun. Might it not be better to attempt to bring differing parties to the table than to intervene and botch relationships further because of the ignorance of or insufficient and deficient understanding of participating parties? It is most difficult to find constructive examples of lethal military intervention in history that are beneficially contributing and long-lasting generators of non-lethal, non-conflictual peace. While Walzer goes to great lengths to justify the unconditional surrender required by the Allies of Nazi Germany, there lingers a heavy burden of proof of moral justification for war on the very Allies themselves who bear significant responsibility for fomenting the conditions that made the Nazi's so powerful. Violence merely begot further violence.[61]

CONDITIONS APPLICABLE AFTER COMMENCING JUST WAR, & THE REAL WORLD

Let us now turn to the practicality of *jus in bello* and analyze the conditions therein. While the two conditions of the Church noted above, namely, proportionality and discrimination of non-combatants, political scientists and military planners also use the same, but from a different perspective. Proportionality, for example, is negatively defined by Henry Sidgwick such that the conduct of hostilities is not permitted when "any mischief which does not tend materially to the

---

61 Walzer, *Just and Unjust Wars*, pp. 111 - 117. Walzer wisely cautions against waging wars whose objectives are total victory and unconditional surrender. These wars border on, if are not identical with, religious crusades and wars of absolutist ideology wherein one side paints unrealistic world views of clear black and white options, emphasizes the punitive character and chastisement, aims not at defense or enforcement of laws, but at creation of a radically restructured world order and mass conversion—thus, it becomes a means to persecute and extract the last pound of flesh. It oft fails to permit or view a world in which the defeated continue to be participants in the world order.

end [of victory], nor any mischief of which the conduciveness to the end is slight in comparison with the amount of the mischief."[62] While the moralist theorizes on the aspect of proportionality, the military planner in fact elevates victory well over the interests of individuals and the ramifications upon society at large. Proportionality is not only difficult to apply in real world terms, but the moral considerations therein are secondary to military strategy.[63] Whatever it takes to win with intelligent, economic, and efficient use of force (in a utilitarian approach) is permitted in military action; lethal violence remains an implicit given, unless threats prove sufficient for military objectives. This begs the question on the morality of engagement in war, but retains the central importance of ends—reducing the total amount of suffering and the avoidance of reprisals and bitterness that necessitate a perpetuation of détente after hostilities end.[64]

Discrimination in *jus in bello* is the most pliable and permissive condition, yet remains the most morally abused condition and difficult to apply. As noted above, given that today the overwhelming majority of persons maimed, injured, and killed in war are non-combatants, whether intentionally targeted or not, by any of the adversaries, the military participants in war have to be culpable. Let us consider the

---

62   Henry Sidgwick, *The Elements of Politics* (London: 1891), p. 254, cited by Walzer, *Just Wars and Unjust Wars*, p. 129. Walzer notes that Sidgwick proposes two criteria: (1) the purpose of war is victory, i.e., military necessity, and (2) proportionality, whereby one weighs the mischief done against individuals and society at large in proportion to its contribution to attaining victory, thereby diminishing the importance of individuals and society to that of the victory.

63   How does one adequately and accurately evaluate and compare either in economic terms analogous to cost-benefit analysis the economic costs of waging lethal conflict, or in spiritual terms that ascribe value to damage, cost, and the expected good as the US Catholic bishops advocate? The level of subjectivity required to undertake such would seem to undercut the veracity of the analytical results. This remains the perpetual problem of cost-benefit analysis, as good as it can attempt to be, though.

64   Citing Sidgwick, Walzer notes that the end of war must result in a reasonable termination of bitterness among rivals which behooves the victor to avoid consequences that the defeated interpreted as unjust in their favor, as excessive brutality in the attainment of victory.

various issues related to application of this condition of discrimination.

Although soldiers are subject to attack at any time, unless wounded or captured, according to previously established conventions ratified at the Hague and at Geneva, non-combatants and civilians are proscribed from being targeted for death. Military necessity may seek to constrict these requirements. Having jumped onto the slippery slope of accepting the necessity of war, it is increasingly difficult to curtail interpretation of these conditions, unless one is on the manifestly superior and victorious side. Might makes right! In traditional and conventional war, non-combatants and civilians increasingly become intertwined with, intermingled in, and implicitly essential to combatants, and not just supporters of one warring group or another. Conventional war today requires a significant part of the population to be involved in military-related industries, not just suppliers of provision of food, clothing, and medical support; war is both military and economic activity. This is not only true with regard to conventional war, but guerrilla war, sieges, blockades, and terrorism. As Mao and Clauswitz have noted, military activity in the manner of war is merely an extension of political activity, political assassinations inclusive.

As if the rules of war meant anything meaningful to non-combatants, they permit militaries to disregard non-combatants and to refuse to come to their aid. Walzer, citing indirectly John C. Ford, SJ, lists four conditions related to the double effect, namely, one is permitted to perform an act likely having evil consequences, such as killing civilians who cannot be extricated from military targets, when the following four conditions are met.

1. The act is good in itself or at least indifferent, which means for our purposes, that it is a legitimate act of war.
2. The direct effect is morally acceptable—the destruction of military supplies, for example, or the killing of enemy soldiers.[65]
3. The intention of the actor is good, that is, he aims narrowly at the acceptable effect: the evil effect is not one of his ends, nor is

---

65 John C. Ford, SJ, "The Morality of Obliteration Bombing," in *War and Morality*, ed. Richard Wassertrom (Belmont, California: 1970), cited by Walzer, *Just and Unjust Wars*, pp. 153 and 155.

it a means to his ends, and, aware of the evil involved, he seeks to minimize it, accepting costs to himself.[66]

4. The good effect is sufficiently good to compensate for allowing the evil effect; it must be justifiable under Sidgwick's proportionality rule.[67]

The double effect, namely the unfortunate evil effected on civilians and non-combatants when attacking military targets, can be deemed nothing other than a spurious, justifying, and legitimizing rationale to assuage the consciences of military participants in circumventing the prohibition of killing non-combatants. No doubt, the separation of non-combatants and civilians from the military theatre is often realistically nigh impossible. When the US in Vietnam attempted forced resettlement of rural villagers from targeted areas, people naturally returned to their homes and their livelihood either out of necessity or once they, rightly or wrongly, perceived the danger past. Non-combatants and civilians invariably became part of the targeted villages. Not only was it unreal to think that the US could provide the necessary means of livelihood through forced resettlement, but it was through perverse logic, myopic reasoning, unrealistic planning, and pursuit of its own vested interests that the US justified its intervention in Vietnam. The aforenoted conditions leave open many unanswered questions. Is the act of even killing another soldier good in itself? How can one be indifferent to killing? This is insensitive and inhuman. Does the intended effect justify the means and make killing and destruction acceptable? While the intent might not be to kill non-combatants, does the consequence of war make it acceptable? This is surely callous reasoning. Finally but not least, the rationale of proportionality permits the good effect (i.e., killing of enemy soldiers or destroying their fighting base, if some form of perverted logic can understand this as good, although it is not Christian morality) to compensate for the evil effect of killing civilians and non-combatants and destroying their livelihood. It is only the most perverse and spurious moral logic that

---

66   Walzer, *Just and Unjust Wars*, p. 155, revised Ford's third condition only.

67   Ford, "The Morality of Obliteration Bombing," cited in Walzer, *Just and Unjust Wars*, p. 153.

can condone the total evil and its effects in war. Again, this becomes none other than the perverse moral logic of might makes right.

The violence inflicted upon civilians and non-combatants rather than on military personnel becomes even more apparent in wars of the past century, particularly of the past half century, but then maybe only our consciousness of such has been aroused. One cannot help to note that the siege of Leningrad by the Nazis killed more non-combatants through famine, disease, and weapons than the massive, immoral fire bombings of Tokyo, Dresden, Hamburg, and the two nuclear attacks on Hiroshima and Nagasaki combined. Roughly one million of the three million temporary and permanent civilian residents died because of the siege. Precedents and the practice of internationally agreed war conventions cannot be counted on to assure the enactment of moral conscience, because the principle of military expedience takes precedence and is accepted under the just war thinking. Civilians who either attempted to flee through the German lines, because that was their only exit before winter, or were expelled from Leningrad by the Russian army, because they taxed the remaining provisions of the besieged Russian army, were trapped in the city until January 1942 when escape became possible across frozen Lake Lakoda. The German army fired on the fleeing civilians and forced these refugees back into the city to overburden their adversary forces. Thus, when the German general, Field Marshal von Leeb, was tried at the Nuremberg war tribunal, he was acquitted of all charges because, under precedent in international law and military convention, the attacker is permitted to deter any benefit to the besieged army. With little doubt, besieged forces as well as attacking armies will take and use for their own provisions whatever is materially necessary; non-combatants are used forcibly to feed, clothe, shelter, and provide medical help to the forces of violence before caring for themselves. Because of what is termed military necessity and expediency, militaries provide for themselves first and the general populace is left to survive on the remainder. Even though permitted under convention and due to the pliability of just war theory, it can hardly be considered moral, as if war itself were moral. Just as Walzer condemns Britain as morally culpable for starving the German civilian populace to get to the military with its expansive blockade in World War I, so too we must condemn the US strategy as immoral for destroying the Iraqi water and sewer works and prohibiting the Iraqi import of materials to restore those works to prevent the deaths of more than 500,000 children. (Walzer, 2000, 174)

Although war conventions and international law may permit attacking civilians, as well as just war theory in terms of double effect, it is doubly immoral to consider the allowance for refugee flight as satisfactory for justifying moral action. Is life better off for the civilian alive, but lacking food, shelter, medicine, work etc. when they as refugees have fled the brutality of war? Is that really living or are we just kidding ourselves? Opportunity might remain, but how many years or decades does it take before some semblance of normalcy returns while starvation, sickness, emotional and mental trauma, miscarriage and abortion, collapse of social and religious morals and order, etc. run ramped? Thus, it is only to be expected that civilians and non-combatants will refuse to flee as refugees, and, thus, by war convention and approved by international law they perversely remain legitimate targets.[68]

GUERRILLA WAR: CONTEMPORARY PREDOMINANT MODE OF WARFARE & ITS MORAL ISSUES

Finally, one needs to consider the moral issues connected with guerrilla warfare and terrorism that is employed by both guerrillas and right-wing militias and militaries. Contrary to the conventions of war, guerrillas attempt to remain one amongst the population that supports them and, therefore, refrain from using customary symbols of soldiers in the form of garb. They do not hide in the general populace, but the populace is part of the guerrillas' base; the war becomes a people's war, with the

---

68   Walzer, *Just and Unjust Wars*, p. 168. One is reminded of the citizens of Mosul, Iraq, in 2004, slightly more than one-quarter of a million people, who either stayed and were killed in the US attack on the city, or fled to a life of greater hardship while their city was leveled. To which life do these refugees have to look forward? Where can one find justifying rationale in the incipient lethal destructiveness of these wanton acts of institutional terror and murder?

To Walzar's credit, he acknowledges that soldiers have an obligation to help civilians leave the target area of a battle, despite the adjudications of Nuremberg.

war from below and within the guerrillas' home base and within their own people, not restricted to uniformed military carrying identifiable weapons.[69] Thus, conventional military forces fighting against guerrillas find themselves in a war with the general civilian populace, noncombatants inclusive, and, contrary to war convention, conventional forces never become safe amongst civilians then. Scholars like Walzer are mistaken in their evaluation of guerrilla war and its morality when they get caught in the trap of acknowledging that resistance may be legitimate and, thus, punishment of resistance is too. This, however, demonstrates the extrapolation that might makes right, but in fact the punishment of resistance is usually effected by an imposed power, an occupier or usurper, who self-proclaims legitimacy of rule even though the general populace may oppose such. It must also be indicated that guerrillas often employ terrorist-like tactics of killing targeted civilians whom they deem are collaborating with their enemy or are sympathetic to their adversary and oppose their own overthrow by the guerrillas. These must be interpreted as political killings; admittedly, unrelated bystanders and others are harmed in the violent process of political assassination often. Guerrillas may also attempt to cause disruption and disorder in society to influence the general populace in favor of the guerrillas. Because guerrilla warfare is a struggle for the hearts and minds of the people, these tactics may prove disastrous, no different than when the occupation forces or nationally standing government through the police or its army oppress the general populace to deter their support for the guerrillas. This does not justify the morality of

---

69   Walzer, *Just and Unjust Wars*, pp. 182-183, mistakenly criticizes guerrillas because they are largely indistinguishable from the civilian population with whom they identify and who supports them. Strategically and tactically the guerrillas use the military means of surprise to dishearten, tire, and demoralize their stronger adversary and in catching them off guard attack them when they are weakest and least expect. Fighting against superior and more powerful forces, the guerrillas have little else to compensate for their weakness and attempt to even the playing field. This has nothing to do with the moral logic employed by Walzer who possibly seems to view war in chivalrous terms of fighting under a gentlemen's agreement according to war conventions that seek to support status-quo powers.

political assassination and suppression of the people's aspirations and desires for an opposing government.

As an ancillary subtopic, what is the morality of killing non-combatant civilians associated with a guerrilla war? Further, despite the aforenoted war conventions and the moral teachings of Jesus, may guerrillas, whether engaged in political assassinations effecting civilians or not, be killed even when captured, under or outside of just war thinking? If one would apply the conventions of war fairly in spirit, it would seem that guerrillas, who are effectively citizen soldiers, should also benefit from the war conventions, despite the guerrillas' lack of identity (clothing, insignias, weapons, etc.) as conventional soldiers. Extrapolating this principle to the next step, one can reason that political assassination by guerrillas, even when injuring or killing other non-combatants, should not disqualify guerrillas from rightfully receiving the benefits of these war conventions.[70] The civilian population which supports or is pressed not to oppose (through terror, persuasion, neutrality, etc.) the guerrilla movement, thereby, increasingly puts itself into a status fraught with liability and danger, not least of which is presenting seemingly valid cause for attack and retribution, but then guerrilla war is for the hearts and minds of the general populace. The onus of influence for winning these hearts is forced into the laps of the counter-insurgents. Walzer shows how a counter-insurgent war becomes immoral if and when the general populace cannot be isolated from the guerrillas precisely because the target of the war is then directed against the society, not just the guerrillas.[71] As noted above, it is nigh impossible to deport,

---

70   Walzer, *Just and Unjust Wars*, p. 183, counters, though, that most legal interpreters opine that guerrillas are excluded from protection under these covenants, for acts related to political assassinations, lethal attacks, and social disruption effected by guerrillas. In the end, Walzer , p. 185, contests that guerrillas should receive protection from these war conventions because, like soldiers, they acquire their rights not as individuals but as political instruments of their communities, who are complicit in their support and involvement in the cause of the guerrillas.

71   *Ibid.*, p. 187. The burden of anti-guerrilla warfare placed on the counter-insurgents may be seen as possibly insurmountable because the forces fighting the guerrillas are in a no-win-no-win situation. To attack the guerrillas and/or their civilian base of support—i.e., its locus amongst the civilian population— either becomes more immoral because it places

relocate, evacuate or extract all civilians from the guerrillas' base for innumerable reasons—limitation of language, inability to provide logistics, deficiency in providing comparable living standards (housing, food, job, healthcare, etc.), unreal expectation that all citizens will be warned of pending attacks in advance, inability to distinguish fighting and support personnel amongst the guerrillas, etc. Any attempt to accomplish these tasks by an occupying army is little more than a pipe dream or casuistic justification for the nominal benefit of occupying forces and their supporters. Should such actions be attempted, in the real world the proportionality of evil and miserable living conditions for the evacuated, relocated, or deported civilians far outweighs the intended good of discrimination for civilians' benefit. To justify such attacks on civilian populations in areas controlled by or supportive of the guerrillas on the basis of political evaluations of the loyalty or friendliness of non-combatants toward the guerrillas does not qualify because these areas also include children and non-supporters of the guerrillas. While much of just war theory related to discrimination and proportionality in *jus in bello* allows great leeway for attack on both guerrillas and non-combatants who are part of the guerrilla area, we can hardly consider it moral for the reasons noted above.

One cannot fail to be conscious that proponents of just war rationale, inclusive of Walzer, promote bellicose treatment of conflict, inclusive of invasion and preemptive strikes, for the central purpose of avoiding further war or worsening a state's present position. Woodrow Wilson attempted to validate the US' entry into World War I under the rationale of embarking on a war to end all wars. This remains no exception. Just as the war to end all wars failed to resolve political or military disputes and conflicts, so too no can expect any war to end future confrontation between belligerent parties. Once a state embarks on militarist means to resolve conflicts, it becomes increasingly difficult to back away from the brink of copying the same model at other times in other situations.

---

the greatest hardship and loss on the civilians or it hardens and broadens the resolve of the guerrillas' base of support as was seen in the Philippines in the 1940s and in Vietnam in the 1960s and 1970s. To refrain from attacking the guerrillas' base allows the guerrillas to embolden and broaden their attack on the counter-insurgents.

Just war rationale, then, can hardly be considered moral in either a Christian context or in the real world. Beginning with the earliest crusades, those initiated by the Christianized Romans who sought to defend or take back land from invading groups in the fifth century and the Crusades against Moslems in the Holy Land of the eleventh and twelfth centuries, the Church has mistakenly proclaimed justification for embarking on the lethal violence of war. The carnage, rape, and exploitation have proven anything but moral, though. Augustine initiated the thinking of just war practice as a defense of the Christianized Roman Empire because of his Manichean past, his partition of inner practice of Christian living from a perceived outer, sinful world, and as an apologetic for the Empire's religion that had become symbiotic with government, contrary to the clear guidance of the fathers of the Church. Aquinas, basing his thinking on Augustine who heavily used natural law theory, further theologically sought to underpin the validation for just war, but left a loophole that allowed the subjugation of natural law thinking to divine law, the law of the Spirit, and the teachings of Jesus, and, possibly in so doing, acknowledged the primacy of the beatitudes and the Sermon on the Mount which clearly forbid the exercise of violence by Christians, inclusive of just-war implementation. The Church has mandated that various criteria be precedent before implementing just war thinking either as validating the entrance into just war or in the practice of war itself. These conditions hardly seem applicable to justify war itself in contemporary society and, in fact, do disservice to the teachings of Jesus, not just because they are difficult to discern and implement, but because contemporary practice of war requires war on society and not combatants. Nevertheless, society today has attempted to secularize and definitely to politicize the morality of war, be it conventional, nuclear annihilation, or guerrilla war. The rules and conventions of war can hardly be considered moral and, like the weakness and hollowness of just war theory, increasingly tolerate harm inflicted on civilians through the double effect. Given the fact that the vast majority of deaths in war are non-combatants, the undertaking and exercise of war remains undeniably futile and immoral. Even in the secularization of the morality of war, war as a means of conflict-resolution fails to become an acceptable or semi-lasting approach to peace.

CHAPTER 6

UNDERSTANDING WAR & VIOLENT CONFLICT-RESOLUTION:

THE CHRISTIAN PROBLEM OF LIVING IN THE TWENTY-FIRST CENTURY

How are we to understand war and violent, lethal conflict-resolution if we are to live as responsible persons, not just followers of Jesus, in the twenty-first century? To answer this, it behooves us to explore the thinking of relatively contemporary social commentators, social philosophers, and moral theologians who have offered key and valuable insight inspired by the teachings of the Hebrew and Christian scriptures.

HYBRID CHRISTIAN MORALITY TOLERATING SPECIFIC & LIMITED WAR

Jürgen Moltmann established a basis for discussing and living non-violence in a world fraught with the threat of nuclear holocaust and the pervasive feeling of danger imposed through terror from non-mainstream groups, without recognizing the incipient and omnipresent existence of institutionalized terror of militarist societies posed by large, industrialized nation-states. The ethical problem in political theology for Moltmann arises from his own forced conscription into the Nazi military during the second World War. Moltmann, after the end of that war, confesses that, although he vowed never to bear arms or engage in war again, he would, nevertheless, never allow a tyrant to come to power and be prepared to murder a tyrant.[1]

Moltmann raises an issue that was addressed within oppressed classes in developing countries, the dilemma of use of revolutionary violence by oppressed peoples finding no other authorized means of alleviating their plight within domestic legal systems, which are generally

---

1 Cited by Rasmusson, *The Church as Polis*, from commentary on "to Bear Arms," p. 136.

skewered in favor of ruling classes. Moltmann initially accepted that, given the case of oppressed blacks in apartheid South Africa, use of inter-group lethal violence in such situations was justifiable. Resistance, whether violent or not, and revolution then are least best solutions to peaceably unsolvable and oppressive situations, though not to be considered desirable.[2] The use of violence must be proportionate to the terms of the human aims of the revolution and depends on the level of social transformation expected.[3] The aim of the revolution, according to Moltmann, does not just include the right to murder tyrants, but also the right to overthrow tyrannical social and political systems that oppress peoples, inclusive of Western societies that economically, politically, and militarily oppress third world countries.[4]

Ernesto Cardenal, the Trappist priest who became Minister of Culture in the Sandinista government under Daniel Ortega in Nicaragua during the 1980s, dealt with this same issue in one of the shared homilies in the archipelago community of Solentiname.[5] Cardenal seems to approve also of revolutionary violence when discoursing on the Kingdom of Heaven and violence discussed in Mt. 11:12-19 and Lk. 16:16-17.

> … the violent ones that conquer the kingdom are the ones that do violence to themselves by means of asceticism, with sacrifices, penitence, and fasting, doing violence to their natures in every way,

2 Moltmann emphasizes that it is usually the powerful that usually emphasize non-violence while the powerless and oppressed do not give up the use of revolutionary violence to resolve their oppression. This observation rings of clarion truth and cannot be denied. It remains a fundamental problem and difficult dilemma in the treatment of violence in Christian morality.

3 Jürgen Moltmann, *Religion, Revolution and the Future* (New York: Scribner, 1969), p. 143.

4 Rasmusson, *The Church as Polis*, p. 137. Moltmann raises the issue that starvation in less developed countries attributed to the exploitive trade and investment policies of developed countries kill more people than the wars of the twentieth century.

5 Ernesto Cardenal, *The Gospel in Solentiname*, vol. 3, translated by Donald D. Walsh (Maryknoll, NY: Orbis Books, 1979), pp. 219-220 and 224.

that idea we should reject. It has been the traditional interpretation for many centuries, but Jesus didn't talk about such things. Instead, right here, a few verses later, Jesus contrasts the lifestyle of John the Baptist (who 'neither ate nor drank'), with his own life style (who 'eats and drinks, and you say he's a glutton and a drunkard'). That's the individualistic and purely spiritualistic interpretation of people who don't want to interpret the Gospel politically. It seems to me that he must be talking about political violence: either the political violence of the kingdom of heaven or that of the guerrilla fighters, who in one way or another want to enter the kingdom, with arms or by laying down arms, or the violence of the enemies of the kingdom of heaven: Herod, the Sanhedrin, the Romans.... He (John the Baptist) told them: 'Now is the revolution.' And that's why since John came violence came. Earlier, when they talked about the kingdom, there was no conflict. They (Jesus and his followers) talked about a future society. Now we must expropriate private property and all that, and now comes violence. The violence that we ourselves must make, and the external violence, as Mayra (another parishioner who participated in this shared homily) says.

Although Moltmann recognizes the non-violence of Jesus as an eschatological hope, not dissimilar from the thinking of Reinhold Niebuhr seen above, he gives priority particularly in the case of revolutionary situations to use violent means of political dispute resolution, but advises non-violent resolution with respect to resolving political disputes amongst industrialized societies, inclusive of threats from nuclear and other mass-destruction weaponry. Rasmusson clarifies Moltmann's position on the eschatological hope with non-violence, "The eschatological hope of a world without violence becomes in the face of the necessary use of violence a transcendental ideal that always questions the necessity of every use of violence and challenges to use as little violence as possible."[6]

Moltmann applies three criteria for determining whether violent resistance is warranted: continuous violation of law, violation of the constitution, or violation of human rights that is legitimized by the constitution or law. Similar to the position of the Catholic Church,

---

6 Rassmusson, *The Church as Polis*, p. 138. The issue is not violence or non-violence, as Rasmusson observes, but the criteria for the use of power—namely, human rights.

Moltmann contends that nuclear weapons and their effect make nuclear war not only immoral, but impractical.[7] This leaves open the moral question of use of nuclear and fissile materials in low-grade nuclear weapons. It would appear that Moltmann would not oppose such, but would condemn the use of nuclear weapons causing mass destruction by either terrorists or conventional powers. Given the proliferation of weapons, inclusive of nuclear weapons of mass destruction, amongst conventional powers and the potential for state subgroups and trans-state powers to obtain and use such, Moltmann calls for (1) the governance of conflict and the maintenance of social order by international organizations, not by self-interested state powers, and (2) for unilateral nuclear disarmament as the only sane way to break the cycle of spiraling proliferation. Finally, although Moltmann concludes from the 1980s and thereafter that violence in international wars is immoral and that international conflicts should be resolved by non-violent and pacifist means, precisely because of the successful precedent witnessed in Eastern Europe, he does not relinquish his acceptance of the morality of revolutionary violence against local tyranny and can be accused of employing a double standard and conflicting use of natural law theory. Suffice it to be said that Moltmann's premise for requiring relinquishment of violence in international conflict but allowing lethal violence in revolution, confusing though it may be, lies in his basic, but conflicting, belief that mankind has it in its power to change and chart the course of history, though not devoid of the power of God as seen in the crucifixion and called for in the Sermon on the Mount, and that power is exercised in political action.

Prophetic Suffering, as Opposed to Violence, as the Means of Conflict Resolution

But, does violence have to be undertaken by the Christian to bring the kingdom? "The lamb that was slain is worthy to receive power and riches, wisdom and strength, honor and glory and blessing," (Rev. 5:12) presents an image of the Christian that seems more in tune with the teachings of Jesus. Not only does Jesus practice non-violence as

---

7 As in encyclicals of Popes John XXIII , Paul VI, and John Paul II and according to *Gaudium et Spes*, there can be neither just nuclear war nor just nuclear armament, something to which Moltmann accedes.

noted in a previous chapter, but the Jews in the first century ce practiced non-violent resistance in the face of Roman attempts to commit sacrilege of their holy sites.[8] Suffering is the required and expected practice of exercising non-violent resistance as seen in not only Jesus, but in the apostolic and patristic communities, and necessarily in the followers of Jesus. Suffering is the result of obedience to carrying out the message of Jesus, there is no getting around it in a world seeking satisfaction upon the suffering of others. "If they persecuted me they will persecute you." (John 15:20) John Howard Yoder indicates that this is not a pastoral counsel, but a normative message about the obedience to the messianity of Jesus, while both renouncing violence as the naturally expected means of redressing wrong and necessitating active involvement in correcting that wrong. Hostility to this type of response may be expected.[9]

Yoder further provides us with important insights into understanding the teachings of Jesus in the way Jesus lived his life with respect to non-violent social interaction in order that we might affect Jesus' messianic morality. Thus, the Jesus of history, living in radical obedience to his God, really sought to commence the kingdom of God now through non-violent overturning of injustice; this was not merely the retroactive interpretation of the Jesus of memory by the early Church or the scriptural and kerygmatic reconstruction of Jesus. As Christians we are called to act prophetically in terms of not just declaring, but working to end violence, to bring peace, hope, freedom for captives, elimination of impoverishment, and to free the burdens of people such that people are permitted to make new beginnings periodically—the

8 John Howard Yoder, *The Politics of Jesus: Vicit Agnus Noster* (Grand Rapids, MI: Wm. B. Eerdmans Publishing, 1994), pp. 90-92.

9 *Ibid.*, p. 96. Yoder adds later, "When Jesus wrestled repeatedly with the tempter, from the desert at the beginning to the garden at the end, this was not a clumsily contrived morality play meaning to teach us that kingship was not temptation; it was because God's servant in this world was facing, and rejecting, the claim that the exercise of social responsibility through the use of self-evidently necessary means is a moral duty." (Pa. 98.) The scriptural and historical Jesus faced repeatedly the temptations either to redress social injustices through what is considered justifiable revolution using lethal violence or to withdraw socially. The latter never seemed to influence him.

jubilee commencing now and continuing forward. Unlike the understanding of Christian action proposed by Reinhold Niebuhr, the reign
of God does not occur in a future eschaton, but is gradually built by
Christians in a new and just social order of the jubilee beginning right
now.[10] Contrary to Niebuhr's contention that "prophetic Christianity ... demands the impossible; and by that very demand emphasizes
the impotence and corruption of human nature," (Niebhur, 1979,
97) Yoder correctly assets that we are called to a realistic prophetic
role in which we stumble and learn on the way, but we must remain
prophetic nevertheless and from such we work out justice, inclusive
of non-violent conflict resolution. Just as Jesus stumbled through the
diversities of complex political, social, and religious issues and refused
either to divorce himself from their political solutions or to assume
violent and authoritarian power to implement his solutions, so too
we as Christians must actively engage in the working out of political
solutions without conceding that "those in power represent an ideal,
a logically proper, or even an empirically acceptable definition of
what it means to be political."[11] Finally, Yoder reminds us that the
Jewish Jesus was not an individualist nor was he engaged in radical
personalism, but, as in the Matthean Sermon on the Mount and the
Lukan Jesus, the Jesus we are called to follow proclaimed healing and
forgiving within the social novelty of a healing community. While
judgmental like Amos in being critical of his own people, Jesus also
like Amos in the prophetic tradition calls the people back to the high
moral and religious demands of YHWH's revelation.

---

10   Reinhold Niebuhr, *An Interpretation of Christian Ethics*, pp. 97-123.

11   Yoder, *The Politics of Jesus*, p. 107. Yoder further adds that Jesus effectively did not say, "'you can have your politics and I shall do something else more important'; he said, 'your definition of *polis*, of the social,
of the wholeness of being human socially is perverted.'" He also cites
Millard Lind's comment on Jesus approach to social, political, and religious change, "This denial that the human exercise of violent power is
necessary to existence was not a withdrawal from political concerns....
Yahweh's leadership in history had to do with political order, both for
the community's external and internal relationships." "The Concept of
Political Power," *Annual of the Swedish Theological Institute in Jerusalem*,
VII, p. 4 ff.

Non-violence practiced by Jesus is also expected to be used by his followers. Jesus directs his followers in Mk. 10:42-45 and Mt. 20:25-28 to substitute the incentive of dominion over others to a practice of suffering servanthood. This does not pertain simply to individual intentionality and private purpose, but relates, as Yoder indicates, to the political sphere which, in Jesus' world, meant to refrain from promoting a world of anti-Zealot and anti-Roman opposition.[12] Jesus, in fact, was critical of political authorities because they sought to exert their weight over others, partially for their own recognition. The practice of non-violence for Jesus, of suffering for the cause of justice, was neither an objective of Jesus nor was it for enduring persecution on behalf of one's faith. Rather, there can be no division between religious and social ethic; Jesus was engaged in effecting a political ethic that often undermines the political leadership and its actions because they are in fact immoral. The suffering and dying with Jesus are neither the intent of Jesus nor the Gospel writers; they also not meant to be mystical or an inwardly spiritual experience. The suffering of Jesus is meant to center on the vulnerability of enemy love, the renunciation of lordship, the abandonment of earthly security, and the uncomfortable threat to political powers with expected antagonism from political powers. (Yoder, 1994, 127) Real power and influence comes in suffering that effectively changes the hearts of adversaries, although the endurance of time is required.[13] "Servanthood replaces dominion, forgiveness

---

12 *Ibid.*, p. 123. Yoder adds, "Jesus is not simply telling his disciples to be servants. He is pointedly contrasting this command with any way of being 'lord' which his listeners are assumed to have in mind. The contrast is meaningful only if the desire for lordship is assumed to be real, as it was in the request of James and John to which he is responding."

13 It is not our intent, nor do we have the time or space, to digress on the meaning of power and Jesus' relationship with the powers, particularly social, political, or religious leadership. Yoder explains in great detail and add insightful commentary in this regard in The Politics of Jesus, pp. 134-161, especially in his interpretation of the Pauline perspective on pp. 143-144. Suffice it to note that Yoder claims that God will save creation in its humanity from the Powers of subordination, not by destroying these Powers, but by breaking their sovereignty over immoral and unjust oppression in his refusal to recognize their injustice, although he remained subject to them in his political death. "But morally he broke their rules by

absorbs hostility. Thus—and only thus—are we bound by the New Testament thought to 'be like Jesus.'" (Yoder, 1994, 131)

The moral dilemma faced by Christian-baptized, political, military and social leaders in so-called "Christian" societies center on whether these individuals can continue to exercise their offices in the face of the expectation that they must authorize and are expected to direct military forces engaged in lethal violence. Maybe, as Hauerwas suggests, the Christian baptized necessarily must remove themselves from such leadership and become part of a counter-culture, a remnant faithful to the teachings of Jesus, because the secular polis has no tolerance for Christian witness and norms. The rationale for supporting and living non-violence is not because of some respect for human life, but because Jesus taught and commanded us to live in this manner. If Christian baptized really live according to the teachings of Jesus, then, even as a minority, they will influence social actions of others far beyond their paucity of numbers. Precisely because of their fidelity to Jesus' command of non-violence in enemy love, they were able to change the whole thinking of the dominant cultural values of the Roman Empire. Such can reoccur even within the militarism of the US.

HAUERWAS' THINKING ON
CHRISTIAN ENACTMENT OF PEACEFUL KINGDOM

Let us look at the thinking of Stanley Hauerwas with regard to the moral treatment of war. Hauerwas, influenced by John Yoder, demonstrates a thoroughly complex understanding and appreciation of the

---

refusing to support them in their (i.e., the weighty representatives of Jewish religion and Roman politics) self-glorification; and that is why they killed him. Preaching and incorporating a greater righteousness than that of the Pharisees, and a vision of an order of social human relations more universal than the Pax Romana, he permitted the Jews to profane a holy day (refuting thereby their own moral pretensions) and permitted the Romans to deny their vaunted respect for law as they proceeded illegally against him. This they did in order to avoid the threat to their dominion represented by the very fact that he existed in their midst so morally independent of their pretensions." What pertains to the theme of this work is the breaking of the sovereignty of these unjust, self-oriented Powers was done with no lethal violence on the part of Jesus and we as Jesus' followers are expected to do the same, even if it also entail our suffering.

problem of judging the morality of war within a Christian context. In a 1984 lecture, Hauerwas appears to accept that war is acceptable for maintaining and attaining certain social goods of particular peoples in a divided world, what he calls "the moral case for war," and correctly acknowledges that war is seldom, if ever, fought for the preservation and protection of a people and their existence, but more for the attainment of certain political advantage. He skillfully twists his argument to demand that Christians respond to a theological imperative that war be eliminated.[14] Hauerwas rightly emphasizes the dilemma of contemporary Christianity in noting that Christians say they want peace, but seem destined for war.

Despite his respect for recent statements of Paul VI, John XXIII, and John Paul II with regard to the official Vatican pronouncements concerning war and armaments and the pronouncement of the US Conference of Catholic Bishops in "The Challenge of Peace," Hauerwas correctly calls them to task for their ambivalence on the treatment of war.[15] While the aforenoted pronouncements of the Catholic Church call for peace, they continue to hold war as a moral possibility permissive of Christian participation, if not Christian duty, in spite of the horrors, irrationality, and brutality of war. Hauerwas, in contrast to the theologians who hold that the natural law makes war a morally permissible institution, accepts that war is always a result of sin (with similarities to Augustine), the breach of human relations, human fail-

---

14   Stanley Hauerwas, *Should War Be Eliminated?* (Milwaukee, WI: Marquette University Press, 1984), p. 47.

15   *Ibid.*, p. 65. Hauerwas further notes that although the bishops "urge non-violent forms of resistance in the interest of justice they always hold out the possibility of violence if non-violence does not work. Yet they fail to give any indication how we are ever to know if non-violence has not worked and thus we can turn to violence. I suspect behind their failure to press this issue is the assumption that war is of the essence of state action so the ability of a state to use non-violence is extremely limited.... For the 'innocent' that we defend cannot be defended 'justly' if the form of the defense belies our conviction, based on Jesus' way of dealing with the world, that the enemy is to be loved even as they attack. Peace and justice are not equal 'means' for the building of God's kingdom, but rather the justice that required the forgiveness of enemies that makes peace possible is the kingdom."

ure, and brokenness, but requires that peace be made real now within community, an eschaton that is happening presently and not on the edge of history. This approach is not based on illusory idealism, but calls Christians to courageous enactment of their belief in realizing a history that opposes the history of nation-states engaged in war for preservation of those very states' meaning.[16] While Hauerwas argues that "war is part and parcel of societies' histories, a necessary part which provides them with their sense of moral purpose and destiny," (Hauerwas, 1984, 52) he underscores that the moral rationality for such, as being not devoid of moral substance, draws on a different assumption of history and its relationship to God's kingdom. These histories, he claims, are not the "way God would have his kingdom present in the world."[17] In stating such, Hauerwas demonstrates that he too accepts and practices the recent trend in ethical and moral theory that it is important to secure a foundation "unfettered by the contingencies of our histories and communities,"[18] particularly when he accepts the moral imperative to choose the mandate of Jesus in realizing the eschaton that is a part of God's history.

Like Lohfink, Yoder, et al., Hauerwas correctly interprets the distinctness of Christian living as something that distinguishes it, differs

---

16   *Ibid.*, p. 57, Hauerwas does not avoid the quicksand which sucked in Augustine when he questions the commitment to Christian faith in the belief of a different history, but he continues to acknowledge the unresolved tension between justice and non-violence. He calls for Christians to collapse the all ready but not yet realization of the eschaton by daring to live the life of non-violence demanded by Jesus. He asks, "… do they (Christians) follow the Augustinian solution noting that the two histories are hopelessly mixed together on this side of the eschaton so we are required to use the means of violence to support the history of the world?"

17   *Ibid.*, pp. 52-53. Hauerwas astutely asks, "For what is war but the desire to be rid of God, to claim for ourselves the power to determine our meaning and destiny? Our desire to protect ourselves from our enemies, to eliminate our enemies in the name of protecting the common history we share with our friends, is but the manifestation of our hatred of God."

18   Stanley Hauerwas, *The Peaceable Kingdom: A Primer in Christian Ethics* (Notre Dame, Ind.: University of Notre Dame Press, 1983), p. 7.

it, from secular culture and the world. To live and act as a Christian is to truly be a contrast society.[19] "They (Christians) are required to be nothing less than a sanctified people of peace who can live the life of the forgiven."[20] Because of this, Christian ethics differ significantly from human ethics that are based on the assumption of the legitimacy of the natural law, inclusive of the deductive aspect of self-defense. Like Reinhold Niebuhr, Hauerwas is conscious of the role of sin in inducing the use of violence. Just as the world in rebellion to God, we too can be in rebellion by acting "as if this is not God's world and therein lies our fundamental sin." (Hauerwas, 1983, 30) So too, we can act as if we are the sole determinants of history, that God has no bearing, direction, influence, or intervention. Hauerwas adds, "Just to the extent I refuse to be faithful to God's way, to live as part of God's life, my life assumes the character of rebellion. Our sin is not merely an error in overestimating our capacities. Rather it is the active and willful attempt to overreach our powers. It is the attempt to live *sui generis*, to live as if we are or can be the authors of our own stories. Our sin is, thus, a challenge to God's authorship and a denial that we are characters in the drama of the kingdom." (Hauerwas, 1983, 31) Niebuhr too acknowledges the contingency of the human situation and subscribes that our impatience with such may breed insecurity that induces us to accede to a will to power that uses force, inclusive of lethal violence, to affect that which we want, peace and other desired

---

19 Hauerwas implicitly criticizes moral theologians like Richard McCormick, Timothy O'Connell, and Joseph Fuchs because they assume that the primary task of Christians is to support human values, based on their premise of natural law theory. "This assumption presumes that Christians will never be radically anti-world—that is, aligned against the prevailing values of their cultures. In fact behind the emphasis on the 'human' character of Christian ethics is a deep fear that there might be a radical discontinuity between Christians and their culture." Hauerwas, *The Peaceable Kingdom*, p. 59. Hauerwas, thus, criticizes McCormick because McCormick refrains from emphasizing the difference of Christian values in the public debate because that debate is already too confusing as it is.

20 Hauerwas, *Peaceable Kingdom*, p. 60. Natural law ethics legitimate survival as the source of moral principles, notes Hauerwas, but this foundational desire may run in contrast and opposition to the good news of peace and reconciliation mandated by Jesus. (p. 161)

goals.[21] Unlike Niebuhr, though, Hauerwas does not accept the tenet that peaceableness and non-violence are unrealizable tenets.

To understand the thinking of Hauerwas with regard to war and the waging of peace, it is important to realize that for him "nonviolence is not just one implication among others that can be drawn from our Christian beliefs; it is at the very heart of our understanding of God."[22] As noted above, the coming of the kingdom of God, as interjected by the life of Jesus, has interrupted a history of war and violence, imposed a history based on peace that requires a new set of convictions for a particular kind of people (i.e., a community of non-violence), and commenced a working out of a new history in an eschaton that is already but not yet. The teaching of Jesus and the Church should not be subsumed in a narrative, or ideological system, in which the state is the primary actor—this is not the history of the God of Jesus and his followers.[23]

---

21 Reinhold Nieburh, *The Nature and Destiny of Man* (New York: Charles Scribner's Sons, 1957), p. 178.

22 Hauerwas, *Peaceable Kingdom*, p. xvii. Hauerwas substantiates the importance of peace in Christian ethics by further noting "a position of nonviolence entails, for example, a different understanding of the significance of Jesus' life, death, and resurrection than that offered in other forms of Christian ethics…. (P)eaceableness as the hallmark of Christian life helps illumine other issues, such as the nature of moral argument, the meaning and status of freedom, as well as how religious convictions can be claimed to be true or false…. (F)or Christians peace is not an ideal known apart from our theological convictions; rather the peace for which we hunger and thirst is determined and made possible only through the life, death, and resurrection of Jesus Christ." (p. xvii)

23 Rasmusson, *The Church as Polis*, p. 309, relates the thinking of Hauerwas to that of Jean Bethke Elshtain, *Women and War* (Chicago: University of Chicago Press, 1987) with regard to subjection of God's history to that of the state. "The discourse of national armed virtue is not only carried by conservative nationalists, or Fascists and Nazis, but in societies like the USA by the 'progressive' liberals, for whom 'schools and the army became the great engines of the nationalization of America.' The aim is Americanization, the means are the schools telling about the good wars America has fought, and the homogenizing effect of universal military

"Indeed, nonviolence is not just one implication among others that can be drawn from our Christian beliefs; it is at the very heart of our understanding of God…. For Christians peace is not an ideal known apart from our theological convictions; rather the peace for which we hunger and thirst is determined and made possible only through the life, death, and resurrection of Jesus Christ," (Hauerwas, 1983, xvii) claims Hauerwas. In the resurrection, Hauerwas finds the seed of hope for realization of a peaceful kingdom of God. Jesus initiated the kingdom of God, radically interrupted the history of war and violence, and inserted an alternative history, a contrast society to be developed and witnessed by his followers. Non-violence is the risk that true followers of Jesus are willing to take because they too believe that death is not the end but, as witnessed in the faithful obedience of Jesus, resurrection may follow; it is a risk that these followers are willing to take to bring about the rule of God; it is a risk to realize a new city of God, something that Augustine actually undercut because he was unwilling to go the full way. Non-violent resistance, which is necessary for the Christian in an unjust world, necessarily must confront in the political arena the powers of history that thwart the alternative history of the contrast society attempting to make all things whole and rectify injustice by taking a preferential stand with the oppressed.[24] It

conscription, and thereby the strengthening of the state. Dissent is seen as disloyalty."

24 Rasmusson, *The Church as Polis*, p. 318, cites Hauerwas' encouragement for Christians to become involved in the political process. "Rather than disavowing politics, the pacifist must be the most political of animals exactly because politics understood as the process of discovering the goods we have in common is the only alternative to violence. What the pacifist must deny, however, is the common assumption that genuine politics is determined by state coercion." Stanley Hauerwas, *Against the Nations: War and Survival in a Liberal Society* (Notre Dame, Ind.: University of Notre Dame Press, 1982), p. 7.
Hauerwas also stresses that "Peacemaking requires the development of the processes and institutions that make possible confrontation and resolution of differences that violence can be avoided. The problem with politics, at least as politics is currently understood, is not that it involves compromises but that it so little believes in truth. As a result, it becomes but a form of coercion without due acknowledgment that it is so." Stan-

is all about convictions and practices. In the alternative history of the contrast society, neither the state nor any specific civilization can be the primary actor, but only the community in working out the rule of God with Jesus as the focus.

This alternative history, based on the non-violence and pacifism of Jesus, poses a dilemma for the powerful nation state because it threatens its very weakness, namely the nakedness of armed society that has unjustly oppressed other states and peoples for the advancement of consumerism and narrow national interests. It threatens Western powers because they have relied on the mistaken rationale of just war since Augustine. In fact, Hauerwas would correctly identify the idolatry used by Christians in support of so-called just wars as the nation state itself, the replacement for God in a new rule, a new history.[25] The crusading

---

ley Hauerwas, "Peacemaking: The Virtue of the Church," in John Berkman and Michael Cartwright, eds., *The Hauerwas Reader* (Durham, NC: Duke University Press, 2001), p. 326.

25   Rasmusson, *The Church as Polis*, p. 309, opines that Elshtain's interpretation of Hauerwas' claims therein make "significant that the discourse of national armed virtue is not only carried by conservative nationalists, or fascists and nazis, but in societies like the USA by the 'progressive' liberals, for whom 'schools and the army became the great engines of the nationalization of America.' [Jean Bethke Elshtain, *Women and War* (Chicago: University of Chicago Press, 1987), p. 117] The aim is Americanization, the means are the schools telling about the good wars America has fought, and the homogenizing effect of universal military conscription, and thereby the strengthening of the state. Dissent is seen as disloyalty."
     It is amazing to observe proponents of just war theory when one questions them on the morality of war. They tend instinctively to respond to criticism of wars, inclusive of wars deemed by religious leaders as unjust, with a defense of war-making on the basis of just war. They remain unconscious that they have substituted the nationalism and militarism of the nation state for the tenets of the centrality of God and they seem to find the rule of God identical with those of the nation state.
     Tucker Foehl, "What Kind of Freedom?," *Mother Jones. Com*, Jan. 28, 2005 has not misunderstood, however, the substitution of nationalism of the nation-state for religion. " … (T)here is an entire segment of the population who are so ideologically committed to a racist, often religious, American nationalism that they do not care what the facts are, and ac-

ethos of today has reappeared in the militarism of the nation states.[26] Hauerwas has definitively distinguished the underlying assumptions about history in relation to God's kingdom by correctly linking just war with the ethos of the nation state (the primary agent for God's care) while Christian pacifism claims that the Church should be the sign that war is excluded from God's providential care. (Rasmusson, 1995, 311)

What sets Hauerwas apart from theologians like Moltmann lies principally in his advocacy for non-violent resistance wherein the Church as a contrast society in making an alternative history offers an alternative to the state that Moltmann *et al* seek to change through revolution, and secondarily in his conviction that, unlike Moltmann, survival is not the basic motivating factor, but the exercise of peace with consciousness about effecting justice and based on a belief in new life. The Church, i.e. the followers of Jesus, however, has no plans or

---

tively don't want to hear any facts that contradict their worldview of the U.S. as a righteous victim that goes out and helps people. But, by and large, most Americans don't know, don't understand, and don't know how to figure it out."

26 One cannot fail to see this realization in the statements made by George W. Bush in response to the tragedies of Sept. 11, 2001 when he launched a "crusade" against terror on other states and social groups.

Hauerwas peaks our consciences when he asks, "Whose just war is it?" With regards to the US invasions of Iraq, for example, Hauerwas considers them demonstrations of hegemonic power claiming "universal morality that is meant to create a social and historical amnesia that is intended to make us forget how the dominant achieved power in the first place." Stanley Hauerwas, *Dispatches from the Front: Theological Engagements with the Secular* (Durham, NC: Duke University Press, 1995), p. 145. Insightfully, Hauerwas emphasizes that for leaders to persuade their people that they are engaged in just war, they must create a virtuous people and the means to do that is with crusade language.

In a similar vein, he comments on the moral status of US Christianity. "While appearing to be a resurgence of 'traditional' religious conviction, some of these movements in fact give evidence of the loss of religious substance in our culture and in ourselves. Christianity is defended not so much because it is true, but because it reinforces the 'American way of life.'" Hauerwas, *Peaceable Kingdom*, p. 12.

designs to change the state, only to rectify social injustices and to avoid violence based on forgiveness and reconciliation, something that the state, engaged in its own idolatry, finds difficult to accept. While the institutional Church only gives witness to this alternative history, it is the church as the people who realize this contrast society in active political involvement that is non-violent and pacifist.

Peacemaking necessitates confrontation and conflict. For the Christian, confrontation without inflicting lethal violence is a challenge that separates Christian pacifists from most other methods of conflict resolution. No small measure of physical restraint is required to overcome the temptation to resort to physical violence in winning the peace.[27] Conflict and confrontation therein may be non-violent and, as such, become redeeming for the conflicting parties who reach a more lasting and truer accord. Hauerwas also reminds us that peace-making enables moral excellence in the Church and calls one to enact justice on many fronts. Peace-making is a virtue that needs to be practiced in community and not just by isolated individuals.[28] Mt. 18: 15-22 gives us a good example on one way to resolve conflicts; further, it demonstrates that, even though, a conflict might continue to ensue without resolution and we remain personally injured therein, the follower of Jesus is called upon ceaselessly to forgive, but must continue *in community* to work for resolution. "No doubt peacemaking … is a demanding business…. (I)t is impossible to sustain it if it is thought

---

27   Hauerwas provides us with a key insight into the issue of resorting to the use of power, inclusive of violent power, when, in The Peaceable Kingdom, pp. 78-79, he interprets the second temptation of Jesus (according to Luke 4, the third temptation in Matthew 4) to be a king that can force all to his will against their own, to make peace through coercion. But, God's kingdom will not bring peace through coercion and domination. Hauerwas adds, "Jesus thus decisively rejects Israel's temptation to idolatry that necessarily results in violence between peoples and nations. For our violence is correlative to the falseness of the objects we worship, and the more false they are, the greater our stake in maintaining loyalty to them and protecting them through coercion." Servanthood, not domination, is the basis of Jesus life and ministry.

28   Stanley Hauerwas, "Peacemaking: The Virtue of the Church," in John Berkman and Michael Cartwright, eds., *The Hauerwas Reader* (Durham, NC: Duke University Press, 2001), p. 318.

to be a virtue of heroic individuals. Rather, peacemaking must be a virtue of a whole community... ."[29]

Peacemaking obviously in no way implies withdrawal from society to find peace within oneself or one's community; nor does it mean bringing peace through violence. Jesus had both of these options before him: side with the zealots in a revolution against Rome to restore the God of the Israelites to God's former position and bring about the kingdom of God, or side with the pious, ascetical, religious disciplines that sought withdrawal from the complexities and tainted evils in the world into an illusory world where one perceives that God's will dominates miraculously without resistance—but also without thought or personal involvement. While Jesus shared in the reformist traits of the Pharisees, he radically divorced himself from them with regard to their "detailed code of observance, careful selectiveness in the company they kept, and a concern for the authority of the tradition in which they stood."[30] Finally, God's kingship and power do not consist of coercion, but the willingness to forgive. Thus, Jesus, claims Hauerwas, challenged the militarist and ritualistic notions of God's kingdom by denying violence and refusing exclusion of what are considered ritualistic impurities.[31]

NIEBUHR'S CONTRASTING TREATMENT OF THE MISTAKEN CHRISTIAN PRACTICE OF LOVE

With the risk of over-simplification of the basic tenets of Reinhold Niebuhr and of admittedly avoiding the challenging questions that he raised with regard to relative moral aspects of radical social change stemming from war and revolution, it behooves us to consider Niebuhr's thinking on violence because of the influence that it has on contemporary social thinking with regard to war, lethal violence, and social change and because it poses a striking contrast to that reviewed above. Reinhold Niebuhr, a US pastor and moral theologian at Union Theological Seminary, who wrote challenging moral perspectives from

29 *Ibid.*, p. 326.

30 A.E. Harvey, *Jesus and the Constraints of History* (Philadelphia: Westminster, 1982), p. 51, cited in Hauerwas, *The Peaceable Kingdom*, pa 84.

31 Hauerwas, *The Peaceable Kingdom*, p. 84.

the early 1930s into the last half of the twentieth century, presents us with moral positions that radically differ from the positions of Yoder and Hauerwas reviewed above, but not necessarily with those of Moltmann.[32] Niebuhr goes further than Moltmann in that he views, from the perspective of social ethics, war and lethal violence in conflict societies as part of the human condition and not something that falls within the realm of divine-oriented morality (religio-ethics or, as he terms it, religio-morality).

He interprets the readings from Matthew 5 as directives from the gospel writers that focus the attention on how God would view morality and how the Christian should think morally in relation to God. Niebuhr describes this as "predominant vertical religious reference of Jesus' ethic," not the horizontal reference or focus of the ethic that would be inter-human activity. (Niebuhr, 1979, 55) While Niebuhr posits his assertion that an "ethical system must base its moral imperative in an order of reality and not mere possibility," he views the Gospel directives for self-sacrifice, practice of Christian virtues, etc. as being only rewarded in a future eschaton. He goes further by emphasizing that the ethical demands of Jesus "are incapable of fulfillment in the present existence of man." (Niebuhr, 1979, 59) Thus, fulfillment of the dicta outlined in the teachings of Jesus are not expected to be employed in this world but are part of a mythical approach having fulfillment in a future eschaton and some other means for living out one's Christianity that needs to be found—an approximation of the Christian ideal based on rationality, the basis of natural law a la Ulpian.[33] Niebuhr,

---

32   Reinhold Niebuhr, *An Interpretation of Christian Ethics*, p. 52. Moltmann observes a premise that acts as the basis for his argument that those who are impoverished and oppressed may have no other choice than violent and lethal overthrow and, thus, Moltmann supports this reasoning of revolution violence, but those persons having social status, power, and wealth can act differently and advocate non-violence. Niebuhr remarked similarly, but several decades earlier, "This is the pathos of the espousal of Christian pacifism by the liberal Church, ministering largely to those social groups who have the economic power to be able to dispense with the more violent forms of coercion and therefore condemn them as un-Christian."

33   *Ibid.*, p. 46. Niebuhr demonstrates his basic thinking when he says, "The very basis of self-love is the natural will to survive." He goes on to

therefore, notes that there was a lack of urgency for fulfillment of the rewards for acting according to Jesus' teachings in Acts, although Paul for a short period seemed to share a different perspective based on historical illusions, not unlike the historical illusions shared by Jesus.[34] Mankind must find some means of dealing with the reality of the historical situation and avoid falling into historical illusion of attempting the impossible, inclusive of the commandment of love in an imperfect world. Niebuhr, therefore, directs us as follows:

> Confronted with this situation humanity always faces a double task. The one is to reduce the anarchy of the world to some kind of immediately sufferable order and unity; and the other is to set these tentative and insecure unities and achievements under criticism

---

note that the gospel ethic fails to make concessions to natural, self-regarding human impulses. In response to Mt. 6:25-32, wherein Jesus prohibits concern about maintaining one's physical existence, he witnesses that a "prudent conscience will have an immediately unfavorable reaction to these words. No life can be lived in such unconcern for the physical basis of life," and indicates that the literal living of these words would have been more possible, but very imperfectly, in a community-based agrarian society of first century Palestine, but not today.

34 Niebuhr, *An Interpretation of Christian Ethics*, pp. 59-60. Niebuhr clarifies his understanding by stating, "If stated rationally the world is divided between the temporal and the eternal and only the eternal forms above the flux of temporality have significance. To state the matter mythically is to do justice to the fact that the eternal can only be fulfilled in the temporal. But since myth is forced to state a paradoxical aspect of reality in terms of concepts connoting historical sequence, it always leads to historical illusions. Jesus, no less than Paul, was not free of these historical illusions. He expected the coming of the Messianic kingdom in his lifetime; at least that seems to have been his expectation before the crisis in his ministry."

It is important to note that Niebuhr did not just believe that early Christianity erred from the historical illusions on the coming of the parousia or eschaton and, thus, required, mistaken ethical application of Gospel mandates, but he also acknowledges that the early Church made unnecessary compromises and adjustments with the relativities of politics, economics, and actual living situations that imperiled the genius of Jesus' teachings. (Pp. 60-61.)

of the ultimate ideal. When they are not thus challenged, what is good in them becomes evil and each tentative harmony becomes the cause of a new anarchy. With Augustine we must realize that the peace of the world is gained by strife. That does not justify us either in rejecting such a tentative peace or in accepting it as final. The peace of the city of God can use and transmute the lesser and insecure peace of the city of the world; but that can be done only if the peace of the world is not confused with the ultimate peace of God." (Niebuhr, 1979, 62)

In classical theory of international relations, Niebuhr would have to be termed a realist. He accepts the world as is and works to bring order and unity, but can only be frustrated if he attempts to realize the illusions of the Gospel in the here and now. He is, nevertheless, willing to struggle (i.e., engage in strife) to improve upon it, but it does not appear that his ethic necessitates an absolute attempted realization of Gospel ideals, as reviewed above under the morality of war in the Christian scriptures, for he is willing to wage war for the attainment of peace, temporal though it may be. He retains, as the basis for his recommended mode of action, faith in transcendence in order to be saved from capitulation to the culture, even a culture of death, of any age.

Niebuhr validates his ethical approach on the basis that Jesus could offer no concrete, moral guidelines for every foreseeable human problem and nothing in the Christian scriptures directs specifically how Christians are to act with regard to war and lethal inter-group conflict. Moreover, he claims, Jesus makes no clear and distinct comments concerning the way Christians are to engage in the political process or in any economic system. (Niebuhr, 1979, 45)

Specifically with regards to relationship with one's enemies, Niebuhr interprets the fifth and sixth antitheses of Matthew 5 as ones wherein Jesus' "attitude toward vindictiveness and his injunction to forgive the enemy reveals ... his intransigence against forms of self-assertion which have social and moral approval in natural morality."[35] He

---

35 *Ibid.*, p. 49. In a note of caution, Niebuhr stresses that excessive vengeance and subtle vindictiveness destroy justice. As in just-war conditionality, he, therefore, stresses the importance of intent (moral attitude) in engaging in war and that there are both unrighteous moral attitudes and

admonishes, however, that "enemy love" and limitless forgiveness should be premised with the understanding that such ethical demands remain impossible for natural man in real world situations. Therein, these demands must be considered in the light of purely religious and not socio-moral terms; "the points of reference are vertical and not horizontal." (Niebuhr, 1979, 50) Along this line of reasoning, Niebuhr naturally observes that non-resistance, while possibly shaming an enemy into retrenchment and less belligerent reaction, may also induce enemies to embolden their aggression. He, therefore, concludes that it is impossible to construct a social-moral or politico-moral policy from Jesus' religio-moral statements.[36]

Because the religio-moral ideal of love is impossible to realize in this world, except in minimal approximations, Niebuhr emphasizes that one is left necessarily to recognize both (a) one's own sinfulness in the cause of human, inclusive of inter-group, violence, and (b) mutual responsibility, something beyond the consciousness of collective man. While implicitly accepting just war rationale on the basis of an obligation to affirm and protect the life of others, not just for oneself, though, Niebuhr correctly cautions that it also behooves participants in war to assure that all parties have a right to secure the goods which sustain life.[37]

---

righteous moral attitudes ("righteous in the sense that they defend their interests no more than is permitted by all the moral codes of history.") (Pa. 108.)

36 Ibid., pp. 50-52. Niebuhr deduces, therefore, that "The order of human existence is too imperiled by chaos, the goodness of man too corrupted by sin, and the possibilities of man too obscured by natural handicaps to make human order and human virtue and human possibilities solid bases of the moral imperative." (Pa. 52.)

37 Ibid., pp. 100-101. Niebuhr adds that, because of finiteness of human perspective, in physical and belligerent conflict, "every appeal to moral standards thus degenerates into moral justification of the self against the enemy. Parties to a dispute inevitably make themselves judges over it and thus fall into the sin of pretending to be God." (Pa. 116.) When religio-moral rationale is introduced into conflicts of war, generally, the conflict rises to new heights as religion itself becomes the incendiary demon in what actually becomes an attempt to escape relativity and reality and seek to understand one's action from the eternal, thereby becoming the most

In his book, *Moral Man and Immoral Society: A Study in Ethics and Politics*, published in 1932, Niebuhr acknowledges the Russian revolution as both a promise and peril in Russian society and the world as well and recognizes that many viewed, not just the Russian revolution, but revolution in general with ambivalence of hope and fear, particularly in light of the Great Depression that was then burdening international society. As to criticism of revolution from the business community and from middle classes, Niebuhr responds that violence is not intrinsically immoral, provided ill-will does not accompany the violence—i.e., the importance of right intention.[38] In consideration of the social goal which the moral intent of the actor seeks as a consequence, Niebuhr opines that revolutionaries, particularly Marxian, seek equal justice. The means or instruments to attain those objectives, though, should be considered more political than ethical. Therein, Niebuhr seems to accept implicitly that undesirable consequences, such as the death of innocent people and children, may accompany the attainment of morally acceptable and desired social goals—e.g., social justice for a number of people greater than that of innocent victims. Although he does not indicate a priority of moral values, he recognizes that moral values are not absolutes and that one moral value may have to be sac-

---

brutal weapons in the conflict. Niebuhr also astutely and correctly observes that all moral judgments pushed by "peaceful countries" on some countries come from countries who are secure and powerful, and possibly imperialist.

38   Reinhold Niebuhr, *Moral Man and Immoral Society: A Study in Ethics and Politics* (New York: Charles Scribner's Sons, 1948), pp.169-170, perceptively draws the reader's attention to the fact that the intentions and morality of proletarian revolutionaries probably differ little in their purity and openness from those who defend special privileges (who often use more covert means of coercion than proletarians can muster).

While he seems to accept and acknowledges violence as an acceptable means to attain morally desirable ends, he remains cautiously dubious about political possibilities of establishing justice through violence because of the dilemmas of becoming indiscriminate with regard to violent and non-violent coercion and the possibility of subordinating ethics to politics. "If a season of violence can establish a just social system and can create the possibilities of its preservation, there is no purely ethical ground upon which violence and revolution can be ruled out." (Pa. 179.)

rificed for other moral values—as when one must decide to sacrifice the life of one person or group for those of others.[39] Although Niebuhr, drawing on his analysis of Marx, Engels, and Lenin, does not clearly delineate the criteria for morally justifiable violence, in his thinking, or for a morally acceptable revolution, he eminently clarifies the complexities of successfully undertaking a revolution. The increased impoverishment and starvation of the majority of the working classes seems to be a critical element for him not only in instigating a successful revolution, but certainly in providing morally justifiable underpinning. (Niebuhr, 1948, 186-188) Insightfully, Niebuhr bothers the conscience of his readers when he observes that it is necessary to mount crises in order to foster change through deconcentration of wealth on behalf of a more equitable sharing of the goods and services of society, thereby transmuting society toward a stable relationship between classes and peoples with mutual benefits for all. The position of the middle classes are critical in determining either the advancement of revolution or incensed stagnation. On the other hand, Niebuhr seems to have miscalculated the neutralizing schemes of the privileged classes to emasculate any progress in revolution. Although he wrote *Moral Man and Immoral Society* nearly three quarters of century ago, his prediction, based on Marxian analysis, that imperialist states with capitalist systems, increasingly involved in external and larger wars, would induce revolutions either by shattering the authority of various states or by fomenting chaos that would lead to revolution. He identifies massive impoverishment of the poorer classes as a principle cause for revolution, but this is not always so, as we reviewed in the first chapter. After allowing for the use of coercion

---

39 Why morally Niebuhr does not consider this as playing the role of God, he never explains, but, based on his premises, Niebuhr implicitly empowers the state actors, authorities, or their designates, to implement this power in his *realpolitik. Ibid.*, p. 174-175. "The more inclusive the ends which are held in view, the more the immediate consequences of an action cease to be the authoritative criteria of moral judgment. Since society must constantly deal with these inclusive ends, it always seems to capitulate to the dangerous principle that the end justifies the means. All morality really accepts that principle, but the fact is obscured by the assumption, frequently though not universally justified, that the character of immediate consequences guarantees the character of the ultimate end."

in either overt or covert forms and the use of lethal violence as a way
to attain equality and mutuality and possibly continue such, provided
the ends can and are reached, he analyzes that such need not necessarily be the case in Western and industrialized society. With respect to
Communist-based revolutions, he wisely cautioned already in 1932
of the dangers inherent in the concentration and centralization of
economic power within the state as a basis leading to concentration of
political power within the hands of a few individuals, and warned of
the possible dangers leading to severe limitation on ethical restraints
on abuse of power therein.[40]

40   With great regret because of the limitation of space, we are unable to
     delve further into the theological thinking of Niebuhr, particularly as it
     pertains to his unique treatment of the problem of evil, his analysis of the
     strengths and weaknesses of orthodox Christianity in contrast to liberal
     Christianity, his interpretation of the centrality of the ideal of love in
     the Christian ethic. Although he greatly criticizes liberal Christianity, he,
     nevertheless, equally condemns orthodox Christian treatment of social
     justice because it pays greater reverence to the principle of order rather
     than the attraction of love and it compromises "with the necessities of
     politics (that) are chiefly drawn from two sources, the Pauline conception
     of the divine ordinance of government (Rom. 13) and the Stoic concep-
     tion of the natural law … the law of reason." Niebuhr, *An Interpretation
     of Christian Ethics*, pp. 131-132. Niebuhr correctly acknowledges that
     orthodox Christianity has given equal validity to the natural law and the
     ideal of Christian love as laws of God. He, thus, notes, "The theory of
     the natural law is thus the instrument by which the orthodox Church
     adjusted itself to the world after the hope of the *parousia* waned. This
     was natural enough since the love perfectionism of the gospels, with its
     implied anarchism and universalism, was obviously not applicable to the
     arbitration of conflicting interests and the choice of relative values re-
     quired in an imperfect world. The development of natural law theories in
     Christianity has been criticized as an apostasy from the Christian ideal of
     love. But all such criticism are informed by a moral sentimentalism which
     does not recognize to what degree all decent human actions, even when
     under the tension and inspiration of the love commandment, are in fact
     determined by rational principles of equity and justice, by law rather than
     by love."
         Suffice it to say that Niebuhr bases his interpretation of Christian eth-
     ics and morality on the distinction between *jus naturale* and *jus gentium*

CHRISTIAN CONFLICT RESOLUTION THROUGH
NON-VIOLENT RESISTANCE

When we consider the practical ramifications of non-violent resistance
in confronting lethal warfare and the threat of such, several observa-

and on the perceived unrealistic inability of humans to realize in the
world of the here-and-now the perfect implementation of the highest
perceived virtues in the natural law of freedom, first, and equality, second. He explains this position as follows. "The ideal is an impossibility
because both the contingencies of nature and the sin in the human heart
prevent men from ever living in that perfect freedom and equality which
the whole logic of the moral life demands.... The ideal equality will be
relativized ... not only by the fortuitous circumstances of nature and
history, but by the necessities of social cohesion and organic social life,
which will give some men privileges and power which other men lack;
and finally by human sin, for it is inevitable that men should take advantage of privileges with which nature or necessity has endowed them and
should enhance them beyond the limits of the one and the requirements
of the other." *Ibid.*, pp. 134-135. Finally, one should be conscious that
Niebuhr considers the law of love as being the perfect fulfillment of the
laws of equality and justice and as applicable in a perfectly transcendent
state, i.e., the *parousia* or the *eschaton*, when the exigencies of the present
strife and difficulties of this world no longer constrain the finiteness of
being. But, Christian social ethics did not evolve, he claims, in the early
Christian communities, until Christians attempted to incorporate the
natural law of the Stoics into the Christian message because of the unrealizable implementation of the law of love in this world. With this premise,
one can easily understand Niebuhr's mistaken interpretation of the Jesus'
commandment of and practice of love and Nieburh's acceptance of lethal
violence and war, especially because of the need to preserve social order
and social cohesion, even through coercion, as per Luke 22:25-26 and the
comments of Iranaeus.

     The above critique of Niebuhr focused on his treatment of orthodox
Christianity because, we believe, the essence of Niebuhr's theology and
ethics is so highly critical of liberal Christianity as being unrealistic ideal,
as demonstrated in the main text, that further explication is unneeded.
Good will cannot implement basic justice, maintains Niebuhr, because,
as society increasingly focuses more on economic rather than political
power, economic mechanisms will automatically create disproportionate
social power and privilege capable of checking and then overcoming political forces that seek to control and morally regulate economic power.

tions are in order. Non-violent resistance to war and tyranny assumes forms such as civil disobedience, street protests, general strikes, non-cooperation, boycotts, etc. and turns a potentially lethal attack into a political confrontation, at best. Many commentators, such as Liddell Hart et al., have commented that non-violent resistance only succeeds at best in situations where the invader, occupier, colonizer, tyrant or terrorist is governed by a set of cultural, religious, moral, or legal norms that are akin to those of the non-violent resister. Lacking a common moral code, it is interpreted as a disguised form of surrender or a way to uphold communal values in the face of defeat. On the other hand, Gandhi in colonial India and Martin Luther King in the US, it is asserted, were successful in their objectives in struggling against total systems of oppression that possessed the military and police force to seemingly dispel their resistance. But, commentators have asserted, non-violent resistance as in the case of the Jewish persecution by the Nazis, for example, could not have been successful precisely because the German leadership sought decisively to exterminate those whom it opposed, inclusive of the three million Soviet citizens and soldiers taken after 1941. Many too have cited (a) the tyrannical persecution of megalomaniacs like Joseph Stalin and his brutal murder of as many as 20 million Soviet citizens who were accused of opposing the Stalin-ist system or his supporters or (b) the millions of Chinese killed by kangaroo courts of the Cultural Revolution initiated by Mao Zedong and the Gang of Four, particularly Jiang Qing. On the other hand, one should not lose perspective of the time frame nor restrict the terms of successful resistance to immediate obstruction and collapse of the lethally oppressive forces. Recalling the persecution of the primitive Christians, particularly in the late third and early fourth centuries, one cannot fail to conclude that resistance for even several centuries was essential in order to turn the hearts and actions of their oppres-sors. The death, suffering, hardship, revilement, and agony born by these martyrs and sufferers was not insignificant. The non-violent resistance enacted by the Czechoslovakians in 1968 and 1969 in the face of overwhelming force of their Soviet invaders, who stole their freedoms and rights of self-determination, definitely seemed like failure, but collapsed in the end three decades later. While the latter two cases may not match the loss of more than nine million lives to the genocidal tyranny of the Nazi power, they demonstrate that time is required to effect the consciences of the oppressor. Why were the primitive Christian communities so willing to endure persecution and death for so long? Walzer, accepting Hart's premise, stresses that non-violent resistance only works on a significant scale if the oppressed people are mobilized and prepared before oppression begins but is no defense at all in the face of tyrants or conquerors.[41] Admittedly, this surely can be concluded to be the case if one's time frame and world scope concentrates on a short horizon. The Christian perspective, however, views the transience of time and considers the reward for waiting while actively engaged in non-violent resistance worth the effort, even if suffering or death is the outcome.

One can draw from the above the following reflections on contemporary, Christian moral thinking with regard to issues of violence affecting us in our lifetime. Although leading moral and systematic theologians of the twentieth century reluctantly accepted limited application of just-war type logic in specific occasions, this thinking remains self-contradictory, counters the essential teachings of Jesus, and leaves open a Pandora's box of slippery-slope ethical application. The real-world experience of the second World War and the debilitating and exploitive remnants of colonialism (inclusive of internal colonization) present harsh awareness of the emotional roughness that would seem naturally to foster violent response when confronted with abusive power. Moltmann and Niebuhr, not to mention many other commentators, correctly acknowledge that individuals in situations of power or wealth can easily relinquish or call for relinquishment of violence as an appropriate response in these situations, and they note that people living in these stark situations are not so easily swayed. This still does not justify temporary or situational suspension of the Christian ethic of love. Francis Bok, a young Sudanese captured and enslaved at seven years of age until his escape ten years later, presents a real world model for the exercise of Christian love and forgiveness, despite the suffering he endured. The Gospel mandates clearly call

---

41   Walzer, *Just and Unjust Wars*, pp. 330-334. Although Walzer recognizes non-violent resistance as a possible approach to war and lethal conflict, he scarcely gives credence to its realization and questionably considers it a viable approach to force and oppression.

for a contrast society, the creation of an alternative history that, while recognizing the evil in the dominant history and preponderance of natural reaction of peoples in that history, seeks to build through active involvement another way to realization of the kingdom of God, an eschaton that is becoming but not yet here in this world now.

CHAPTER 7

PRACTITIONERS & MODELS OF CHRISTIAN MORALITY WITH RESPECT TO VIOLENCE & WAR

Heretofore, we have reviewed a broad array of aspects of issues and tenets related to the morality of war and lethal violence. It behooves us now to consider contemporary models for implementing and living out the ethical and moral aspects of Christian understanding of violence and war. In this regard, several leading and recent models shall be considered briefly.[1]

Since Jesus, the most profound implementer and model of the Christian virtue of realistic love and the practice of non-violence can best be demonstrated in modernity in a non-baptized Indian, Mohandhas Karamchand Gandhi. His influence on Western Christianity for most people probably draws reactions of spurn or disinterest because, as Howard Zinn would tend to indicate,[2] Gandhi is not in the mainstream of the history of exploitation, wealth, and power. Nevertheless, for seeking true implementation of the teaching of Jesus, it is difficult to find such a contemporary precedent that turned the once powerful imperialist Britain to relinquish its control over its dominion because of the powerful effectiveness of peoples united in non-violent resistance. Despite the disinterest of most Christians, this Indian leader cannot be forgotten or cast aside. He led a disunited people with the second largest national population in the world to peacefully overthrow the reign of the mighty imperialist British who exploited that subcontinent for centuries. It is both an inspiration and

---

1 Although far more many persons than are actually considered herein could be offered, time and space restrict ourselves to a brief survey of four.

2 See Howard Zinn, *A People's History of the United States: 1492-Present* (New York: HarperCollins, 2003).

188 JESUS THE WARRIOR?

an embarrassment that a non-baptized person has best demonstrated the teaching of Jesus.[3]

What then does Gandhi have to teach us about non-violence? How did he come to accept this means of involvement and what motivated him to exercise political interaction in this manner?

Gandhi learned several key points from his experiences in South Africa that helped him when he returned to India.[4] From lawyering, he learned that it is better to bring adversaries together and find points of commonality than to seek redress in the courts of law or engage in conflict in the public domain. The struggle for respect and representation takes not a month, but years and decades as it took for

---

3 See comments of G.K. Chesterton and Gandhi noted above in Chapter 3. Gandhi was pressed in South Africa by Roman Catholics, Quakers, and Protestants, but the book that most influenced him in regard to religious convictions was Tolstoy's *The Kingdom of God Is Within You*. While the aforenoted sects taught him the essence of Christianity, he neither wanted redemption from the consequences of his own sin nor believed that Jesus was the most perfect man who was better than other great men of other religions or that Christianity was better than any other religion. He wisely sought redemption from sin itself, though. Gandhi comments on Christianity, "I could accept Jesus as a martyr, an embodiment of sacrifice and a divine teacher, but not as the most perfect man ever born.... The pious lives of Christians did not give me anything that the lives of men of other faiths had failed to give. I had seen in other lives just the same reformation that I had heard of among Christians. Philosophically there was nothing extraordinary in Christian principles." Louis Fischer, ed., *The Essential Gandhi: His Life, Work, and Ideas: An Anthology* (New York: Vintage Books, 1962), p. 41. In the same manner, Gandhi could not accept Hinduism as the greatest religion either because of its acceptance of the tenets of untouchability that made it "a rotten part or an excrescence" of Hindu. He acknowledged that if the Vedas (Hindu scripture) were inspired, the Bible and the Koran could also be.

4 Bhikhu Parekh, *Gandhi* (Oxford: Oxford University Press, 1997), p. 1, notes that Gandhi was influenced by his father whose many friends were Jains. The Jains practiced strict non-violence and self-discipline. Gandhi's sense of equitable and fair treatment of all seemed to be influenced by the religious practice of his mother, who was a member of the Pranami sect, which combined Hindu and Muslim religious beliefs and practices, of the devotional Hindu cult of Vishnu that required fasting and asceticism.

him to assist the Indians of South Africa to get representation in their legislature. He learned that secrecy is the enemy of freedom. Non-violent resistance is best determined by the time, the place, the issue, the adversary, the public psyche, etc. and should be used judiciously, but one should not wait passively for either "the wrong to be righted" or "till the wrong-doer has been roused to a sense of his iniquity."[5] It would seem prudent to wait actively by working to create the right moment and situation to force ultimate change. Gandhi never sought to immerse himself in politics, but picked issues to push through legitimate means. His practice of non-violent resistance overshadows his greatness of conscious toward righting social injustice and his modus operandi of community organizing.

Gandhi was moved to political activity because "the still small voice within you must always be the final arbiter when there is a conflict of duty."[6] It is important to note that Gandhi was keenly aware that hate debilitates one's thinking and political interaction; hate was the passion that deterred India, whose people felt weak and helpless in the face of the powerful British, from strong and self-reliant force against the tyrant. Non-violent self-resistance, he believed, would make Indians both end their hate for the British colonizers and give them the confidence to have strength and self-reliance. The strength of which Gandhi speaks, though, is not that of physical capacity and the brute force that the West has historically used to conquer and subjugate, but, he says, strength "comes from an indomitable will."[7]

Terrorism and deception, the hallmarks of both major powers and those seeking dominance, he proclaimed, are the tools of the weak, but Indians even without using those methods felt themselves weak because of the hate within them against a domineering British.[8] Thus, Gandhi called on his fellow Indians to overcome their hatred by restraining their feelings through the use of non-violence. Only love can overcome hatred and remove the blinding post in one's eye. Thus, he wrote:

5 Mohandhas K. Gandhi, *Young India*, (a Gandhi-edited nationalist journal), June 16, 1920 cited in *The Essential Gandhi*, p. 154.

6 Ibid., p. 152.

7 Ibid., p. 157.

8 Ibid., p. 154.

[The] force of love ... truly comes into play only when it meets
with causes of hatred. True Non-violence does not ignore or blind
itself to causes of hatred, but in spite of the knowledge of their existence, operates upon the person setting those causes in motion....
The law of Non-violence—returning good for evil, loving one's
enemy—involves a knowledge of the blemishes of the 'enemy.'
Hence do the Scriptures say ... 'Forgiveness is an attribute of the
brave.'[9]

Gandhi acknowledged that violence in the form of defense of another
person or in defense of an oppressed nation is superior to cowardly
reaction of doing nothing, turning from the oppression. Nevertheless,
he adamantly counters, "I believe non-violence is infinitely superior to
violence, forgiveness is more manly than punishment ... But ...for-
giveness only when there is the power to punish."[10]

What prompted Gandhi to embark on a course of non-violent
resistance? *Swaraj* [self-rule] and equality. Self-rule, though, was
necessitated by the lack of self-sufficiency. He therefore sought to
rectify the unjust economic structures that fostered the dependency
of Indians on foreign goods, the basic goods of living, and make Indians self-sufficient (the weaving—textile and garment industry—and
the salt from their shores) and self-reliant, thereby giving them the
self-respect that induced their will which gave them the strength to
forgive and the courage to become non-violent. Justice lies at the basis
of non-violent resistance; justice requires that every person have both
work and food.[11] Gandhi astutely realized that attainment of *swaraj*

---

9 Ibid., p. 198.

10 Ibid., p. 157. Ibid. p. 216, Gandhi acknowledged the deep force within
us to reach out and strike in defense of oneself, but continued to maintain
the importance of striving for higher ground of non-violent reaction. "I
do not want to live at the cost of the life even of a snake. I should let him
bite me to death rather than kill him. But it is likely that if God puts me
to that cruel test ... I may not have the courage to die but the beast in me
may assert itself and I may seek to kill the snake in defending this perish-
able body."

11 Gandhi writes in *Young India*, Oct. 13, 1921, cited in *The Essential
Gandhi*, pp. 160-161, "To a people famishing and idle the only acceptable form in which God can dare appear is work and promise of food as

through violence would only result in a violent *swaraj*, something that political leaders of major international societies today refuse to accept because they are willing to tolerate the consequences as long as they believe that they maintain the upper hand. Violence begets violence! Thus, Gandhi declared, "Truth [*satya*] is my God. Non-violence is the means of realizing Him ..."[12] Gandhi would sacrifice neither truth nor non-violence for the sake of any movement. Both went hand in hand.

Non-violent resistance is implemented through civil disobedience, *satyagraha*, the non-violent civil disobedience to unjust laws and unfair

wages. God created man to work for his food and said that those who ate without work were thieves. Eighty percent of India are compulsorily thieves half the year. Is it any wonder if India has become one vast prison."

It is reported that Gandhi said that poverty is the greatest violence, effectively because even work in poverty cannot provide enough sustenance for a person to work his way out, thereby becoming nothing other than economic slavery.

12 Ibid., p. 199. Glyn Richards, *The Philosophy of Gandhi: A Study of His Basic Ideas* (London: Curzon Press Ltd., 1982), p. 1, observes that Gandhi, although not consciously as an academic exercise, pursued metaphysical and philosophical truth through existentialist engagement with and living out the truth. Like in theology, wherein one acts and then in a dialectic reflects upon the act before acting again to pursue the meaning and existence of God, so too Gandhi created and made truth based on his observation of and experience with the reality of truth about God. In this way, Gandhi was faithful to his Hindhu tradition which "affirms the isomorphism of Truth (*Satya*) and Reality (*Sat*). He refers to reality as Truth ... For him nothing is, or nothing exists, except Truth, and where Truth is there also is true knowledge, (*cit*), and where true knowledge is, there also is bliss, (*ananda*). Truth then is *Saccidananda*, being, consciousness, bliss." (Pa. 1.)

Gandhi had no difficulty in regarding truth (*Satya*) as the most perfect term to be used for God and, thus, accepted that Truth is God. He accepted, however, that the expression of God could be anthropomorphized and expressed as such in *Isvara*. But, Gandhi considered Truth to be the best description of God because, for example, even the atheist seeks truth. Thus, one can say that in Truth, even in reality (*sat*), Gandhi found God, as the absolute expression of formless Truth.

social and political practices being based on truth, literally "firmness in truth,"[13] or "truth-force."[14] By civil disobedience, Gandhi did not mean the unorganized violence of the people against the government, nor did it infer "a state of lawlessness and license but presupposes a law-abiding spirit combined with self-restraint."[15] Gandhi describes civil disobedience in the following way:

> Complete Civil Disobedience is rebellion without the element of violence in it. An out and out civil resister simple ignores the authority of the state.[16] He becomes an outlaw claiming to disregard every unmoral state law. Thus, for instance, he may refuse to pay taxes.... In doing all this he never uses force and never resists force when it is used against him. In fact, he invites imprisonment and other uses of force ... This he does because ... he finds the bodily freedom he seemingly enjoys to be an intolerable burden. He argues to himself that a state allows personal freedom only in so far as the citizen submits to its regulations. Submission to the state law is the price a citizen pays for his personal liberty. Submission, therefore, to a state wholly or largely unjust is an immoral barter for liberty.... Thus considered, civil resistance is a most powerful expression of a soul's anguish and an eloquent protest against the

---

13   While in South Africa, Gandhi was heavily influenced by Henry Thoreau's *On the Duty of Civil Disobedience*. From this work, he began to search for ways to apply this mode of political action and resistance in a non-violent way, that he ultimately perfected and used upon his return to India in several focused strikes in 1914. The use of civil disobedience to achieve representation for Indians living in South Africa required more time of him than he originally thought—twenty-one years versus the one year he initially estimated.

14   Parekh, *Gandhi*, p. 51 and Mohandhas K. Gandhi, *Young India*, Mar. 32, 1921, cited in John Somerville and Ronald E. Santoni, eds., *Social and Political Philosophy* (Garden City, NY: Doubleday & Co., Inc, 1963), p. 501.

15   Gandhi, *Young India*, Nov. 17, 1921, cited in *The Essential Gandhi*, p. 165.

16   The thinking of Gandhi with regard to civil disobedience in the face of unjust and immoral laws or government in order to reform such is akin the early Greek philosophical concept of *epikaia*, the need to reform the law by breaking it because of its unjustness or immorality.

continuance of an evil state. Is this not the history of all reform? Have not reformers, much to the disgust of their fellows, discarded even innocent symbols associated with an evil practice?[17]

... Civil Disobedience ... becomes a sacred duty when the state has become lawless or, which is the same thing, corrupt. And a citizen who barters with such a state shares its corruption or lawlessness.[18]

Non-cooperation is a protest against an unwitting and unwilling participation in evil.[19]

Like Jesus who, contrary to Jewish law and custom, picked grain from the fields with his disciples and ate it on the Sabbath (Mk. 2:23-28, Mt. 12:1-8 and Luke 6:1-5), frequently cured people of their infirmities on the Sabbath or persons who were connected with the despised, foreign Roman occupiers or hostile to the Jews (Lk. 6:6-10, Lk. 4:31-35, Lk. 7:1-10, Lk. 14:1-5, Mk. 5, Mk. 7:24-35), associated with women and ostracized persons (Lk. 8:1-3, Lk. 17:11-19), etc., Gandhi also judiciously practiced civil disobedience because of the evil and corrupt system around him. Unlike Gandhi, though, Jesus did not engage in non-cooperation on an institutional level, although he definitely set a precedent for such and apparently roused people's consciences to act contrary to Jewish law. One can observe that the results of civil disobedience both with respect to Jesus and with respect to Gandhi were the same—the actions of non-cooperation spoke loudest because of the action and not the protest. Jesus' actions led to a change of heart and practice in the way of living of many people outside Israel, even though it was not called public opinion then; Gandhi induced a change in the treatment of Indians in South Africa and the overthrow of the British in India, precisely because of the swaying of international public opinion. By effectively not recognizing the so-called validity of the authorities who were engaged in maintaining oppressive and evil practices, both Gandhi and Jesus brought about radical change in the thinking and, to a certain extent, in the actions of the oppressors.

17 Gandhi, *Young India*, Nov. 10, 1921, cited in *The Essential Gandhi*, p. 165.

18 Ibid, p. 166.

19 Ibid.

Unlike Jesus, Gandhi cultivated public opinion and public support. This seemed to matter little to Jesus because he was not attempting to force change upon anyone, but he certainly was influencing change by both his actions and his teachings. Jesus and his disciples clearly demanded self-sacrifice and, as Paul often testified, even willingness to die in non-violent resistance to the evil inflicted unwillingly upon oneself. Gandhi not only willingly used this self-sacrifice (his own beating, assassination attempts, etc.) as a tool for change, but used this as a means to induce others to act similarly to force societal change.[20] "As larger and larger numbers of innocent men come out to welcome death their sacrifice will become the potent instrument for the salvation of all others, and there will be a minimum of suffering. Suffering cheerfully endured ceases to be suffering and is transmuted into an ineffable joy."[21] Suffering, nevertheless, can be expected to be an essential part of acting non-violently. "Suffering in one's own person is ... the essence of non-violence and is the chosen substitute for violence to others."[22]

A.L. Herman has identified four essential elements of *Satyagraha*. They are:

> 1. Like the Greek concept of *epikaia* (the breaking of bad law to reform the law), *Satyagraha* must be used against unjust laws that

---

20 While in South Africa, Gandhi was also heavily influenced by John Ruskin's *Unto This Last*, a work that lead Gandhi to undertake a life of harsh austerity and a sense of communal living that he actually lived in two communes in South Africa. Even after returning to India, one can say that he effectively attempted to live in a commune wherein the members become self-sufficient and every member of India he considered as part of his family.

21 Gandhi, *Young India*, Oct. 8, 1925, cited in *The Essential Gandhi*, p. 199. He further wrote that he himself could countenance the terrible voluntary loss of lives in the practice of non-violent resistance because, from the situation of India in the 1920s, it would result in the least loss of life and would ennoble those who sacrificed their own life.

Gandhi previously noted that the only sacrifice worthy of such requires joy. "Sacrifice and a long face go ill together ..." (Gandhi, *Young India*, June 25, 1925, cited in *The Essential Gandhi*, p. 205.

22 Ibid., p. 168

fail to respect human dignity and foster human suffering. The laws, therefore, must be broken in order to reform and correct the laws.

2. Civil disobedience must be conducted with non-violence and love.

3. The practitioners of civil disobedience must be willing to suffer physically, mentally and emotionally and offer such to God.

4. More so than the laws, Gandhi sought to change the hearts and minds of the oppressors. Thus, as in US school desegregation, it can be observed that little changed in substance, but only in appearance, as laws changed segregation practices, but the heart and mind of segregation remained entrenched.[23]

These four elements tell us much about the external and internal objectives of civil disobedience, the required prerequisites for engaging in it, and the expected, immediate results of it while forcing the desired outcome. These elements also demonstrate Gandhi's understanding that the head and the heart must be united; he was aware of the limitations of human argument as a persuasive means for effecting social change and the scant historical precedents therein.

Gandhi's emphasis on non-violence stems from his respect for any person and every person. Like Jesus, he refuses to destroy individuals and people, but attacks social systems and restraining laws and prohibitions.[24] For Gandhi, he perceived a two-way movement between Truth (*Satya*) and non-violence (*Ahimsa*).[25] Influenced by the Bhagavad-Gita, the Hindu scriptures, that called one to action, he understood that the endless cycle of birth, death, and rebirth necessitated a disciplined and desireless action, "action where there is no hankering after the fruits of action, if liberation is to be achieved." (Richards, 1982, 8) Gandhi correctly believed that *himsa*, or violence,

23 A.L. Herman, *Community, Violence, and Peace: Aldo Leopold, Mohandas K. Gandhi, Martin Luther King, Jr., and Gautama the Buddha in the Twenty-First Century* (Albany, NY: State University of New York Press, 1999), pp. 80-81.

24 Gandhi, *Young India*, May 25, 1921, cited in *The Essential Gandhi*, p. 170. "[Whilst] we may attack measures and systems we may not, must not, attack men. Imperfect ourselves, we must be tender toward others and be slow to impute motives."

25 Richards, *The Philosophy of Gandhi*, p. 8.

can never lead to Truth, but that non-violence always leads to it, and that "the same moral demands apply to the means as to the ends in the quest for Truth," no matter what difficulties are certainly to arise in the process. (Richards, 1982, 8) Gandhi also believed, rightly or wrongly, that the world was developing from *himsa* to greater practice of *Ahimsa*.[26] To practice *Ahimsa* is to realize Truth and vice-versa. It is important to realize that Gandhi also felt that all truth was relative; thus, to use lethal violence in pursuit or practice of truth may result in mistaken lethal, irreversible consequences of the death of another person because of misperception of truth.[27] Thus, the pursuit of truth necessarily required the exercise of non-violent means.

Glyn Richards indicates that, because for Gandhi means and ends are convertible and effectively the same thing, "our ideals not only inform the ends we aim at but also the means we employ to reach them…. If this is the case, then means and ends amount to the same thing since the same moral demands apply to both in the quest for Truth." (Richards, 1982, 31) Aldous Huxley observed similar to Gandhi that "For the means employed inevitably determine the nature of the results achieved; whereas, however good the end aimed at may be, its goodness is powerless to counteract the effects of the bad means we use to reach it."[28] Precisely because of this thinking, Gandhi stressed *Ahimsa* in order to attain the objective or goal of Truth, *Satya*. Non-violence is the only acceptable means to attain Truth. Richards deduces that the self-revelation, i.e., self-truth, lies at the heart of the pursuit

---

26   Parekh, *Gandhi*, p. 52. contests that Gandhi accepted spontaneous violence when born out of frustration with entrenched injustices attributable to morally blind and myopic dominant groups, but that he could not condone violence as a deliberate method of social change.

27   Gandhi, *Young India*, Mar. 23, 1921, cited in *Social and Political Philosophy*, p. 500, stated that *Satyagraha* demanded non-violence, "It excludes the use of violence because man is not capable of knowing the absolute truth and, therefore, not competent to punish." How different this attitude is compared to the self-righteous certitude that major international governments employ!

28   Aldous Huxley, *Ends and Means* (London: Chatto & Windus, 1941), p. 52 and cited by Richards, *The Philosophy of Gandhi*, p. 32.

of truth and correspondingly necessitates non-violence as the means
to pursue truth of self and, as a result, God.

> … the Self within man is at one with the essence of reality, which
> is truth or God. But if the kernel of an individual, the higher self,
> is the *Atman* (i.e., the Self) which is at one with Truth or God,
> then to inflict deliberate violence on another is to injure God or
> undermine Truth, and to cause suffering to another is to violate
> one's higher Self or *Atman*.[29]

The Self for Gandhi is engaged in a monumental struggle of self-
ishness against unselfishness. One should prefer unselfishness and
cultivate selflessness, but this can be achieved only through sacrifice,
self-discipline, and devotion to and service of others. Non-violence
remains at the heart of this struggle because it is the disciplined means
to attainment of Truth. Tolstoy's writing influenced Gandhi to help
Gandhi realize that "non-violence involved not only the negative
attitude of freedom from anger and hate but also the positive attitude
of love for all men," claims Richards.[30] Thus, the *Ahisma* promoted
by Gandhi required not just the prohibition of inflicting physical
harm upon another person but also refraining from wishing ill of
another. Ahimsa means loving those who hate you, do ill or have ill
will against you, and reacting to them in the same way as one would

---

29   Richards, *The Philosophy of Gandhi*, p. 32. Gandhi effectively identifies
the Self with no distinction from Truth or God. Further, he underscores
the importance of faith and belief in God in order to exercise *Ahimsa*
when he states, "In the last resort it does not avail to those who do not
possess a living faith in the God of Love." Nirmal Kumar Bose, *Selections
from Gandhi* (Ahmedabad, India: Navajivan Publishing House, 1948), p.
154, cited in Richards, *The Philosophy of Gandhi*, p. 36.

30   *Ibid.*, pp. 33-34. Although this work focuses more particularly on the
issue of war and lethal physical violence, Gandhi, and indirectly Tolstoy
(*The Kingdom of God Is Within You*), as well as Jesus, do not separate or
diminish the necessary linkage between internal attitude and expressive,
external action. One may be schizophrenic in refraining from external
oral and physical violence, but retain tremendous internal violence with
hatred and anger within. As such, it is difficult to attain Truth.

respond to one's kin with forgiveness and compassion and not with
vindictive retribution.

Is the non-violence promoted by Gandhi absolute in all situations?
Richards, contrary to the actual practice and known history of Gandhi,
conjectures that, because Gandhi is aware that we live in world devoid
of order and imbued with severe violence, *himsa*, there may be situations that necessitate the use of violence. Although, as noted above,
Gandhi suggested that, if his son had a choice, between acting violently
or cowardly by doing nothing in reaction to exploitation, he preferred
him to act with violence, Gandhi recommended that non-violence
is the only preferable way and that it requires extraordinary courage.
Richards, nevertheless, notes that Gandhi never wanted *Ahimsa* to
become a fetish, and raises the hypothetical cases wherein Gandhi
would kill (a) his son if he had an incurable disease in order to end
his suffering and (b) his daughter if she were to be threatened to be
violated in order to save her from such.[31] Therefore, Richards contended
that there are situations in which moral dilemmas would have induced

---

31   Richards, *The Philosophy of Gandhi*, pp. 36-37. (Gandhi had no daugh-
     ters.) Gandhi, "The Doctrine of the Sword," *Young India*, Aug. 11, 1920,
     cited in *Social and Political Philosophy*, p. 529 wrote the following.

     I do believe that where there is only a choice between cowardice and
     violence I would advise violence. Thus, when my eldest son asked
     me what he should have done, had he been present when I was
     almost fatally assaulted in 1908, whether he should have run away
     and seen me killed or whether he should have used his physical force
     which he could and wanted to use, and defended me, I told him
     that it was his duty to defend me even by using violence. Hence it
     was that I took part in the Boer War, the so-called Zulu rebellion
     and the late War. Hence also do I advocate training in arms for
     those who believe in the method of violence. I would rather have
     India resort to arms in order to defend her honour than that she
     should in a cowardly manner become or remain a helpless witness
     to her own dishonour.

     But I believe that non-violence is infinitely superior to violence,
     forgiveness is more manly than punishment. (Forgiveness adorns a
     soldier.) But abstinence is forgiveness only when there is the power
     to punish; it is meaningless when it pretends to proceed from a
     helpless creature …

Gandhi to yield his principle of *Ahimsa* and, engaging in violence, he surmises, Gandhi would have retained his intent, even though it could not have been implemented. The violence would still remain as evil and the act wrong, but possibly must be acknowledged as the least worse result of a resolution of a moral dilemma. Bhikhu Parekh also questions the total, successful applicability of *Satyagraha* because, he claims, it rests on the decency of the conflicting parties. Where such does not exist, especially in the case of pathological or distorted intent, *Satyagraha* is like a dog barking up the wrong tree.[32]

These conjectures seem to contradict Gandhi's basic thinking, though, because Gandhi himself never resorted to violence and spent his time building the courage to do so and because Gandhi is not known to have spared either his wife or children from hypothetical and possibly real sexual threat. While Gandhi allowed for exceptions to his rule of *Satyagraha* and *Ahimsa*, he himself developed the courage, suffering, and self-discipline to pursue truth through non-violence and must be considered a model practitioner, though admittedly a fallible and imperfect one, of these principles.

Richards also indicates the idealism of Gandhi in the implementation of *Ahimsa*. When Gandhi was questioned what he would do when informed that an aircraft would drop an atomic weapon on him, he responded that he would let the pilot see that Gandhi harbored no ill-will against the pilot. This response must be taken, not as if in a hypothetical situation, but as demonstrating (a) the conviction of Gandhi to practice *Ahimsa* even when faced with overwhelming odds of destruction, (b) the commitment of Gandhi to turn the continual use of *himsa* to a different and more humane way of interacting amongst conflicting parties, and (c) the interlinkage between all people which necessitates the welfare of all.

One must realize that Gandhi grew in his understanding of *Ahimsa* and that he placed primacy on religious values and their practice in everyday and exceptional living. During the First World War, for example, he acted as an army recruiter of ambulance work on behalf of the British in India. The Indian people who had listened to him preach home rule, non-violence, and *Satyagraha* questioned him on his recruiting on behalf of the foreign Raj and colonizers, particularly

---

32   Parekh, *Gandhi*, pp. 59-60.

in light of his reputation for non-violent struggle to benefit Indians in South Africa. He acknowledged that there was no defense for his conduct and, in fact, there could be no distinction between ambulance work for the military and those engaged in actual lethal combat and that both were guilty of war crime, but cautioned that moral dilemmas were not easily evaluated in black-and-white principles, and due to their complexity required time to analyze.[33]

At the start of World War II, Gandhi commented that he did not consider Hitler with the disdain that others held; he maintained these views because of the horrific deaths that were suffered in the first World War did not seem to occur with early World War II German tactics, but also because it was not known then that Hitler had embarked on a systematic extermination of Jews, Gypsies, and Russians. By the end of the Second World War, he had clearly cemented his disgust for violence as a means of conflict resolution in war and stated, "What is a war criminal? Was not war itself a crime against God and humanity, and, therefore, were not all those who sanctioned, engineered, and conducted wars, war criminals? War criminals are not confined to the Axis Powers alone. Roosevelt and Churchill are no less war criminals than Hitler and Mussolini, England, America and Russia have all of them got their hands dyed more or less red—not merely Germany and Japan."[34] One can understand by this that Gandhi interpreted war itself as a crime because of the lethal violence. As such, it is impossible to accept the aforenoted analysis of Richards that Gandhi would accept the use of violence in certain moral dilemmas. Louis Fisher, Gandhi's biographer, reported that Gandhi enigmatically stated to him in 1946 that, although Hitler killed five million Jews and perpetrated the greatest crime of the twentieth century, the Jews

33 Mohandhas Gandhi, *All Men Are Brothers* (Unesco, 1958 and 1969), pp. 175-176, compiled and edited by Krishna Kripalani, cited in Richards, *The Philosophy of Gandhi*, p. 42.

34 www.military quotes/quotations. Gandhi, given his early education and work in Britain and his knowledge of Western culture and civilization, inclusive of imperialist oppression in India and elsewhere, held Western society in very low esteem and the practice of Christianity there no different. "I consider western Christianity in its practical working a negation of Christ's Christianity."

should have offered themselves to the butcher's knife.[35] This can only be interpreted to mean that, in the face of such terrible violence by grossly evil practitioners as Hitler, one should not submit to reacting in turn with violence. Gandhi clarified his position on violence in no uncertain terms, "I am prepared to die, but there is no cause for which I am prepared to kill."[36] He was fully aware that, while India was capable for reasons of years of non-violent resistance and other important political and economic factors of throwing off oppressive British colonial rule, in other situations non-violent civil disobedience would be met with different, if not brutal, reaction, given the events of Germany during the second World War, for example.

Gandhi viewed the world as a community, an enlargement of his Ashrams of South Africa and those of India, and as such considered there to be a oneness of humanity. The practice of Satyagraha through Ahimsa was intimately linked to the welfare of all the people, i.e., *Sarvodaya*, the welfare of all. Contrary to utilitarianism which pursues the greatest good for the greatest number of people, *Sarvodaya* is totally inclusive and pursues the welfare of all.

Religion has been one of the root causes for fomenting war. Gandhi reacted against the fanaticism of religious righteousness and theocratic purity promoted at one time or another by many religions. He acknowledged that, even though he was Hindu, all religions are true and all hold some errors. He prayed that, whatever religion a person held, that person would become a better practitioner; and he avoided the hope for successful proselytizing and conversion.[37] Gandhi was

---

35 This should not be considered a slight of Jews by Gandhi. While in South Africa, a wealthy Jewish friend and South African immigrant, financed one of Gandhi's earliest communes, Ashram, which was called the Tolstoy Farm, a farm of about 1,100 acres where the *Satyagrahi* lived and worked. It must be noted that Gandhi identified the Indians of South Africa with Jews of Europe. Both were oppressed unjustly. See Mohandhas K. Gandhi, *Harijan*, Nov. 26, 1938, cited in *Social and Political Philosophy*, p. 535.

36 www.wikipedia.

37 *The Essential Gandhi* quotes Gandhi with regard to religion, "True religion being the greatest thing in life in the world, it has been exploited the most." (p. 214, from *Old Letters*, Apr. 25, 1925, p. 42.) He further acknowledges that morality supercedes any and all religion.

keenly conscious that the crimes which believers committed in the name of their religion generally used the end to justify their means. He was all too conscious of antagonism between Hindus and Muslims in India, that later erupted with devastating consequences.

DOROTHY DAY

The peace movement in the US owes much to the socialists and other left-wing activists during the First World War. Dorothy Day was one of them. Although born in Brooklyn, New York in 1897, and raised mostly in Chicago, her return to New York in 1916 launched her, not only in the trade of her father as a journalist for a Socialist paper, *The Masses*, and for *New York Call*, but also as an activist for human rights such that in 1917 she was arrested with the Wobblies (Industrial Workers of the World) for protesting in front of the White House against the brutal treatment and arrest of women suffragettes and for demanding their release. At twenty, she herself was first imprisoned one month for this arrest, but was released early with the other prisoners by President Woodrow Wilson because he thought that the hunger strike undertaken by the prisoners would adversely affect the war effort. Her life as a journalist was shaken when the US government closed *The Masses* under the spurious "Espionage Act" because the government claimed that *The Masses* was printing material injurious to the government when *The Masses* criticized and lampooned the US' entrance into the First World War against the Central Powers. Dorothy Day like other journalists at *The Masses* believed that competing imperialist systems had caused the war and, therefore, the US should remain neutral.

Day studied nursing in Brooklyn in 1918 and embarked on a searching personal journey wherein she had several experiences with different men, leading to the birth of her only child, Tamar Theresa, and her separation from her common-law husband in 1927 because of her independent decision to baptize their child and for her to convert to Catholicism. Prior to that, her search led her on this spiritual journey wherein her introduction to Catholicism helped her through the psychological trauma of an illegal abortion. She was influenced amongst other reasons by the difficulty of unemployment of her father in Chicago, Upton Sinclair's *The Jungle*, Dostoyevsky, Eugene O'Niell's recitation of "The Hound of Heaven," the frequent walks through the impoverished south Chicago with her younger brother in a baby carriage, and personal religiosity of her roommates and their parents. She came to see the Church as the protector of immigrants and the poor.

On December 9, 1932 she was introduced to Peter Maurin, an immigrant from France and ex-Christian Brother, who was living according to the teachings of St. Francis, was working at a Catholic boys' camp, and who strongly influenced her in her convictions against war. On the previous day, the feast of the Immaculate Conception, she had prayed fervently at the Shrine of the Immaculate Conception in Washington, DC for some way that she could live her life helping her fellow workers and the poor. She had been in Washington, DC to report for *Commonweal* and *America* on the Hunger March organized and led by the Communists. Maurin, after reading her articles, showed up at Day's door with the introduction of the editor of *Commonweal*.[38] He advised Day that she should start a paper that would inform people of Catholic social teachings on social justice and promote peaceful social change. Five months after meeting Maurin, Day and Maurin on May 1, the feast of St. Joseph the Worker, launched the *Catholic Worker*, a newpaper that to this day still sells for one penny and focuses on issues pertaining to poverty, social injustice, violence and war. Peter Maurin influenced Day in countless ways, not just the establishment of the paper, but also (a) with a belief that the Catholic social teachings could be united with the Wobblies to start a new "green," communitarian revolution that sought commonality and worked through non-violence, (b) the introduction to papal encyclicals on "The Condition of Labor," etc. which condemned the misery of the masses working under the yokes of a few wealthy men, (c) the critique

---

38 Jim Forrest, "A Biography of Dorothy Day," *The Encyclopedia of American Catholic History*, Liturgical Press, 1994), writes, "Day watched the protesters parade down the streets of Washington carrying signs calling for jobs, unemployment insurance, old age pensions, relief for mothers and children, health care and housing. What kept Day in the sidelines was that she was a Catholic and the march had been organized by Communists, a party at war with not only capitalism but religion."

of finance capitalism and the preparation for war as an established disorder, and (d) the establishment of communal farms.[39]

The success of the paper was soon apparent with its circulation of 100,000 copies. Articles by Maurin on the impoverishment and hunger of people eventually brought the homeless to the door of Day's apartment where the paper was edited. She and Maurin first rented an apartment for six women and then another for men. This led to establishment of the first Catholic Worker house in New York in 1934, followed by the rental of two buildings in Chinatown. By 1936, there were 33 Catholic Worker houses around the US serving the needs of the homeless and unemployed caused by the Great Depression.

When in 1935 the *Catholic Worker* published an article on a dialogue between Christ and a patriot, who protested that the non-violent teachings of Jesus, while noble, were impractical, few paid heed of its pacifist tendencies. In 1936 Spain was rent with civil war between the Fascist insurgents led by General Francisco Franco and the nationalist loyalists supported by the Communists. The US supported the Fascists, but the *Catholic Worker* cautioned its readers on Franco's alignment with and support from Hitler's Nazi Germany that was systematically persecuting the Jews, refused to align with either side, and remained neutral. This caused nearly two-thirds of its readers to cancel their subscriptions because Spanish priests and nuns were being attacked, churches burned, and the Church in Spain supported the Fascists. Day and Maurin stuck with their belief in the teachings of Jesus, though, and declared their pacifism, opposed class warfare and hatred, and opposed imperialist wars.[40]

Day made a telling observation with regard to non-violence and pacifist actions at the time of the Spanish Civil War. She compared

---

39   Eileen Egan, *Peace Be with You: Justified Warfare or the Way of Nonviolence* (Maryknoll, NY: Orbis Books, 1999), p. 267.

40   Day wrote in *The Catholic Worker*, in 1936 on the courage and suffering that pacifists must deal: "A pacifist who is willing to endure the scorn of the unthinking mob, the ignominy of jail, the pain of stripes and the threat of death cannot be lightly dismissed as a coward afraid of physical pain…. A pacifist even now must be prepared for the opposition of the mob who think violence is bravery. A pacifist in the next war must be ready for martyrdom." Cited by Egan, *Peace Be with You*, p. 271.

the difficulty that the apostles of Jesus had with accepting Jesus' comment that both Jesus and they must lay down their lives for their friends. She wrote, "Christians, when they are seeking to defend their faith by arms, by force and violence, are like those who said to Our Lord, 'Come down from the Cross. If you are the son of God, save yourself."[41] Renown, European, Catholic scholars and writers, such as Jacque Maritain, Emmanuel Mounier, Georges Bernanos, and Francois Mauriac held similar neutral positions that opposed the violence perpetrated by either side in that civil war.

The Catholic Worker in the 1930s began to picket at the German consulate in New York to protest Germany's persecution of the Jews and dissidents and carried signs proclaiming, "Spiritually we are Semites." The *Catholic Worker*, nevertheless, retained its staunch pacifist stance of non-violence even after Japan attacked the US at Pearl Harbor on Dec. 7, 1941 and the US declared war.[42] Nearly half of the Catholic Worker houses closed in response to Day's stringent pacifism and emphasis of non-violence. Day along with another Catholic Worker, Joseph Zarrella, went to Washington, DC in 1940 to protest in committee against the US government's proposed legislation on military conscription because the said legislation failed either to include Catholics as a group that was permitted conscientious-objector status in addition to the Quakers, Mennonites, etc. or to recognize those who claimed objection because they did not acknowledge just war

---

41   Robert Ellsberg, ed., *Dorothy Day: Selected Writings* (Maryknoll, NY: Orbis Books, 1983), p. 78, cited by Egan, *Peace Be with You*, p. 271.

42   Egan, *Peace Be with You*, p. 261, quotes Dorothy Day's statement in the *Catholic Worker* (Jan. 1942) after the US declared war: "Our manifesto is the Sermon on the Mount, which means that we will try to be peacemakers. Speaking for many of our conscientious objectors, we will not participate in armed warfare or by making munitions, or by buying government bonds to further the war effort, or by urging others to these efforts.... Love your enemies and do good to those who hate you." Egan reports that the US government in 1941 considered Day so threatening that it placed Day on a list to be removed to custodial detention in the event of national emergency.

rationale.[43] Draft boards, based on this legislation, refused to recognize those who opposed war or just war theory. Many Catholic Worker men were either imprisoned or forced to work in rural work camps when they refused induction into the US military.[44]

As Dwight D. Eisenhower was later to criticize the US' military-industrial complex, Day and the Catholic Workers were prescient in their understanding of the threat of a militarist state. When the US, relying on its dominant world power and the threat of its nuclear force, sought to counter the hegemonic spread of the USSR's military might, strengthened by its own nuclear capabilities, Day and *The Catholic Worker*, influenced by the *Satyagraha* of Gandhi, refused to participate in the mandatory civil defense drills in New York city precisely because the US government was attempting to convey that people could be protected from a nuclear attack. They peacefully protested outside City Hall each time these drills were conducted in preparation for war because they contested that the US was embarked on a policy of undertaking nuclear war that it believed that it could win, in spite of the expected mass destruction of countless numbers of civilians. Day was arrested and imprisoned several times for this.[45]

Day acknowledged the important contributions of fellow Catholic Workers, particularly Ammon Hennacy and Bob Ludlow, to support and clarify the position of pacifism in the Church, even to the

---

43 Day had written in *The Catholic Worker*, September 1939, that "We must choose sides now; not between nations at war but between the world's way and Christ's way." Cited by Egan, *Peace Be with You*, p. 274.

44 Unlike in World War I, when as many as 20 or more persons refused to accept conscription and were later hung, draft boards in World War II are not known to have resulted in capital punishment, but they continued to refuse to recognize the conscientious objection to war or just war and refusal to fight. Selective objection was disregarded by the draft boards.

45 Day wrote in *The Catholic Worker*, September, 1945, her strong opposition and loathing of these weapons of mass destruction. "We can only suggest one thing—destroy the two billion dollars worth of equipment that was built to make the atomic bomb, destroy all the formulas, put on sackcloth and ashes, weep and repent." Cited by Egan, *Peace Be with You*, p. 280.

amazement of other long-time Catholic Workers.[46] Both men as well as many other Catholic Workers considered themselves anarchist, if not anarcho-syndicalists, who staunchly opposed the violence of war and were shamed by the centuries of Christian belligerence and support of aggressive Western governments.

The history of the Church in its compromising alignment, if not capitulation, with powerful military forces in the West and its complicity with just-war thinking since the fifth century posed a problem to Day and the Catholic Worker. Day and many of the Catholic Workers were pacifists. Egan reports that, when confronted with this issue, Day responded that "the Church was the cross on which Christ was crucified. One needed ... to be in permanent dissatisfaction with the Church." (Egan, 1999, 288) While Day was a sponsor and mentor of the US' Pax, the non-violent peace movement originated in the UK in the 1930s which finally came to the US in 1962, she also aligned possibly more closely with the Fellowship of Reconciliation. In the former, just-war activists were involved, but the latter was strictly non-war, non-violent objectors.[47]

In April 1963, Pope John XXIII issued his encyclical *Pacem in Terris* ("Peace on Earth") that roundly condemned the use of weapons of mass destruction, particularly nuclear weapons that threatened the annihilation of a good part of humanity. This was a welcomed position taken by the leader of the Church on behalf of the church of humanity. It provided sustenance to the fledgling US peace movement against a government dependent on violent means of conflict-resolution, even in the face of massive destruction. US Catholics, heavily involved in opposition to USSR threats because of the place of religion in Communist states and the history of harassment of believers throughout these states, had a hard time swallowing criticism against nuclear deterrence, particularly because so many of them had been duped by the ideologi-

---

46   Dorothy Day, "War Is the Health of the State," in *The Long Loneliness* (New York: Harper and Brothers, 1952), pp. 265-267.

47   Egan poignantly remarks on Day's visit to the grave of Karl Marx and in consideration of Marx's statement carved on the tombstone and taken from his *Theses on Feuerbach* that theologians and philosophers have interpreted and commented on just war in numerous and diverse ways, but that the point is to change the world to one of gospel nonviolence.

cal beliefs that wrapped the flag around the cross. With the guiding position of John XXIII and later further supported by Pope Paul VI's beseeching at the United Nations ("No more war, war never again") on October 5, 1965 and in Paul VI's later encyclicals, the second Vatican Council that was meeting in Rome thrashed out a key document that set about to restore a leadership role for the church in contemporary life, "*Gaudium et Spes*," or "Pastoral Constitution on the Church in the Modern World," and issued it one and one-half years after *Pacem in Terris*. *Pacem in Terris* and *Gaudium et Spes* both sought to restore the original peace position of the early Church and the fundamental teaching of Jesus on non-violence after fifteen centuries of distorted Christian practice, thereby bringing to an end the Constantine era of perverted Christianity.[48] The latter document saw many drafts (*schema*) and was severely challenged by some US Catholics and not too few of their bishops (led on a late charge by Cardinal Francis Spellman of New York and Archbishop Phillip Hannan of New Orleans) on the

---

48 Pope John XXIII, *Pacem in Terris*, April 11, 1963, clearly states in paragraphs 109-117 and 126-129 the Church's disapproval of the violent world that we have created, roundly criticizes the wasteful and spirally arms race, deplores the Armageddon threat of nuclear war and the weapons that support it, decries the millstone of fear sucking life out of everyday men and women, demands an urgent end to the arms race and elimination of nuclear weapons, calls to reason the hopeless dependence on weaponry, demands the banning of nuclear weapons, and invites states to engage in diplomatic discussion and basic human reasoning.
In *Gaudium et Spes*, December 7, 1965, paragraphs 77-82, the Church identified the meaning of peace and highlighted its basis in the enterprise of justice which people must constantly and continually be building up, called for Christians to join with all peacemakers in bringing about peace, deplored the increasing savagery of war and its modern iterations, indirectly called for an effective and authoritative international body to deter war and advance peace, criticized the military and economic exploitation of nations by powerful states, suggested that wasteful expenditures in arms races by many countries be reconsidered in finding a better way to restore peace, demanded that all efforts be exhausted to end and outlaw all wars, required that conscientious objection be the norm and not the presumed rightness of the warring state, and beckoned all people to exert themselves to avoid hostility, contempt, distrust, and hatred.

issue of nuclear armaments.[49] Six, lay Catholic members of the Arms Control Subcommittee of the Catholic Association for International Peace ("CAIP") are reported to have drafted and issued in October 1964 a document entitled, "Morality, Nuclear War, and the Schema on the Church in the Modern World," which urged the Council not to ban nuclear weapons; they privately sent copies to certain Vatican Council participants and influenced debate on the issue of nuclear weapons and nuclear war. The Arms Control Subcommittee strongly suggested that if the Council called for a ban on nuclear weapons, and thereby a ban on nuclear war, it would impose a dilemma on US Catholics to choose between the directives of the Vatican Council and the assurances of the US government on its policy of nuclear deterrence as the sound basis for deterrence and international stability. The Council chose a position more in keeping with the teachings of Jesus; the US Catholic community would seem to demonstrate that they chose the position of their government over the moral guidance of the Church. The Catholic Association for International Peace clearly was seeking to thwart the influence of European pacifists and the advocacy against war taken by the Fellowship of Reconciliation and Pax, inclusive of Day who had gone to Rome in October 1965 to counter the bellicose influence of CAIP at the Council and undertake a water fast for the success of the Council's interpretation of peace and opposition to war.[50] The peace proponents won the day against the bellicose US-led clerics on the last day of the Council.[51]

49 Dorothy Day, *Loaves and Fishes* (New York: Harper & Row, 1963), p. 60, records how the New York Chancery also summoned her to retract a call in *The Catholic Worker* urging men not to register for the draft and encouraging conscientious objection. The institutional Church is replete with cases such as this in its ties with preservation of the state, even militarist states.

50 In *The Catholic Worker*, in a special edition of July 1965, in which Day and Eileen Egan amongst others collaborated, John L. McKenzie, SJ, wrote, "If the warfare based on the deterrent is not immoral warfare, then there is no immoral warfare. George H. Dunne, SJ, totally condemned nuclear weapons and warfare, writing "Neither the manufacture nor the use of nuclear or other indiscriminate weaponry could be morally justified." Cited by Egan *Peace Be with You*, p. 173.

51 Egan indicates that not since the twelfth century had the Church condemned specific weapons. In the twelfth century, it condemned as im-

On August 6, 1976, US Catholics celebrated as part of the bicentennial of the US with an International Eucharistic Congress in Philadelphia. Day along with Mother Theresa and other women were invited. Day had been invited to be a keynote speaker. Her speech matched her consciousness of the horrible anniversary of the immoral bombing of Hiroshima and the complicity of Christians in military involvement at the cathedral's mass. While the mass at the Catholic cathedral was celebrated to honor the US military, simultaneously Day addressed the Congress. She did not hesitate either to chide the Congress for failing to acknowledge the atrocities inflicted upon Hiroshima in 1945 or to prick the consciences of the Church for honoring the US military on a day that liturgically was to have been the celebration of the Transfiguration.

Martin Luther King, Jr.

Like Dorothy Day, Martin Luther King, Jr. found inseparable linkage between his consciousness of social injustice and the violence inflicted on the disenfranchised and marginalized, whether it be the violence of economic injustice or the violence in forcing these people to engage in international warfare.[52] King drew his sustenance from his belief in a God who was both all good and all powerful. Anyone who believed in such a God, he considered, was part of a beloved community of that God and should reflect the same in the way it lives, not just in an interiorized spirituality.

> Any religion that professes to be concerned about the souls of men and is not concerned about the slums that damn them, the economic conditions that strangle them and the social conditions that cripple them, is a spiritually moribund religion waiting burial."[53]

moral the crossbow because of the mortal wounds that it inflicted; the second Vatican Council condemned the immorality of atomic weapons because they indiscriminately killed. As if there is a moral way to kill another person!

52 Mohandhas K. Gandhi had correctly condemned economic disparity when he noted that poverty is the greatest form of violence.

53 Martin Luther King, Jr., "Pilgrimage to Nonviolence," in James Melvin Washington, ed., *A Testament of Hope: The Essential Writings and Speeches of Martin Luther King, Jr.* (San Francisco: Harper & Row, 1990), p. 38.

The power of love was the power of the almighty God, but this power symbiotic with love had to be not only efficacious, but also concrete in relieving people of their misery and the injustice committed against them. King initially believed that on a personal level this was more easily accomplished, but, when racial and national groups were in conflict, a more realistic approach than simply turning the other cheek was required. Reinhold Niebuhr had influenced King that the individual by him/herself was moral but the group was more often immoral. His reading of Gandhi changed his thinking such that he came to believe that Christian love used in conflict with the practice of non-violence was a realistic means that the oppressed and poor had to win their freedom.[54]

While working on his dissertation in systematic theology at Boston University, King accepted a pastorship at Dexter Avenue Baptist Church in Montgomery, Alabama in 1954. With the 1954 US Supreme Court's ruling that racial segregation of the schools in Topeka, Kansas was unconstitutional because it created a sense of inferiority that affects the hearts and minds of African-Americans, the stage was set for desegregation in other areas as well. Thus, when Rosa Parks in December 1955, with her week's work done, was returning home from her seamstress' job in Montgomery and refused to relinquish her seat to a white male, she was arrested and imprisoned. Four days later with King as the newly elected president of the Montgomery Improvement Association and in alignment with other African-American leaders directed a boycott of Montgomery's city buses which lasted nearly thirteen months until the city enacted the US Supreme Court ruling that declared segregation of Montgomery buses illegal and unconstitutional. King's old friend in Baton Rouge, Louisiana had successfully led a similar boycott two years prior. Like Gandhi previously, non-violent African-Americans with nearly 100 percent participation successfully boycotted public transportation and arranged alternative means of transportation for themselves, but not without arrest on trumped-up charges of loitering, hitchhiking, and the breaking of antiquated anti-boycott laws, and the bombing of King's own residence. The forty-two year old Rosa Parks

54   King, "Pilgrimage to Nonviolence," *A Testament of Hope*, p. 38.

and the African-Americans', united, non-violent boycott succeeded in ending this historical injustice of discrimination in Montgomery.[55]

With the formation of the Southern Christian Leadership Conference, King was elected its first president and instilled in the Conference members the practice of non-violent civil disobedience that he had learned the previous year in Montgomery. He used this *Satyagraha* approach as the means to combat racism, poverty, hatred and war because, as Gandhi and Day also experienced, it disarmed the violence of the oppressor by enacting the teachings of Jesus. He outlined five key observations pertaining to the difficulty, but possible success, of non-violent resistance or civil disobedience as a means to right injustice, particularly related to racial discrimination.

> First, this is not a method for cowards; it does resist. The nonviolent resister is just as strongly opposed to the evil against which he protests as is the person who uses violence. His method is passive or nonaggressive (*sic*) in the sense that he is not physically aggressive towards his opponent. But his mind and emotions are always active, constantly seeking to persuade the opponent that he is mistaken. This method is passive physically but strongly active spiritually; it is nonaggressive (*sic*) physically but dynamically aggressive spiritually.
>
> A second point is that nonviolent resistance does not seek to defeat or humiliate the opponent, but to win his friendship and understanding. The nonviolent resister must often express his protest through noncooperation (*sic*) or boycott.... The end is redemption and reconciliation. The aftermath of nonviolence is the creation of the beloved community, while the aftermath of violence is tragic bitterness.
>
> A third characteristic of this method is that the attack is directed against forces of evil rather than against persons who are caught in those forces. It is evil we are seeking to defeat, not the persons victimized by evil.... The tension is at bottom between justice and injustice, between the forces of light and the forces of darkness....

---

55 Success of non-violent desegregation of the Montgomery bus lines spurred the desegregation of the Woolworth's and Kress' lunch counters in their respective department stores in 1964 in Montgomery, Alabama. It was achieved by four college freshman, roughly 18 years in age and attending Alabama Agriculture and Technical College, an all black college, in the same town.

A fourth point that must be brought out concerning nonviolent resistance is that it avoids not only external physical violence but also internal violence of spirit. At the center of nonviolence stands the principle of love. In struggling for human dignity the oppressed people of the world must not allow themselves to become bitter or indulge in hate campaigns. To retaliate with hate and bitterness would do nothing but intensify the hate in the world. Along the way of life, someone must have sense enough and morality enough to cut off the chain of hate...

Finally, the method of nonviolence is based on the conviction that the universe is on the side of justice. It is this deep faith in the future that causes the nonviolent resister to accept suffering without retaliation. He knows that in his struggle for justice, he has cosmic companionship. This belief that God is on the side of truth and justice comes down to us from the long tradition of our Christian faith... (King, 1990, 7-9)

King began to be criticized by African-Americans in the mid-1960s because, while he focused on racial discrimination and poverty, he had refrained from identifying any linkage with the war raging in Vietnam and the high proportion of African-Americans involved in fighting that white man's war. On April 4, 1967, he acknowledged his failure of betrayal to speak out on this topic at Riverside Church in New York. Although questioned by others on the dubious linkage between civil rights and war and peace, he had the courage to step forward and identify the evil in war itself, not just the discriminating aspect of racial oppression in fighting an unjust war. King acknowledged that he too experienced that "men do not easily assume the task of opposing their government's policy," not unlike Day and others before him.[56] He continued, "(T)his is the first time in our nation's history that a significant number of its religious leaders have chosen to move beyond the prophesying of smooth patriotism to the high ground of a firm dissent based upon the mandates of conscience and the reading of history." (King, 1990, 231) He connected the dots and identified the culprit of inability to address the social injustices of everyday men and women. " ... I knew that America would never invest the necessary funds or energies in rehabilitation of its poor so

---

56 Martin Luther King, Jr., "A Time to Break Silence," *A Testament of Hope*, p. 231.

long as adventures like Vietnam continued to draw men and skills and money like some demonic destructive suction tube. So I was increasingly compelled to see the war as an enemy of the poor and to attack it as such." (King, 1990, 233)

Not only does King correctly identify the causes and effects of war as immoral, but he admits the linkage between social injustice of impoverishment and discrimination of human rights with the immorality and evils of war itself. For a country as bellicose as the US, one cannot attempt to correct the evil of one without attempting to address and correct the evil of another. In this sermon at Riverside Church, he did not make the leap in identifying the probable mutual causality of social injustice with war, though. He did, however, name the evil of manipulation of the poor for the exploitive desires of national injustice of concentrated power, achieved through "massive doses of violence." But, it was just not the exploitation of the US' poor, the US government deprived the Vietnamese of their freedom and continued to keep them in their poverty. The colonizer easily uses the traits of slavery that he practices at home in the colonized country. King identified the lies that deny the truth, the *Satya*, when he implicated the duplicity in war— not uncommonly, the US, "the most powerful nation of the world speaking of aggression as its drops thousands of bombs on a poor weak nation."[57] In his last speech to the Southern Christian

---

57   *Ibid.*, p. 238. King further added the duplicity of US hegemonism and the exploitation of US citizens. "We are adding cynicism to the process of death, for they (US troops) must know after a short period there that none of the things we claim to be fighting for are really involved. Before long they must know that their government has sent them into a struggle among Vietnamese, and the more sophisticated surely realize that we are on the side of the wealthy and the secure while we create a hell for the poor.

Somehow this madness must cease. We must stop now. I speak as a child of God and brother to the suffering poor of Vietnam. I speak for those whose land is being laid waste, whose homes are being destroyed, whose culture is being subverted. I speak for the poor of America who are paying the double price of smashed hopes at home and death and corruption in Vietnam. I speak as a citizen of the world, for the world as it stands aghast at the path we have taken.... The great initiative in this war is ours. The initiative to stop it must be ours."

Leadership Conference that he delivered after his sermon at Riverside Church, King held nothing back and clearly linked the three social evils of the 1960s in the US. "Now when I say question the whole society, it means ultimately coming to see that the problem of racism, the problem of economic exploitation, and the problem of war are all tied together. These are the triple evils that are interrelated."[58]

King, however, did not yet condemn war itself but seemed headed in that direction when he recognized that, one day, people will see the sense of this value and rationality of non-violence.[59] Like Reinhold Niebuhr, Dietrich Bonhoeffer, Jürgen Motmann, and others, he was still unable to make the leap to perfect love and accepted violent revolution of those who had been burdened by oppressive and exploitive colonialism and had arisen to defend with force their right of equality

---

58 Martin Luther King, Jr., "Where Do We Go from Here," (1967) *A Testament of Hope*, p. 251.

59 King, "A Time to Break Silence," p. 241. In his dream of a future world in which the value of love and the avoidance of international capital exploiting the poor of the world, King hinted his acknowledgement that a revolutionary change of peoples' thinking and acting will end war itself. "A true revolution of values will soon look uneasily on the glaring contrast of poverty and wealth. With righteous indignation, it will look across the seas and see individual capitalists of the West investing huge sums of money in Asia, Africa and South America, only to take the profits out with no concern for the social betterment of the countries, and say: 'This is not just.' It will look at our alliance with the landed gentry of Latin America and say: 'This is not just.' The Western arrogance of feeling that it has everything to teach others and nothing to learn from them is not just. A true revolution of values will lay hands on the world order and say of war: 'This way of settling differences is not just.' This business of burning human beings with napalm, of filling our nation's homes with orphans and widows, of injecting poisonous drugs of hate into veins of peoples normally humane, of sending men home from dark and bloody battlefields physically handicapped and psychologically deranged, cannot be reconciled with wisdom, justice and love. A nation that continues year after year to spend more money on military defense than on programs of social uplift is approaching spiritual death."

and justice.[60] His sermon at Riverside Church would seem to indicate an implicit acceptance of just war rationale. He certainly deplored the inhumanity and terrible atrocities of war. He demonstrated the spirit that is required of Christians facing the war in Vietnam when he said in response to criticism of his involvement in anti-war questioning, "What then can I say to the 'Vietcong' or to Castro or to Mao as a faithful minister of this one? Can I threaten them with death or must I not share with them my life?" (King, 1990, 234) He truly wanted a realization of an all-embracing and unconditional love for all men and women, not a sentimentality but a force at the basis of life itself, and realized that it had become a necessity for the survival of humanity.

What King offered the US was the identification of the truth, the reason that the US had engaged in countless counter-insurgency movements, not just in Vietnam, but in multiple countries on several continents. "The need to maintain social stability for our investments accounts for the counter-revolutionary action of American forces in Guatemala. It tells why American helicopters are being used against guerrillas in Colombia and why American napalm and green beret forces have already been active against rebels in Peru. It is with such activity in mind that the words of the late John F. Kennedy come back to haunt us. Five years ago he said, 'Those who make peaceful revolution impossible will make violent revolution inevitable.'" (King, 1990, 240)

Criticism against a standing militarist and expansionist government is not taken lightly by the government or those in the institutional Church. Not unlike Gandhi and Day, King too was criticized for engaging in non-violent civil disobedience. When he as leader of the Southern Christian Leadership Conference went to Birmingham, Alabama in 1963 was invited by a Birmingham affiliate of the same organization to come and participate in a civil rights demonstration and in non-violent civil disobedience, he was arrested. Eight prominent, local, white, liberal clergymen (four bishops, one rabbi, and three pastors) publicly criticized King for outsider involvement and use of civil disobedience in demonstrations. King responded to them that

---

60 *Ibid.*, p. 242, King proclaimed, "The shirtless and barefoot people of the land are rising up as never before. 'The people who sat in darkness have seen a great light.' We in the West must support these revolutions."

he, like Paul of Tarsus, was compelled to carry the gospel of freedom to this locale and questioned why these clergymen failed to show concern for the conditions that prompted the demonstrations. King outlined four principle steps required to engage in non-violent civil disobedience: "collection of the facts to determine whether injustices exist; negotiation; self-purification; and direct action."[61] He and his staff had meticulously gone through each of these steps and could arrive at no morally responsible method of action besides civil disobedience, other than complicity in the evil of affirming the status quo through non-action. He stressed that freedom is never given by the oppressor, but it must be demanded by the oppressed, and preferably through non-violent means, inclusive of legal methods and civil disobedience in the face of intransigent resistance to correcting social injustice. With regards to civil disobedience and breaking the law, King chided his critics that, because there are two types of laws (just and unjust), one has a legal and moral responsibility to obey just laws, but one also has a moral responsibility to disobey unjust laws.[62] He identified that "an unjust law is a code that is out of harmony with the moral law... not rooted in eternal law... Any law that uplifts human personality is just. Any law that degrades human personality is unjust." (King, 1964, 84-85) As to the liberal interpretation of morality and Christian ethics with regard to social change and righting injustice, King further rightly castigated them because they focused on and emphasized the importance of order over justice, preferring a "negative peace which is the absence of tension to a positive peace which is the presence of

---

61   Martin Luther King, Jr., "Letter from Birmimgham Jail," *Why We Can't Wait* (New York: Harper and Row, 1964), p. 77-100.

62   In fact, King noted, the precedent for breaking unjust laws was set in the Hebrew scriptures when Shadrach, Meshach, and Abednego refused to obey the laws of Nebuchadnezzar on the ground that a higher moral law ruled and the precedents set by the early Christians who were willing to suffer death by persecution. King astutely outlined for his critics that Hitler functioned according to the laws of the land and that the Hungarian freedom fighters of 1956 acted illegally in fighting the Communist government in power.

justice."[63] Finally, King addressed in his letter that the alternative to
non-violence was either (a) continual waiting and complicity in the
toleration of injustice or (b) the evil of violence itself that many opponents of injustice were calling for because of their tiredness at waiting
for those who for decades recommended moderation and gradualism
that brought no liberation and perpetuation of injustice.

By Christmas of 1967 in a sermon that he delivered at Ebenezer
Baptist Church, King seems clearly to have made the jump condemning war and calling for the full realization of the teaching of Jesus. "
… (T)he Christmas hope for peace and good will toward all men can
no longer be dismissed as a kind of pious dream of some utopian. If
we don't have good will toward men in this world, we will destroy
ourselves by the misuse of our own instruments and our own power.
Wisdom born of experience should tell us that war is obsolete. There
may have been a time when war served as a negative good by preventing the spread and growth of an evil force, but the very destructive
power of modern weapons of warfare eliminates even the possibility
that war may any longer serve as a negative good."[64] The loyalties that
nation states, classes, races, etc. create undermine the unifying point of
our humanity that we are citizens of the world. Thus, King called for
ecumenical loyalties that unite, not ones that divide and set humanity
apart from one another because "We are all caught in an inescapable
network of mutuality, tied into a single garment of destiny." (King,
1990, 254) Where conflict exists, non-violent means could be the
only means to resolution. Like Gandhi and Day previously, King
then acknowledged the interconnection between means and ends, as
he had done in his letter from Birmingham jail, that one cannot use
immoral means to achieve a moral end.[65] In concluding that sermon

63 *Ibid.*, p. 87. King corrected his critics that those who engage in non-
violent civil disobedience did not create the tension, that Gandhi also
indicated, but that they merely brought to the surface the hidden tension
that already existed, but was not acknowledged—the admission of the
truth and the contrast of non-practice of moral principles.

64 Martin Luther King, Jr., "A Christmas Sermon on Peace," (1967), *A
Testament of Hope*, p. 253.

65 *Ibid.*, p. 255. King points out the dilemma in using war as the means to
a moral end of peace. "Every time we drop our bombs in North Vietnam,

at Ebenezer Baptist Church, King returned to the essence of Jesus teaching that inspired him for so many years.

> ... (T)he ... thing we must be concerned about if we are to have peace on earth and good will toward men is the nonviolent affirmation of the sacredness of all human life. Every man is somebody because he is a child of God. And so when we say 'Thou shalt not kill,' we're really saying that human life is too sacred to be taken on the battlefields of the world. Man is more than a tiny vagary of whirling electrons or a wisp of smoke from a limitless smoldering. Man is a child of God, made in His image, and therefore must be respected as such. Until men see this everywhere, until nations see this everywhere, we will be fighting wars.[66]

One can only muse at what King would have preached in his powerful, Gospel-based and Gospel-laden, sermons of realization of Jesus' teaching of love had he lived longer.

These three models and practitioners of the Gospel virtue of love and the morality of war according to Christian teachings in the twentieth century offer to us a sense of hope, support, and guidance. These are not the only ones. Scores of other Christians also serve as models too. (See Appendix IV for a statement from prison of another unsung hero of the Christian practice of love and non-violence.) Perfection is difficult in the practice of non-violence. Some achieve it or attempt to achieve it differently under diverse and trying circumstances. One cannot overlook models such as Dietrich Bonhoeffer or Camillo Torres who, although siding with justice and the oppressed, they are purported to have condoned revolutionary violence or violence against systems and people that directed that violence. Others like Daniel and Philip

> President Johnson talks eloquently about peace. What is the problem? They are talking about peace as a distant goal, as an end we seek, but one day we must come to see that peace is not merely a distant goal we seek, but that it is a means by which we arrive at that goal. We must pursue peaceful ends through peaceful means. All of this is saying that, in the final analysis, means and ends must cohere because the end is preexistent in the means, and ultimately destructive means cannot bring about constructive ends."

66   King, "A Christmas Sermon on Peace," *A Testament of Hope*, p. 255.

Berrigan, Elizabeth MacAlister, John Dear, Thomas Gumbleton, etc. have stood non-violently against oppression and war machines and the people who run them only to be imprisoned for their civil disobedience. Nor can we overlook the importance that the Brethren, the Mennonites, the Quakers, and other religions that have been faithful to Jesus' teachings have provided in keeping alive those teachings of Jesus. Countless others like Frank Cordaro, Roy Bourgois, William Slattery, *et al.* have put their values into action to oppose foreign oppression abroad. Some like Thomas Merton have had the courage to speak out against war but have not necessarily suffered abusively for their views. The list is endless.[67]

What can we draw then from our review of these models? Tremendous courage is absolutely necessary to suffer for the sake of the gospel message of love and non-violence. All of the aforenoted persons spent some time in prison or were assassinated for their courageous stand against non-violence and the force of evil in their world. These persons had values that set them apart from their peers. Not one of these models shied from pursuing what they saw as the call to live with integrity and honesty with respect to themselves and their fellow humans. Gandhi provided an exemplary model for others in the twentieth century and thereafter to follow. Like Gandhi, all these models pursued an honest approach to truth and found it difficult to live with themselves if they did not live according to what they perceived as the truth. All of these models were heavily influenced by the teachings of Jesus and in fact

---

67 Henri J.M. Nouwen, *Encounters with Merton* (New York: Crossroad Publishing, 1981), p. 92, cites Merton's commitment to nonviolence and opposition to war in a letter that Merton wrote in the summer of 1968 when racial tension and violence was rampant in the streets of major US cities. "I am against war, against violence, against violent revolution, for peaceful settlement of differences, for nonviolent but nevertheless radical changes. Change is needed, and violence will not really change anything: at most it will only transfer power from one set of bull-headed authorities to another. If I say these things, it is not because I am more interested in politics than in the Gospel. I am not. But today more than ever the Gospel commitment has political implications, because you cannot claim to be 'for Christ' and espouse a political cause that implies callous indifference to the needs of millions of human beings and even cooperate in their destruction."

saw love as an essential basis in the righting of injustice. Based on love, all but conditional Christians, such as Niebuhr, Moltmann, Cardenas, Niemoller, Torres, and Bonhoeffer mentioned above, pursued correction of unjust laws through non-violent civil disobedience. These six unfortunately accept the use of violence only in cases that would either (a) be considered necessary under revolutionary overthrow of oppressive regimes that denied their liberty or (b) unavoidable in the case of tyrannical governance where they considered no other means is possible to right an evil. Except for these six individuals mentioned above, non-violence remains a critical component of the living out the love of one's fellow humans in addressing injustice. Non-violent practitioners consider the means as important as the end goals pursued and, thus, could not endorse immoral means to achieve moral and just ends. To conditionally apply the teachings of Jesus with regard to love was difficult for the aforenoted six individuals. All see action, not complicity with an unjust status quo, as imperative for their conscientious living. Finally, with the conditional exclusion of these six individuals, they all disapproved, if not initially, then over time, of lethal violence and deemed war in contemporary society as both immoral and interlinked with other injustices committed in exploitive societies. That all of them acted on their convictions against personal insult and suffering sets them apart from the rest of contemporary Christendom.

CHAPTER 8

HOW TO LIVE TODAY AS A CHRISTIAN WITH THE MORALITY OF WAR

O Lord, our God, help us to tear their soldiers to bloody shreds with our shells; help us to cover their smiling fields with the pale forms of their patriot dead; help us to drown the thunder of the guns with the shrieks of their wounded, writhing in pain; help us to lay waste their humble homes with a hurricane of fire; help us to wring the hearts of their unoffending widows with unavailing grief; help us to turn them out roofless with their little children to wander unfriended the wastes of their desolated land in rags and hunger and thirst, sport of the sun-flames of summer and the icy winds of winter, broken in spirit, worn with travail, imploring Thee for the refuge of the grave and denied it—-for our sakes who adore Thee, Lord, blast their hopes, blight their lives, protract their bitter pilgrimage, make heavy their steps, water their way with tears, stain the white snow with the blood of their wounded feet! We ask it, in the spirit of love, of Him Who is the Source of Love, and Who is the ever-faithful refuge and friend of all that are sore beset and seek His aid with humble and contrite hearts. Amen.[1]

Mark Twain, in his bitter and satirical criticism of the mis-construed valor of war-making in the aforenoted quote, previously had all too perceptively and accurately described the role of churches and religious authorities in the development and progress of war. Although churches and religious authorities gener-ally condemn war prior to the initiation of hostilities, as the war commences and the populace is drawn into the progression of the war, these same leaders become involved in blessing their citizens' endeavors in the war and on the battlefield and eventually provide the

---

1 Mark Twain, "The War-Prayer," 1916, published posthumously in *A Pen Warmed-up in Hell: Mark Twain in Protest*, ed. Frederick Anderson, publisher unknown, 1972 and cited in Leonard Roy Frank, ed., *Random House Webster's Quotationary* (New York: Random House, 1998), p. 915.

spiritual sustenance to perpetuate its rage in support of their nation. Such could not be truer when we observe the second US invasion of Iraq (in 2003). While the Vatican condemned the invasion as a "crime against peace," and leaders of all major denominations of mainstream Christianity (Catholic, Lutheran, Presbyterian, Methodist, Anglican, etc.) condemned any pre-emptive strike and ensuing hostility as having no moral justification prior to their commencement, once hostilities began and well into the ensuing year in which elections were held, little or nothing was said to condemn these same US hostilities.[2] What

---

2 Bishop Robert Banks, Roman Catholic bishop of Green Bay, when questioned by the local television media about the Church's stance to the pre-emptive US attack on Iraq in 2003, responded that now that war had commenced it was important for Americans to get behind their president. He also prayed for a quick and successful war, in his weekly column in the diocesan newspaper, *The Compass*, Mar. 28, 2003, p. 2. Banks stated in his weekly column, "My hope and my prayer is that, when you read this column next week, the war will be successfully ended with as few casualties as possible among all those involved, especially our own service men and women." He elaborated further with regard to statements regarding the US-pre-emptive planned attack and its pretenses, statements made by various Vatican officials, inclusive of Pope John Paul II, and the United States Conference of Catholic Bishops both groups of which resoundly condemned the war morally and in terms of general humanity, " ... I did not nor do I see a serious problem for the individual Catholic, (a problem that) Catholics might have in choosing between the Pope and the President ... ." One can only wonder where clerical leaders such as these studied Church morality, whether they have the capacity to understand moral guidance by superior ecclesial authorities, or where their allegiance is with respect to the moral teachings of Jesus and the rationale exercised by the state.

Another bishop, when approached and interviewed by this author, stated that "(demonstration against war and working for peace) was not his bag" and that the US "preemptive" invasion was justified "because Saddam Hussein was an evil person." While not totally indicative of ecclesial leadership, these examples demonstrate the shallowness of much of the nationally inspired church hierarchy with regard to their understanding of Church teaching, based on Jesus' teachings, with regard to war, self-determination, inter-state intervention, and the horror or lack thereof of violence and lethal force.

we see is simply the perversion of religious fundamentals and, in the case of Christianity, the undermining of the teachings of Jesus and the practice of religious life as seen in the early Church, those closest to the mentality of and living with Jesus.

Truth is always the first casualty of war just as force and fraud are war's two cardinal virtues.[3] Given the purported lies presented by the US' leadership to justify the engagement of war and given the silence and effective complicity of Church leadership with regard to the morality and justice of this war in the US presidential elections after war ensued, truth (*Satya*) certainly became the major casualty which induced suffering and evil on parties fighting in this war.

The morality of war cannot be divorced from the decisions related to the allocation of scarce resources. The morality of war and lethal inter-group violence is more than the exercise of war itself; it is intimately interconnected with the whole war-making machine. In 1961, Dwight D. Eisenhower as president of the US in his farewell address to that nation singled out the evils and perils of the military industrial complex.[4] The caution is more amazing given his background as a career military officer, but the caution has regrettably proved true. Today, the US military expenditure, for example, exceeds at least more than the next 20 largest national military budgets combined worldwide; by our own calculations, based on the 2004 US Congressional budget,

---

There was supposedly only one report of a US pastor refusing or advising against communion to US military personnel because they were supporting activities defined as mortal sin, but the mainstream press did not report such, although it did not fail to report on many cases, and they were not lacking, of priests and bishops advising and directing excommunication of politicians or their supporters adopting pro-choice positions on the issue of abortion.

3 Quotes taken from Hiram Johnson, California governor and US senator and delivered in a US Senate speech, and from Thomas Hobbes, "Leviathan," 13, as cited in *Random House Webster's Quotationary*, p. 914.

4 Eisenhower stated, "In the councils of government, we must guard against the acquisition of unwarranted influence, whether sought or unsought, by the military-industrial complex. The potential for the disastrous rise of misplaced power exists and will persist. We must never let the weight of this combination endanger our liberties or democratic processes." See *Random House Webster's Quotationary*, p. 916.

annual outlay (on an appropriation basis) for military-related expenditure exceeds US$ 570 billion.[5] The immorality of expenditure dedicated to war-making cannot be overlooked when one considers what the US government spends on social welfare. "A nation that continues year after year to spend more money on military defense than on programs of social uplift is approaching spiritual death," stated Martin Luther King, Jr. in his sermon at Riverside Church in New York on April 4, 1967 and noted in the previous chapter. (See Appendices I through III.)

When one compares, analyzes, and evaluates the US expenditure on armaments and personnel costs, one cannot be anything but appalled, horrified, and morally condemning. It is difficult to understand and appreciate the value of morality with respect to war in the twenty-first century without analyzing the largest contributor and participant in warfare now. The attached Appendices demonstrate that, if we take only the line item for defense in the 2000 budget of US$417.4 billion (Appendix II), this is roughly 90 percent of what the rest of the world spends on their aggregate military expenditure of US$461.6 billion. However, if we include items not incorporated in this number of US$417.4 billion, such as expenses for veterans' administration, military pensions, nuclear-powered submarines and aircraft carriers, foreign aid related to grants for military goods and military training, Homeland Security activities, military-related space operations, etc., or well in excess of that $417.4 billion, real US military expenditure is far more than double the total aggregate military expenditure of the rest of world, according to data maintained by the Stockholm International Peace Research Institute. Again, this number also does not account for the annual outlay for the US' ongoing wars in Iraq and Afghanistan. Even ignoring the real US defense expenditure and using the misreported defense expenditure of US$417 billion, one

5 2004 Congressional Budget. This number accounts for funds allocated for the Department of Defense, Veteran Administration, Military Pensions, nuclear-powered submarines and aircraft carriers, foreign aid related to grants for military goods and military training, Homeland Security activities, military-related space operations, etc. No firm numbers, however, could be garnered for intelligence activities nor does this amount include special allocation for the US war in Iraq whose costs seem to approximate US$ 160 billion in 2004.

can deduce that on a nominal basis only the US and Israel exceed the per capita weighted average defense expenditure of $986 amongst the top 15 defense spending countries.

Moreover, amongst the largest 15 defense-spending countries, the US constitutes more than 40 percent of the total expenditure even on a purchasing-power-parity basis. Compared to expenditure on health and education, based on SIPRI data in Appendix I, amongst countries with the highest military expenditure burden vis-à-vis Gross Domestic Product ("GDP"), the US is proportionately spending about average for education and slightly above average for health care, but the US differs little with proportionate expenditures for education and healthcare compared to countries with lowest defense expenditure burdens. (The reader should not overlook the fact that the basis of these numbers is skewed as per the comments below because all real military and defense expenditures are not included in the numbers that SIPRI uses. If, as per our comments below on real military expenditure of US$840 billion in 2004, actual US defense expenditure to Gross Domestic Product would be about 7.6 percent, more than twice what can be seen in the table of Appendix I.)[6] One cannot forget, however, that, roughly, at least 43 million US residents in 2004 lack health insurance and, thus, either have no healthcare or can scarcely afford such, while virtually all other industrialized countries have universal health care. One should also be conscious that the data in Appendix I compare respective expenditures to GDP. If one analyzes the expenditure of public funds for the public good, namely for goods and services that the private sector either is incapable of or does not undertake for the general good of the population who may not benefit from private goods and services, one sees that US government outlays for military expenditure far exceed government outlays for either or both education and health care for those unable to supply their own benefit. Thus, US health care is concentrated most probably for the benefit of wealthier segments of US society. King's moral criticism of US expenditure for military and war objectives to the detriment of necessary social services is valid and all the more telling then.

---

6 Central Intelligence Agency, *The World Fact Book*, 2004, reports for 2003 Gross Domestic Product of US$10.99 billion.

What makes the aforenoted data more appalling is the mistruth, misperception, and deceit in the reported defense expenditure, the failure to ascertain and seize *Satya*, the real truth. If one observes, for example, Appendix III, one can quickly realize that military expenditure probably is nearly double that reported, as noted above. Analyzing actual funds fiscally allocated and available for use and obligation on defense and military expenditure during 2004, *i.e.*, US$841 billion, they constituted roughly 35 percent of the federal budget.[7] This number does not include more than US$100 billion of funds allocated for the US-instigated war in Iraq or the hidden funds allocated for intelligence gathering (e.g., Central Intelligence Agency, etc.) which are estimated to approximate between US$30 billion and 50 billion. Given the level of unemployment, the number of persons lacking health insurance, the reductions in educational expenses, the increasing disparity in income gaps, the shifting tax burden to less wealthier classes, etc., the context of military expenditure even domestically constitutes an immoral, structural burden inflicted on US society. The use of scarce resources on so large a scale from an economic standpoint clearly deprives (or robs, to use a morally pregnant term) society of greater social benefit, not only domestically but internationally. The greater one country invests in military capability, the more it induces other countries to raise their barriers and expend their scarce resources on instruments whose sole purpose is destruction.

What can we deduce from this morally? Given that all countries' defense would be no more important than that of any other country, (because the security of their human population and livelihoods would be no greater and no worse than those of anyone else), we can surmise that the US considers the defense of its interests to be more valuable and of greater importance than that of the rest of the world. It also becomes more threatening to the good of the rest of the world. One would also find it increasingly difficult to deduce anything other than that the US is undeniably a militarist country. Further, given that

---

7 If fiscally appropriated funds were used as the basis for calculating the actual US military and defense expenditure, not just funds available, the actual expenditure far exceeds the number usually reported by the government and used by analysts who fail to analyze and get the numbers used to support this military-industrial complex.

military expenditure is for the purpose of purchasing weapons and tools to kill, maim, and destroy or to threaten such, and to provide the necessary training for effecting such, the greater the expenditure vis-à-vis the rest of the world, the more immoral the undertaking, particularly in light of the ability to inflict greater damage than comparative adversaries can inflict.

What is the connection between the discussion of the causes of war reviewed in the first chapter with the theoretical, religious, and historical discussion of the morality of war itself considered in the balance of the above material? Certainly, the immediately identified problem of US military expenditure cannot be considered anything other than an important factor related to US bellicosity and its frequent engagement in or threat of war itself. But, are there also deeper problems and other imposing factors outlined in the first chapter that induce war, even war for the US? The answer can only be in the affirmative. The unchecked need and demand for natural resources by processing industries and the companies that own them in industrialized countries cannot be denied as one cause for instigating war. The remnants of classical colonialism and its newer forms of neo-imperialism and neo-colonialism (as per political, economic, and military hegemony) also serve as one of the direct and indirect causes of war. The denial of freedom for not only basic human rights but for competing in the market place has also contributed. Inequitable distribution of income and scarce resources, but not necessarily poverty, drives war too. Unfair and inequitable treaties that one-sidedly benefit those with greater wealth, deeper pockets, more military power, cleverer manipulation of political and business structures, etc. incite feelings of injustice that demand correction; those individuals and states that demand their greater or equitable share of the pie, often also want their pound of flesh and not just pecuniary remunerative retribution. Internal and psychological pressure from changing social mores, structural and class-based changes, population and resource scarcity also drive states to war. Manipulation of the media, *i.e.*, messaging the message or "spin," is a tool increasingly used by both industrialized states and developing countries and is driven by a more interconnected world who can get their news and analyses elsewhere. The failure to legitimize supra-national authority and to provide the means for its effectiveness has contributed to the use of war as a means to conflict resolution just as much as the lack of effective international law itself. But, to what do all of these relate? Are they not connected with the perception of justice, fairness, and liberty and the inter-human practice of justice itself? When injustice is perceived, whether rightly or wrongly makes no difference because justice holds a high degree of subjectivity as well as objective criteria, and the will to right the injustice exists, war and violence unfortunately may be one option.

Morality is born out of context and situation. It is not a theoretical or esoteric subject that is the amusement of academics and ecclesial theoreticians. The morality of war is preceded by moral dilemmas, inclusive primarily of injustice, that are not satisfactorily addressed. [It may also be attributed to hegemonist exploitation, but the injustice is the greed of the (neo-)imperialist exploiter.] Using violence to amend these injustices, whether in desperation or out of perceived self-righteous, might ensue and has been an age-old method of addressing social wrongs. Social injustice and oppression in various forms provide ample cause, though not morally justifiable according to the teachings of Jesus, for stimulating war.

Despite the contemporaneous practice of Israel's neighbors to engage in war and lethal inter-group violence, the Hebrews' acquirement and expansion of a "Promised Land" is recorded in much of the Hebrew scriptures to have been achieved no differently than through lethally violent conquest. The ban and the theological ideology, that the God of the Hebrews was stronger, that the sacrificial annihilation of their enemies was the calling of YHWH, that their federation of tribes was making them into God's chosen people, and that God sanctioned their enslavement of their captives in spite of their own history of enslavement as a minority people, were clearly portrayed in the Hebrew scriptures, but with the intent that it was YHWH who was leading them and protecting them, the oppressed and outsider of the Middle East. Nevertheless, retrospectively, some of the prophets, in interpreting the past while seeking the meaning of their relationship with their God in the present and projecting into their future, remained critical of Israel's pugnacity and theologically sought to attribute their fortuity to the power of YHWH, but did not shy from pricking the Hebrews' conscience on their injustices committed not only against their own people but against foreigners too. Contrary to the belligerence of Israel and their perception of their God as told theologically in Joshua, Judges, Samuel, etc, the prophets Isaiah, Jeremiah, Micah (Micah 4:3; 6:8 and Micah 2 and 3), and Amos singled out Israel's injustices, not just their infidelity, as part of the cause of their unfortunate circumstances leading to their military defeats. The prophets understood the importance of justice towards all. They seemed to have understood the connection between injustice and the use of violence, inclusive of the lethality of war.

The Christian scriptures, however, present a stark, new approach to human interaction which eschews violence and, thereby, war. Not only the Gospels, but the letters of Paul and John clearly portray a God of compassion and love, not one engaged in annihilation. Jesus unquestionably shows a searing keenness for justice toward his fellow humans. He, like the YHWH of the Hebrew scriptures portrayed by the prophets, aligns his interest and concern with the marginalized, the oppressed, the impoverished, the despised, and the weak. He seeks not merely to relieve their suffering but to bring attention to righting the wrong against them and calls his followers to a new consciousness of love and reconciliation in their interactions. The Sermon on the Mount remains with the terribleness of the cross as the core of Jesus life and the call that all of Jesus' followers are expected to live. Suffering for the sake of true love, enemy-love, is an incontrovertible and unconditional element of Jesus' teachings that his followers must implement in doing justice.

Has contemporary society, then, transcended the limitations, application and understanding of morality on peace and physical violence proclaimed in the Christian scriptures? With the vast amount of military expenditure consumed in mostly Western and so-called Christian states and the history of the previous four centuries of Western and Christian colonial, imperialist rule, it is difficult to deny that the Christian morality of peace seems either to have been made irrelevant by a secularized and politicized understanding of just war rationale or to have been perverted in its fundamental essence.[8] Based

---

8 One should ask why Western, and so-called Christian, societies are symbiotic with colonialism and militarist power. Does their superior wealth drive them structurally to protect and defend that wealth against those

on the above historical review, we concluded that, not only secular governments, but Christians themselves have distorted the essential teachings of Jesus on peace, love, violence, justice, and reconciliation in both their domestic policies and in their international relations. The institutional Church, particularly that in various sects within the US, has been an accomplice in the accommodation of violence. Many, if not most, Christians seem to be baptized, non-Christian practitioners. They have readily and sacrilegiously draped the flag around the cross, which is the incontrovertible symbol of Jesus' willingness to endure suffering, even to death, in the living out of his love for humanity and his righting of injustice. Many have made the ideology of the state the disguised practice of their religion. As noted above in Mark Twain's cynical and satirical prayer, US ecclesial leadership, particularly with regard to just war theory and its application, must often be judged for its moral bankruptcy in its leadership, despite its well founded criticism of war and weapons of mass destruction. Although Church statements like *Pacem in Terris, Populorum Progressio, Gaudium et Spes*, "The Challenge of Peace," etc. have deplored the immorality of nuclear and other weapons of mass destruction and their use in war, their proliferation continues unabated because the states possessing them refuse to eradicate their own completely. Ecclesial leaders have not followed through on their own morally laudable directives and, because of such, their followers have dismissed their leadership therein. Moreover, given that the vast majority of persons killed and maimed in wars of the twentieth century are increasingly non-combatants, ecclesial leaders still fail to show leadership, not just in condemning any and all war itself, but in providing the moral guidance to induce their followers to realize the teachings of Jesus and eschew violent conflict-resolution. A few insightful and courageous individuals, though, both Christian and non-Christian, have dared to live with moral integrity, to suffer for their convictions, to call for rectifying injustice and place their lives with those who are unjustly exploited. They continue to act for justice, love, truth and work non-violently as per Jesus' teachings to realize the way of saving humanity from itself.

---

societies and peoples who have been deprived or exploited of such? The Christian should also retrospectively and presently reflect on what in Christianity has induced this behavior amongst Christians.

Christians for millennia have had the millstone of just-war rationale hung from their necks. The reliance on the Greek Stoics' early
development of natural law and its further elaboration by Ulpian
influenced Augustine to the extent that he distorted the essential
teaching of Jesus in the Gospels and set the Church in a dilemma
from which it has never successfully emerged. Augustine clearly went
against the teaching and practice of the fathers of the Church and
the apostolic community. The just-war thinking and the implicit or
direct interconnectedness between the religion of Christianity and
the state have been one of the worst perversions of the teachings of
Jesus that have perplexed and harmed the practice of Jesus' essential
teaching. If, hypothetically, just war teaching ever could have been
deemed moral, in contemporary society it is difficult to imagine that
it retains its legitimacy because wars and violent conflict-resolution
conducted by both entrenched states and revolutionary or insurgent
forces are killing and maiming more civilians and non-combatants
than the lethal casualties of the actual forces engaged in the conflict
at an increasing and alarming rate. Further, the cost to international
and national societies cannot be deemed moral. International society
has become so interdependent that war is no longer even a rational
and moral, if it ever was, means of conflict-resolution.

If Christians are to act truly as Christians, they have a monumental task before them. Militarization and arming, of not just the old
colonizing and imperial powers of the world, but of the developing
world itself, is robbing humanity of the resources and means to bring
domestic and international justice to those crying out for fairness. The
tax burden for financing this development of militarization deprives
all peoples of the social services that are foregone and retains the
incentive to use these funds for their destructive purposes. Increasingly, too, surrogate armies are employed to engage in conflict whose
resolution can doubtfully bring true peace. Structural and systemic
causes of conflict that result in war and physical violence require new
approaches of conflict-resolution, but non-violent resolution is difficult
to implement. States too often respond with violent military strikes
to eradicate the culprits of violence, but, because they fail to address
and correct the actual causes, namely various social injustices, they
thereby perpetuate a cycle of conflict and violence. We fail to realize

234 JESUS THE WARRIOR?

that a moral wrong, *i.e.*, war and lethal violence, cannot make a moral right, the culmination of temporary peace.

Where then is our hope as believers in the teachings of Jesus? It definitely is not the just war theory that has perpetuated and worsened violence, war, and human suffering for the Christian world and its victims since the fifth century. We need the courage to try something different, maybe the practice of Jesus' teachings themselves. Just as Dorothy Day was surprised after fifteen years of publishing *The Catholic Worker* that some members of the Catholic Worker only became aware that Day and the paper were pacifist and opposed to US involvement in World War II, so too it should not amaze us today that, despite over 2000 years of Christianity, Christians still have failed for more than a millennium to realize that Jesus was non-violent and a pacifist.[1] We are no more wiser nor less blind than our ancestors in our faith. What we need is the courage to act upon our convictions as practitioners of Jesus' essential message of love. Non-violence is the only way that we humans can save us from ourselves, particularly if we profess to live according to Jesus' teachings.

---

1 Day, *The Long Loneliness*, p. 264.

APPENDIX I

begins on page 235 and continues on page 236-237 (2 tables).

Burden comparison
Countries with the highest and lowest military burden in
2002; social and military expenditure as a share of gross
domestic product, 2000–2002. Figures are percentages.

Sources for table on page 236: Education expenditure as a share of GDP for 2000/2001: UN Educational, Scientific and Cultural Organization (UNESCO), Institute for Statistics Database Access Statistics, table on Public expenditure on education as percentage of GDP URL <http://stats.uis.unesco.org/eng/TableViewer/wdsview/dispviewp. asp>; education shares for 1998-2000 and health shares: UN Development Programme (UNDP), Human Development Report 2003 (Oxford University Press: New York, 2003), annex table 17, Priorities in public spending and military expenditure shares: SIPRI Yearbook 2004 Armaments, Disarmament and International Security (Oxford University Press, Oxford 2004) appendix 10A, table 10A.4

[ ]=SIPRI estimates.

Burden comparison
Countries with the highest and lowest military burden in 2002; a social and military
expenditure as a share of gross domestic product, 2000-2002. Figures are percentages

High-income countries				Low- and middle-income countries			
Country	Education	Health	Military	Country	Education	Health	Military
Countries with the highest military burden in 2002							
Kuwait	..	2.6	10.4	Eritrea	4.8	2.8	23.5
Israel	7.3	8.3	9.2	Oman	3.9	2.3	[12.3]
Brunei	4.8	2.5	7.0	Saudi Arabia	9.5	4.2	9.8
Singapore	3.7	1.2	5.2	Jordan	5.0	4.2	8.4
Greece	3.8	4.6	4.3	Burundi	3.4	1.6	7.6
UAE	1.9	2.5	3.7	Liberia	..	..	(7.5)
USA	4.8	5.8	3.4	Yemen	10.0	..	7.1
France	5.8	7.2	2.5	Syria	4.1	1.6	[6.1]
UK	4.5	5.9	2.4	Ethiopia	4.8	1.8	5.2
Taiwan	..	..	2.3	Turkey	3.5	3.6	4.9
Average	**4.6**	**4.8**	**4.7**		**4.9**	**2.8**	**9.7**
Countries with the lowest military burden in 2002							
Iceland	5.9	7.5	0.0	Costa Rica	4.4	4.4	0.0
Ireland	4.4	5.1	0.7	Mauritius	3.7	1.9	0.2
Austria	5.8	5.6	0.8	Moldova	4.0	2.9	0.4
Luxembourg	3.7	5.3	0.9	Mexico	4.4	2.5	0.5
Japan	3.5	6.0	1.0	Ghana	4.1	2.2	0.6
New Zealand	6.1	6.2	1.1	Guatemala	1.7	2.3	0.6
Switzerland	5.5	5.9	1.1	Cape Verde	4.4	1.8	0.7
Finland	6.1	5.0	1.2	Honduras	4.0	4.3	0.8
Spain	4.5	5.4	1.2	El Salvador	2.3	3.8	0.8
Slovenia	..	6.8	1.5	Georgia	..	0.7	0.9
Average	**5.1**	**5.8**	**0.9**		**3.7**	**2.9**	**0.5**

Table on world and regional military expenditure, 1994-2003

World and regional military expenditure estimates
1994 - 2003

Figures are in US $b., at constant 2000 prices and exchange rates. Figures in italics are percentages.
Figures do not always add up to totals because of the conventions of rounding.

Region	1994	1995	1996	1997	1998	1999	2000	2001	2002	2003	% change 1994-2003
Africa	(9.2)	(8.7)	(8.4)	8.6	9.2	9.9	10.3	10.5	11.3	11.4	(+24)
North	(4.1)	(3.9)	(4.0)	4.2	4.4	4.3	4.7	4.8	5.4	5.5	(+35)
Sub-Saharan	5.1	4.8	4.4	4.4	4.8	5.6	5.7	(5.8)	5.9	(5.9)	(+15)
Americas	365	347	328	329	321	323	334	339	376	451	+24
North	344	324	306	304	298	299	310	313	350	426	+24
Central	3.5	3.1	3.2	3.3	3.2	3.4	3.5	3.6	3.4	3.3	-5
South	17.6	20.2	18.4	21.2	20.2	20.1	20.7	22.6	22.9	21.8	+24
Asia & Oceania	120	123	127	127	126	128	133	140	146	151	+25
Central Asia	0.4	0.4	0.4	0.5	(0.4)	0.5	..	(0.5)	..	..	..
East Asia	101	103	107	107	105	105	110	115	121	125	+24
South Asia	12.0	12.6	12.8	13.4	13.5	14.6	15.2	15.8	15.9	16.9	+41
Oceania	7.3	7.0	7.0	7.1	7.4	7.7	7.7	8.0	8.3	8.5	+17
Europe	200	187	186	186	184	188	191	191	194	195	-2
CEE	26.4	20.6	19.3	20.1	17.5	18.3	20.0	21.5	22.2	24.5	-8
Western	174	166	166	166	167	170	171	170	172	171	-2
Middle East	47.1	43.8	43.8	48.1	51.9	50.3	58.0	63.1	63.8	70.0	+48
World	742	709	693	699	693	699	727	743	792	879	+18
Change (%)	..	-4.4	-2.2	0.9	-0.8	0.8	4.0	2.3	6.5	11.0	

Source: SIPRI Yearbook 2004, appendix 10A, table 10A.1 and table 10A.3.
Note: Sub-regional totals are presented within brackets when based on country data accounting for less than
90% of the regional total. No data are presented when the estimate would be based on data accounting for less
than 60% of the sub-regional total.
(a) For the country coverage of the regions, see Regional coverage. CEE= Central and Eastern Europe. Due to
lack of consistent time series data, Africa excludes Angola, Benin, Congo (Republic of), Congo (Democratic
Republic of), Liberia and Somalia; Asia excludes Afghanistan and the Middle East excludes Iraq. World totals
exclude all these countries.

APPENDIX II

World's Top 15 Countries with Highest Military Expenditure, 2000

		Nominal Expense					Purchasing Power Parity Rank	
Rank	Country	US$1 BB Level	Per Capita	World Share (%)		Rank	Country	US$ 1 BF
1	USA	417.4	1,419	47		1	USA	417.4
2	Japan	46.9	367	5		2	China (PRC)	(151.0)
3	UK	37.1	627	4		3	India	64.0
4	France	35.0	583	4		4	Russia	(63.2)
5	China (PRC)	(32.8)	25	4		5	France	38.4
Subtotal Top 5		569.1		64		Subtotal Top 5		734.0
6	Germany	27.2	329	3		6	UK	35.0
7	Italy	20.8	362	2		7	Japan	32.8
8	Iran	(19.2)	279	2		8	Germany	30.4
9	Saudia Arabia	19.1	789	2		9	Italy	26.4
10	South Korea	13.9	292	2		10	Saudia Arabia	25.6
Subtotal Top 10		669.3		76		Subtotal Top 10		884.2
11	Russia	(13.0)	91	1		11	South Korea	25.0
12	India	12.4	12	1		12	Iran	(23.7)
13	Israel	10.0	1,551	1		13	Turkey	22.5
14	Turkey	9.9	139	1		14	Brazil	21.0
15	Brazil	9.2	51	1		15	Pakistan	15.0
Subtotal Top 15		723.8		82		Subtotal Top 15		991.4
World		879.00		100				

Source: Stockholm International Peace Research Institute, 2005, web page. Notes: (a) The USA contains only what the federal budget terms as defense expenditure under the Defense Department. (b) Numbers in parentheses are estimates. (c) Purchasing Power Parity is an economic comparison of purchasing power in local currency compared to the purchasing power of US dollars in the USA in 2000.

Appendix III

2004 Actual Defense Expenditures

	(US$1 MM)
Dept. of Energy	19,895
Dept. of Defense	689,624
Veterans Affairs	84,116
Defense Nuclear Facilities Safety Board	23
US Court of Appeals for Veterans' Claims	16
Other Defense-Civil Programs	40,194
State Department	17,316
Homeland Security—Coast Guard et al.	9,048
Total defense budgetary resources available for obligation	840,337

Source: Executive Office of the President of the United States, Office of Management and Budget, *Budget of the United States Government, Fiscal Year 2006*, (Appendix).

Notes:

(a) The above data have been gathered from the 2006 fiscal budget proposal submitted by the US president's Office of Management and Budget and are listed as actual expenditures in 2004. The aforenoted data have been identified from line items for "appropriated budgetary resources available for obligation" therein of the respective listed departments and agencies. Despite the fact that some line items may not use all the appropriated funds, they retain the aforenoted amount of fiscal allocation available for respective obligations. For breakdown by actual appropriation, kindly see the respective appendices.

(b) Data for above line items include, but are not exclusive of:
- Dept. of Energy: nuclear reactors, weapons activities, defense nuclear non-proliferation, defense site acceleration completion, defense environmental services, defense nuclear waste disposal, other.

- Dept. of Defense: military personnel costs for regular forces, National Guard, and reserves; Medicare and health costs; operation and maintenance; defense health program; Iraqi military support; USSR threat reduction; weapons, equipment, and delivery systems procurement; research and development; construction; family housing; working capital fund allocation; other.

- Veterans Affairs: medical services, administration and facilities funds, disability benefits, education benefits, pension benefits, housing programs, allocation for various trust funds, other.

- Other Defense—Civil Programs: military retirement, retiree health care, Medicare eligible retiree health care, other.

- State Department: foreign military financing, non-proliferation, anti-terrorism, foreign military financing direct loan allocation, foreign military sales trust fund allocation, other.

- Homeland Security—Coast Guard: air and marine interdiction, Coast Guard, acquisition, construction, and improvements, retirement pay, bio-defense countermeasure, other.

Although the 2004 budget allocated slightly more than US$400 billion for the Department of Defense, real US defense expenditure far exceeded that amount as seen above. Data associated with the military-related defense of the US for the above can be obtained by reviewing each department's or agency's allocation on an item-by-item basis for each subsection therein.

Appendix IV

In prison for peace:
Consequences, opportunities and blessings
By Frank Cordaro

Some have claimed that I get arrested so I can go to jail. I don't. Jail is hard, and it is intended to be. My jail time is a consequence of being a peacemaker. It is a by-product of speaking my truth about war. Going to jail is no more a goal for me than getting crucified was a goal of Jesus It is a consequence that I accept and embrace. It is also a blessing and an opportunity. I am writing not to complain about the consequence of my actions, but to describe my opportunities and share my blessings.

As a result of a court sentence handed down on Dec. 16 2004, I celebrated Christmas and New Years in jail. Seven of us appeared in Polk County District Court to answer charges of misdemeanor trespass, which occurred on Election Day, Nov. 2, 2004 at the STARC Armory in Johnston, Iowa. Six of us pleaded guilty and took our chances with Judge Brandt. For me, it was the fourth arrest at the Armory since the beginning of the war in March 2003.

The Court sentenced the first-time offenders to their time served. Then, one by one, I listened as the others were sentenced to the maximum 30 days in jail and offered a suspended sentence along with 12 months informal probation and 25 hours of community service. I heard them each, begrudgingly, accept the terms in lieu of jail. I was the last to be sentenced.

A sentence, generally, reflects the nature of the crime committed. In this case, the crime was a simple misdemeanor trespass. We were peaceful and non-violent. We were civil and respectful. We harmed no person and no property. In my three prior trespass cases, we offenders had received sentences of time served, a small fine and/or community service. Clearly, those were sentences that reflected the true nature of our crimes committed.

In my mind, this time was different. Judge Brandt's sentence did not reflect the nature of our crime. Instead, he had transformed the sentence into a political statement on the wars in Iraq and Afghanistan; he supports them, we resist them.

In the 25 years that I have been protesting wars, I have watched our legal system side repeatedly with the war-makers. A decision is made, sometime after each trespass, as to what, if any, charges will be brought. If charges are brought, and they always have been, then each of us must individually decide how to plead. I had already pleaded guilty to the charge and I had heard the sentencing of my friends. Before my sentencing, I was given an opportunity to speak to the Court.

I told Judge Brandt that I believed he was putting the legal system on the wrong side of human history. I said that I agreed with him on one thing crimes had been committed. I just didn't believe that we were the criminals. I suggested that our peace-making heroes of the past have paved a traveled road to peace Gandhi, Martin Luther King, Oscar Romero, Cesar Chavez, Dorothy Day and Phil Berrigan have lit that path. I said that 90 percent of the world's people, and authorities including Pope John Paul II, believe that the U.S. war and occupation in Iraq are unjust, immoral and illegal.

To date, more than 6,000 Iowans have left their communities, their jobs and their families, federalized by the U.S. government, to fight, to risk their lives and to suffer the burden of killing other human beings. Many have returned wounded; 20 have been killed. Their collective personal sacrifices serve as the base for Iowa's support of George Bush's wars.

Our local collective protests constitute a small portion of a much larger national and worldwide campaign to eliminate the scourge of wars in our human family. If we are to achieve peace, I believe the peacemakers must also be willing to make personal sacrifices to serve that peace.

So I told Judge Brandt that I would refuse any community service because I believed what we did at STARC Armory constituted a community service; that I could not pay any fine because I lived as a Des Moines Catholic Worker and received no income; and finally, that I could not in good conscience accept any form of probation, as I could not keep a promise to avoid arrest.

When I finished, the Judge gave me the maximum sentence. I will be here until January 13th. It is no fun to be in jail. I take no delight in the hardship I bring to my family and friends by being here, especially during Christmas and New Years. Ironically, though, I am grateful to Judge Brandt for giving me this opportunity to pay a small price for my efforts at peace. In this season, when we celebrate the birth of Jesus, the Prince of Peace, I count myself blessed to be locked up on his birthday for those efforts.

In jail there are no soft places, only concrete and iron. One sheet, one blanket, no pillow, no privacy. People here are separated from family, friends and familiar settings. Everyone looks the same stripped of their individuality. All movement, and I do mean all, is monitored. All aspects of jail are designed as social punishment and ostracism.

The air in the Jail is recycled. Each cell has a stainless steel toilet/sink, which backs up into the adjoining cell's fixture when the inmate next door flushes. Jail is the only place in the world I have ever heard of a courtesy flush. Use your imagination.

I miss apples the most. There are no fresh foods, just canned items consisting mainly of carbohydrates rice, beans, pasta, cookies and pastries. But there is plenty to eat, and my own weight reflects that. If you have any money, and hardly anyone does, you can get extra stuff at the commissary one day a week coffee (a highly desired commodity), cookies, crackers, and candy. No apples.

And speaking of money, the county jail is a pay-as-you-go operation now. Inmates are charged for their stay. I incur a $48.00 charge per day. If I need a nurse, a doctor or a prescription, I pay extra for it. A call costs $3. If you can't call collect to someone, you can't call. If you can't pay your bill at the time of your release, they garnish your wages. If you have no wages, they take away your driver's license until the debt is paid. It's hard to get work without a car, so this is like a sinkhole for the poor.

One measure of a society is how it deals with its prison populations. We have more than two million Americans behind bars for the purpose of punishment, not rehabilitation. Ninety percent of the inmates in our county jails come from the bottom 10 percent of society's economic class. Poverty is the single greatest factor in recidivism. Adding additional indebtedness to the mix helps to ensure that the cycle of poverty will bring people back to jail.

I am a Catholic Worker. We Catholic Workers built our communities on doing the works of mercy feeding the hungry, sheltering the homeless and clothing the naked. We take to heart the directives Jesus gave in the parable of the Sheep and Goats in Matthew 25: Whatever you do to the least, you do to me. Visiting the imprisoned is also a work of mercy. I am not just visiting.

Whether out of concern for my well being, or to make my stay more difficult, my first assigned cell was the medical unit two weeks on 5 North. There were 16 of us in 12 single cells, four of us doubled up in cells meant for one. Most of the men suffered from some form of mental illness or incapacity. They were there for arson, robbery, burglary, domestic abuse and intoxication. I was there for peace and a whole lot more as it turned out.

The first day, I recognized Larry and he recognized me. Larry is a regular at the Catholic Worker House. He is 67 years old and has lived on the streets for years. Apparently he set fire to the garage he was living in and is doing a year's time for it. A pleasant man with a ready smile, his incapacity is particularly challenging in jail; he frequently soils himself. I mention this only to punctuate the fact that each and every man in the ward went to great lengths to support Larry. They were the first to alert the guards to the problem each day, and the ones who cleaned out Larry's cell while he was being cleaned up. Never did I see them ridicule or take advantage of him. I was impressed.

George was the loudest and most disruptive, but he could not help it. When he spoke, he shook and dominated all conversations, even the ones he was not a part of. While he was on crack he had robbed two guys at knifepoint for $20. His mother kept him in commissary money and he kept the entire unit in coffee in exchange for a cinnamon roll. On Christmas day he gifted the entire unit with a cupcake.

Marty was in for burglary. Because he had begun hearing voices in his head, he was now doing the "Chorazine shuffle," medicated into a stupor. A lot of the guys envied him, saying it is a great way to do time.

Ralph was locked up for domestics. He remembered nothing of the incident; he was drunk. Larry must have told him I was a former priest, because early on he nearly took up residence in my cell to tell me his stories and conspiracies about all the reasons he'd been locked up before. He loved his woman and wanted to talk about it. Each night before lights out, he would appear at my cell to ask me to pray for him and his lady friend, often with tears in his eyes. On Christmas day he proposed and she accepted. The next thing I knew he was hugging me, kissing me and thanking me for my prayers. I was embarrassed but thrilled for Ralph. I hope it lasts.

My cellmate, Tom, is a 28-year-old kid, back in jail for a probation violation. They nabbed him at the courthouse while he was paying fines. His eyes are blue and sit close together, which gives him an angelic younger look. He has a child-like spirit, a heart of gold and talks incessantly. An accident when he was nine years old left him mentally challenged. The very first day I agreed to one game of Sorry each day, no more. In case you don't know, Sorry is not an easy game.

A number of Tom's family members have preceded him in prison. Many are involved in drugs. He says some members of his family framed him. Though never married, he has two children, one with the woman he lives with. He loves her and both children very much and wants to be married.

One night, early in my stay, I retreated into our cell trying to find some alone time, relief from the needs and concerns of the others. Tom was there, and when I told him what I was trying to do, he looked at me very intently and said, "They come to you because you are a pastor, a man of God. They come to you so you can pray to God for them because we really need God's help here. And I really feel lucky to have you as my cellmate. I feel closer to God, and the other guys think so, too.

Tom's comments struck me to the heart and humbled me in spirit. That night, after lock-up, Tom and I prayed together for each inmate on 5 North, one inmate at a time. Tom especially prayed for his children and girlfriend he was missing so terribly. I silently thanked God for allowing me to be where I was, doing what I was doing.

While I would have been content to finish my sentence in this unit, the jail had different plans for me. On Dec. 29, I was moved to the Interim Jail, 2 East Unit. I am in an open bay area with 18 bunks, a dining area with stainless steel tables and stools, a television mounted on the wall, six phones, six showers, sinks and toilets, and 36 men.

246 : "246 Jesus the warrior "

The second night on 2 East I was invited to the nightly prayer circle. Amazing. I thank God for my many blessings. I am also looking for any opportunities to do what Catholic Workers do best the works of Mercy. And at night, before I go to sleep, I pray for the guys I left behind on 5 North, wondering how they are doing.

හ

Frank Cordaro is a peace activist, a former Catholic priest and founding member of the Des Moines Catholic Worker community. He has spent more than four years in jail for protesting for peace and justice. Another member of Des Moines Catholic Worker community, Elton Davis, is currently in the midst of a 90-day sentence at a federal facility in Leavenworth, Kan., for trespassing at Offut Air Force Base, the home of the Strategic Nuclear and US Military Commands in Omaha NE. He is expected to be released in mid-February (2005).

Source: *Pointblank Magazine*, Jan 12, 2005 Des Moines Iowa

BIBLIOGRAPHY

BOOKS

Allen, Joseph L. *War: A Primer for Christians.* Dallas: Southern Methodist University Press, 2001.

Apter, David E. *Choice and the Politics of Allocation* (London: Yale University Press, 1971.

Aquinas, Thomas. "Summa Theologica." *Great Books of the Western World,* Vol. 20. Edited by Robert Maynard Hutchins. Chicago: Encyclopaedia Britannica, Inc., 1975.

Augustine. "The City of God," translated from *De Civitate Dei* by Marcus Dods.

Augustine, Great Books of the Western World, vol. 18. Edited by Robert Maynard Hutchins. Chicago: Encyclopaedia Britannica, Inc., 1952.

Bainton, Roland H. *Christian Attitudes Toward War and Peace: A Historical Survey and Critical Re evaluation.* Nashville, Tenn.: Abingdon Press, 1985.

Barth, Karl. *Church Dogmatics,* Vol. III/4. Ttranslated by A.T. Mackay et al. New York: Charles Scribner's Sons, 1961.

Birch, Bruce. *Let Justice Roll Down: The Hebrew Scriptures, Ethics, and Christian Life.* Louisville, Kentucky: Westminster/John Knox Press, 1991.

Bose, Nirmal Kumar. *Selections from Gandhi.* Ahmedabad, India: Navajivan Publishing House, 1948.

Bravo, Carlos. "Jesus of Nazareth, Christ the Liberator." *Systematic Theology: Perspectives from Liberation Theology.* Edited by Jon Sobrino and Ignacio Ellacuria . Maryknoll, NY: Orbis Books, 1993.

Brown, SS., Raymond E. *The Death of the Messiah: From Gethsemane to the Grave: A Commentary on the Passion Narratives in the Four Gospels,* Vol. 1. New York: Doubleday, 1994.

Brown, SS, Raymond E., Joseph A. Fitzmyer, SJ and Roland E. Murphy, O.Carm. Eds.

The Jerome Biblical Commentary. Englewood Cliffs, NJ: Prentice-Hall, 1970. Joseph A. Fitzmyer, SJ and Roland E. Murphy, O.Carm. Eds.

The New Jerome Biblical Commentary. Englewood Cliffs, NJ: Prentice-Hall, 1990.

Brown, Robert McAfee. *Unexpected News: Reading the Bible with Third World Eyes.* Philadelphia: The Westminster Press, 1984.

Brueggemann, Walter. *A Commentary on Jeremiah: Exile and Homecoming.* Grand Rapids, Mich.: William B. Eerdmans Publishing Co., 1998.

Bramson, Leon and Goethals, George W. Eds.. *War: Studies from Psychology Sociology Anthropology.* New York: Basic Books, 1968.

Ernesto Cardenal, *The Gospel in Solentiname*. Vol. 3. Translated by Donald
D. Walsh. Maryknoll, NY: Orbis Books, 1979.

Catechism of the Catholic Church. New York: Doubleday, 1995.

Central Intelligence Agency. *The World Fact Book*, 2004.

Connors, Jr., Russell B and Patrick T. McCormick. *Character, Choices, and
Community: The Three Faces of Christian Ethics* (New York: Paulist Press,
1998)

Crossan, John Dominic. *The Historical Jesus: The Life of a Mediterranean
Jewish Peasant* . San Francisco: Harper, 1992.

Crossan, John Dominic and Jonathan L. Reed. *In Search of Paul: How Jesus'
Apostle Opposed Rome's Empire with God's Kingdom*. San Francisco: Harpers, 2004.

Crossan , OSM, Dominic M. "Judges." *The Jerome Biblical Commentary*.
Edited by Raymond E. Brown, SS, Joseph A. Fitzmyer, SJ and Roland E.
Murphy, O.Carm. Englewood Cliffs, NJ: Prentice-Hall, 1970.

Day, Dorothy. *Loaves and Fishes*. New York: Harper & Row, 1963.

———. "War Is the Health of the State." *The Long Loneliness*. New York:
Harper & Brothers, 1952.

de Tocqueville, Alexis. "On War, Society, and the Military." *War: Studies
from Psychology Sociology Anthropology*. Edited by Leon Bramson, and
Goethals, George W. New York: Basic Books, 1968.

Dillon, Richard J. and Joseph A. Fitzmyer, SJ, "Acts of the Apostles." *The
Jerome Biblical Commentary* (q.v.).

Dulles, SJ, Avery. *Models of the Church*. New York: Doubleday, 1987.

Eckstein, Harry. "On the Causes of Internal Wars." Edited by Nordlinger,
Eric A. *Politics and Society: Studies in Comparative Political Sociology*. Englewood Cliffs, NJ: Prentice-Hall, 1970.

Egan, Eileen. *Peace Be with You: Justified Warfare or the Way of Nonviolence*.
Maryknoll, NY: Orbis Books, 1999.

Ellsberg, Robert. Ed. *Dorothy Day: Selected Writings*. Maryknoll, NY: Orbis
Books, 1983.

Elshtain, Jean Bethke. *Women and War*. Chicago: University of Chicago
Press, 1987.

Fitzmyer, SJ, Joseph A. "The Letter to the Romans." *The Jerome Biblical
Commentary* (q.v.).

Ferguson, John. *Politics of Love: The New Testament and Non-Violent Revolution*. Cambridge, UK: Jas. Clarke Publishers.

Fischer, Louis. Ed.. *The Essential Gandhi: His Life, Work, and Ideas: An Anthology*. New York: Vintage Books, 1962.

Ford, SJ, John C. "The Morality of Obliteration Bombing." *War and Morality*. Edited by Richard Wassertrom. Belmont, California: 1970.

Forrest, Jim . "A Biography of Dorothy Day." *The Encyclopedia of American
Catholic History*. Liturgical Press, 1994.

Frank, Leonard Roy. Ed. *Random House Webster's Quotationary*. New York: Random House, 1998.

Gandhi, Mohandhas. *All Men Are Brothers*. Unesco, 1958 and 1969.

Gula, SS, Richard M. *Reason Informed by Faith: Foundations of Catholic Morality* New York: Paulist Press, 1989.

Harvey, A.E. *Jesus and the Constraints of History*. Philadelphia: Westminster, 1982.

Hauerwas, Stanley. *Against the Nations: War and Survival in a Liberal Society*. Notre Dame, Ind.: University of Notre Dame Press, 1982.

————. "Jesus and the Social Embodiment of the Peaceable Kingdom." *The Hauerwas Reader*. Edited by John Berkman and Michael Cartwright. Durham, NC: Duke University Press, 2001.

————. *Naming the Silences: God, Medicine, and the Problem of Suffering*. Grand Rapids, Mich.: 1990.

————. *The Peaceable Kingdom: A Primer in Christian Ethics*. Notre Dame, Ind.: University of Notre Dame Press, 1983.

————. "Peacemaking: The Virtue of the Church." *The Hauerwas Reader*. Edited by John Berkman and Michael Cartwright. Durham, NC: Duke University Press, 2001.

————. *Should War Be Eliminated?* Milwaukee, WI: Marquette University Press, 1984.

Hays, Richard B. *The Moral Vision of the New Testament: A Contemporary Introduction to New Testament Ethics*. San Francisco: Harper, 1996.

Helgeland, John, Robert J. Daly and J. Patout Burns. *Christians and the Military: The Early Experience* Philadelphia: Fortress Press, 1985.

Herman, A.L. *Community, Violence, and Peace: Aldo Leopold, Mohandas K. Gandhi, Martin Luther King, Jr., and Gautama the Buddha in the Twenty-First Century*. Albany, NY: State University of New York Press, 1999.

Hobbes, Thomas. "Leviathan." 13. *Random House Webster's Quotationary*. Edited by Frank, Leonard Roy. New York: Random House, 1998.

Hobbs, T.R. *A Time for War: A Study of Warfare in the Old Testament*. Wilmington, Del.: Michael Glazier, Inc., 1989.

Hogins, James Burl and Gerald A. Bryant. *Juxtaposition*. Palo Alto, Cal.: Science Research Associates, 1971.

Howard, M. *The Causes of Wars*.[2nd ed.] Cambridge, Mass: Harvard University Press, 1983.

Huxley, Aldous. *Ends and Means*. London: Chatto & Windus, 1941.

James, William "The Moral Equivalent of War." *War: Studies from Psychology Sociology Anthropology*. Edited by Leon Bramson, and Goethals, George W. New York: Basic Books, 1968.

Janowitz, Morris. "Military Elites and the Study of War." *War: Studies from Psychology Sociology Anthropology*. Edited by Leon Bramson, and Goethals, George W. New York: Basic Books, 1968.

————. "The Military in the Political Development of New Nations." *Garrisons and Government: Politics and the Military in New States*. Edited by Wilson C. McWilliams. San Francisco: Chandler Publishing Co., 1967.

Johnson, Chalmers A. "Civilian Loyalties and Guerrilla Conflict." *Garrisons and Government: Politics and the Military in New States*. Edited by Wilson C. McWilliams. San Francisco: Chandler Publishing Co., 1967.

Johnson, James Turner. *The Quest for Peace: Three Moral Traditions in Western Cultural History*. Princeton, NJ: 1987.

John XXIII, Pope. *Pacem in Terris*. April 11, 1963.

Kaufman, Peter Iver. *Redeeming Politics*. Princeton, NJ: Princeton University Press, 1990.

Keaney, Peter J. "Joshua." *The Jerome Biblical Commentary* (q.v.).

King, Jr., Martin Luther. "A Christmas Sermon on Peace," (1967) Edited by James Melvin Washington. *A Testament of Hope: The Essential Writings and Speeches of Martin Luther King, Jr.* San Francisco: Harper & Row, 1990.

————. "A Time to Break Silence," in *A Testament of Hope* (see above).

————. "Letter from Birmimgham Jail." *Why We Can't Wait*. New York: Harper and Row, 1964.

————. "Pilgrimage to Nonviolence,"in *A Testament of Hope* (see above).

————. "Where Do We Go from Here," (1967) in *A Testament of Hope* (see above).

Lasswell, Harold D. "The Garrison State." *War: Studies from Psychology Sociology Anthropology*. Edited by Leon Bramson, and Goethals, George W. New York: Basic Books, 1968.

Lind, Millard C. *Yahweh Is a Warrior: The Theology of Warfare in Ancient Israel*. Scottdale, Pennsylvania: Herald Press, 1980.

Lipset, Seymor Martin. *Revolution and Counterrevolution: Change and Persistence in Social Structure*. London: Heinemann, 1969.

Lohfink, Gerhard. *Jesus and Community*. Philadelphia: Fortress Press, 1984.

Lonergan, Bernard *Insight*. Toronto: Toronto University Press, 1992.

Mally, SJ, Edward J. "The Gospel According to Mark." *The Jerome Biblical Commentary* (q.v.).

Mao Tse-tung. "Problems of War and Strategy," in *Selected Works*, I (Beijing: Foreign Languages Press, 1964.

McDougall, William. "The Instinct of Pugnacity."' *War: Studies from Psychology Sociology Anthropology*. Edited by Leon Bramson, and Goethals, George W. New York: Basic Books, 1968.

McKenzie, SJ, John L. *Dictionary of the Bible*. New York: Bruce Publishing Company, 1965.

————. "The Gospel According to Matthew," *The Jerome Biblical Commentary* (q.v.).

McSorley, SJ, Richard. *New Testament Basis of Peacemaking* . Washington, DC: Center for Peace Studies, 1979.

McWilliams Wilson C., ed.. *Garrisons and Government: Politics and the Military in New States*. San Francisco: Chandler Publishing Co., 1967.

Meier, John P. *A Marginal Jew: Rethinking the Historical Jesus*, Vol. 1. "The Roots of the Problem and the Person." New York: Doubleday, 1991.

————. *A Marginal Jew: Rethinking the Historical Jesus*, Vol. 2. "Mentor, Message, and Miracles." New York: Doubleday, 1994.

————. *A Marginal Jew: Rethinking the Historical Jesus* , Vol. 3. "Companions and Competitors." New York: Doubleday, 2001.

Moltmann, Jürgen. *Religion, Revolution and the Future*. New York: Scribner, 1969.

New American Bible, The. New York: Catholic Book Publishing Co., 1992.

New Catechism, A: Catholic Faith for Adults. Translated by Kevin Smyth from *"De Nieuwe Katechismus."* New York: Herder, 1969.

New Commentary on the Code of Canon Law. Edited by John P. Beal, James A. Coriden, Thomas J. Green. New York: Paulist Press, 2000.

Niditch, Susan. *War in the Hebrew Bible: A Study in the Ethics of Violence*. New York: Oxford University Press, 1993.

Niebuhr, Reinhold. *An Interpretation of Christian Ethics*. New York: Seabury, 1979.

————. *Moral Man and Immoral Society: A Study in Ethics and Politics*. New York: Charles Scribner Sons, 1932.

————. *The Nature and Destiny of Man*. New York: Charles Scribner's Sons, 1957.

Nolan, OP, Albert. *Jesus Before Christianity: The Gospel of Liberation*. London: Darton, Longman and Todd Ltd, 1977.

Nouwen, Henri J.M. *Encounters with Merton*. New York: Crossroad Publishing, 1981.

O'Brien, David J. and Thmoas A. Shannon. Eds. *Catholic Social Thought: The Documentary Heritage*. Maryknoll, NY. Orbis Books, 1998.

Office of Management and Budget, Executive Office of the President of the United States. *Budget of the United States Government, Fiscal Year 2006*.

Ollenburger, Ben C. "Gerhard von Rad's Theory of Holy War." *Holy War in Ancient Israel.*. Gerhard von Rad. Grand Rapids, Michigan: Wm. B. Eerdmans Publishing Co, 1991.

Parekh, Bhikhu. *Gandhi*. Oxford: Oxford University Press, 1997.

Paul VI, Pope. "Pastoral Constitution on the Church" (*Gaudium et spes*). *The Documents of Vatican II*. New York: American Press, 1966.

Pedersen, Johannes. *Israel: Its Life and Culture*. Vol. 1. London: Oxford University Press, 1940.

Pfaltzgraff, Robert L., Jr. (ed.). *Politics in the International System* . Philadelphia: JB Lippincott Company, 1972.

252   JESUS THE WARRIOR?

Rasmusson, Arne. *The Church as Polis: From Political Theology to Theological Politics as Exemplified by Jürgen Moltmann and Stanley Hauerwas.* Notre Dame, Ind.: University of Notre Dame Press, 1995.

Rejai, M. (ed.) *Mao Tse-tung on Revolution and War* Garden City, NY: Anchor Books, 1970.

Richards, Glyn. *The Philosophy of Gandhi: A Study of His Basic Ideas.* London: Curzon Press Ltd., 1982.

Rubenstein, Richard E. *When Jesus Became God: The Epic Fight over Christ's Divinity in the Last Days of Rome.* New York: Harcourt Brace & Company, 1999.

Sidgwick, Henry. *The Elements of Politics* . London: 1891.

Smend, Rudolf. *Yahweh War and Tribal Confederation.* Nashville: Abingdon Press, 1970.

Sobrino, Jon. "Central Position of the Reign of God in Liberation Theology." Edited by Jon Sobrino and Ignacio Ellacuria. *Systematic Theology: Perspectives from Liberation Theology.* New York: Orbis Books, 1996.

Somerville, John and Ronald E. Santoni. Eds. *Social and Political Philosophy.* Garden City, NY: Doubleday & Co., Inc, 1963.

Spencer, Herbert. "The Military and the Industrial Society." *War: Studies from Psychology Sociology Anthropology.* Edited by Leon Bramson, and Goethals, George W. New York: Basic Books, 1968.

Stolz, Fritz. *Jahwes und Israels Kriege.* Zurich: Theologischer Verlag, 1972.

Stockholm International Peace Research Institute. *Arms Trade with the Third World.* New Jersey: Humanities Press, 1973.

———. *World Armaments and Disarmament: SIPRI Yearbook 1973.* New Jersey: Humanities Press, 1973.

Stuhlmueller, Carroll. "Deutero-Isaiah." *The New Jerome Biblical Commentary.* Edited by Raymond E. Brown, SS, Joseph A. Fitzmyer, SJ and Roland E. Murphy, O.Carm. Englewood Cliffs, NJ: Prentice-Hall, 1990.

Sullivan, Harry Stack. "Toward a Psychiatry of Peoples." *War: Studies from Psychology Sociology Anthropology.* Edited by Leon Bramson, and Goethals, George W. New York: Basic Books, 1968.

Turro,James C. and Raymond E. Brown, SS. "Canonicity." *The Jerome Biblical Commentary.* Edited by Raymond E. Brown, SS, Joseph A. Fitzmyer, SJ and Roland E. Murphy, O.Carm. Englewood Cliffs, NJ: Prentice-Hall, 1970.

Twain, Mark. "The War-Prayer." (1916.) *A Pen Warmed-up in Hell: Mark Twain in Protest.* Edited by. Frederick Anderson. Publisher unknown, 1972.

US Catholic Bishops. "The Challenge of Peace: God's Promise and Our Response," 1983. *Catholic Social Thought: The Documentary Heritage.* Edited by David J. O'Brien and Thomas A. Shannon. Maryknoll, NY: Orbis Books, 1998.

von Clausewitz, Karl. "The Nature of War." Written by Karl von Clausewitz. *On War.* New York: Barnes and Noble, Inc.
von Harnack, Adolf. *Militia Christi: The Christian Religion and the Military
   in the First Three Centuries.* Philadelphia: Fortress Press, 1981.
von Rad, Gerhard. *Holy War in Ancient Israel.* Grand Rapids, Michigan:
   Wm. B. Eerdmans Publishing Co, 1991.
Walzer, Michael. *Just and Unjust Wars: A Moral Argument with Historical
   Illustrations.* New York: Basic Books, 2000.
Wellhausen, Julius. *Prolegomena to the History of Ancient Israel.* Cleveland:
   World, 1957.
Wright, Quincy. *A Study of War* (Chicago: University of Chicago Press,
   1964),
Yoder, John Howard. *The Politics of Jesus: Vicit Agnus Noster.* Grand Rapids,
   MI: Wm. B. Eerdmans Publishing, 1994.
Zinn, Howard. *A People's History of the United States: 1492-Present.* New
   York: HarperCollins, 2003.

CONFERENCES
"The Concept of Political Power." *Annual of the Swedish Theological Institute in Jerusalem,* **VII.**

JOURNALS
The Bulletin of the Canadian Society of Biblical Studies: Craigie, Peter. "War,
   Religion and Scripture." 1986.
Christianity Today: Holmes, Robert L. "A Time for War?," Sept. 21, 2001.
Church History: Helgeland, John. "Christians and the Roman Army A.D.
   173-337." No. 43, 1974.
Concilium: Hauerwas, Stanley. "The Sermon on the Mount, Just War and
   the Quest for Peace." No. 1, 1988.
Journal of Religious Ethics: Langan, SJ, John. "The Elements of St. Augus-
   tine's Just War Theory." 12.1, Spring 1984.
Pointblank Magazine, Jan 12, 2005: Cordaro, Frank. "In prison for peace:
   Consequences, opportunities and blessings."
Sojourner: Zabelka, George. "I Was Told It Was Necessary." Sept. 8, 1980.
VT: Jones, G.H. "Holy War or Yahweh War." 25 (1975).

MOVIES
"Fog of War."

NEWSPAPERS
The Charlotte Observer: Hauerwas, Stanley. "Christianity and War." Feb.
   10, 1991, 1C.

Houston Catholic Worker: Zwick, Mark & Louis. "Pope John Paul II calls
   War a Defeat for Humanity: Neo-Conservatives' Iraq Just War Theories
   Rejected." Vol. XXIII No. 4, July 2003.

WEBSITES

Iraqbodycount
Mother Jones.com
Foehl, Tucker. "What Kind of Freedom?" Jan. 28, 2005.
UNESCO
wikipedia

Index

A

Acts 53, 65, 68, 80, 87, 177, 248
Africa 86, 91, 92, 101, 102, 160,
    188, 192-194, 200, 201,
    215
aggression 17, 22, 24, 113, 124,
    141, 145, 179, 214
Ahimsa 195, 197, 198, 199, 201
Albright, Madeleine 14, 128
Allen, Joseph L. 85, 107, 108, 247
Al Qaeda 137
Ambrose 99, 100, 101, 105
Amin, Idi 137
Ammianus 96
amphictyony 35, 39, 40, 41
ananda 191
anarchy 178
anawim 51
antitheses 59, 86, 117, 179
apartheid 160
Apocalypse 80
apostolic 7, 57, 65, 67, 77, 80, 81,
    89, 93, 99, 104, 118, 163,
    233
appeasement 141
Apter, David E. 16
Aquinas, Thomas 111-116, 124,
    146, 158, 247
Argentina 137
Arian 96, 97, 99, 100, 101
Aristotle 112, 113
Arius 96
Armenia 96
Aron, Raymond 9, 27
Arsenius 96
Ashram 201

assassination 155, 156, 194
Assyrian 35
Athanasius 96, 99
Athenagoras 10
Atman 197
Augustine 10, 84, 91, 93, 100-105,
    109, 110-116, 124, 128,
    130, 131, 133, 143, 146,
    158, 168, 171, 172, 178,
    233, 247, 253
authority 62, 63, 70, 77, 78, 80,
    82, 91, 101, 109, 110, 114,
    116, 119, 121-124, 130,
    132, 147, 175, 182, 192,
    229

B

Babylon 44
Bainton, Roland H. 85-87, 89, 90-
    93, 95, 103, 247
ban 42
Banks, Robert 224
Barth, Karl 120, 247
basileia 56
Beal, John P. 109, 251
beatitudes 55, 60, 75, 117, 158
Bella Americana 49
belligerence 27, 60, 207, 231
Berkman, John 71, 172, 175, 249
Bernanos 205
Berger, Peter 9
Berrigan, Daniel 220, 242
Bhagavad-Gita 195
Birch, Bruce 9, 36
Birmingham 217, 219
Bok, Francis 186

Bonhoeffer, Dietrich 121, 140, 216, 220, 221
Borg, Marcus 10
Bose, Nirmal Kumar 197, 247
boundaries 145, 147
Bourgois, Roy 220
Bowlby, John 22
Bravo, Carlos 69, 70, 82, 247
Brazil 137
Brethren 220
Brown, Raymond 10
Brown, Robert McAfee, 10, 31, 32, 49, 64, 66, 68, 247, 248, 252
Brueggemann, Walter 9, 44, 247
brutality 136, 140, 148, 150, 154, 168
Buddha 195, 249
Bund 9, 48, 52
Burns, J. Patout 86, 249

C

Caesar 69, 81, 82, 88, 98, 105
Cain 91
Canaanites 32, 42, 108
Cardenal, Ernesto 160, 248
Cordaro, Frank 220, 241, 246
Cartwright, Michael 71, 172, 175, 249
catechism 125, 130-134, 248, 251
Catholic Association for International Peace 209
Catholic Worker 122, 203-207, 209, 210, 234, 242, 244, 246, 254
Celsus 87, 89
Central Intelligence Agency 227, 228, 248
Chavan, Gen. 28
Chechnya 137

Chile 137
Chronicles 31, 33, 38, 42, 47, 52
Cicero 112, 113
cit 191
civil disobedience 184, 192, 193, 195, 201, 212, 217, 218, 220, 221
Clausewitz, Karl von 16, 17, 136, 151, 253
Clement of Alexandria 7, 10, 89
Club of Rome 23, 77
coercion 16, 86, 140, 172, 174-176, 180, 182, 183
Colombia University 126
colonial 129, 137, 143, 184, 201, 231
colonization 144, 186
Colossians 80
combatants 35, 126, 128, 134, 151-153, 157, 158
commandment 54, 56, 59, 62, 75, 91, 132, 178, 183
community 57, 58, 64, 67, 71, 74, 75, 78-81, 84, 92, 94, 103, 104, 113, 117, 120, 141, 144, 145, 160, 164, 168, 170, 172, 175, 177, 180, 201, 209, 211, 213, 233, 241, 242, 246
Comte, Auguste 27
Connors, Jr, Russell B. 15, 113
conquest 38, 47, 49, 98, 141, 144, 230
conscience 79, 80, 109, 123, 124, 130, 133, 153, 177, 181, 214, 230, 242
conscription
   universal military 69, 85, 94, 140, 159, 171, 172, 205, 206

Constans 96
Constantine 7, 84, 95-99, 101,
    104, 105, 136, 208
Constantinople 101
Constantius 97, 99
consumerism 172
conventional war 151
Corinthians 57, 65
counter-revolution 123
covenant 35
Craigie, Peter 9, 48
Crispus 96
Crossan, John Dominic 10, 32,
    54, 61, 62, 71, 73, 74, 81,
    84, 248
crusade 107, 108, 173
Cyprian 7, 10, 91, 93

D

Damasus 92, 96
Darwin, Charles 23, 24
Daly, Robert J. 86, 249
David 16, 38, 40, 41
Day, Dorothy 133, 202, 203, 205,
    209, 210, 234, 242, 248
Dear, John 220
death 14, 22, 42, 56, 58, 59, 62,
    64, 66, 71, 73-75, 77, 79,
    84, 103, 118, 119, 135,
    137, 151, 166, 170, 171,
    178, 181, 185, 190, 194,
    195, 204, 214, 215, 216,
    217, 226, 232
Decius 95
dehumanizes 60, 61
destruction 14, 21, 32, 38, 43, 44,
    62, 64, 78, 103, 126, 128,
    135, 140, 142, 148, 151,
    152, 161, 162, 199, 206,
    207, 220, 228, 232

Deutero-Isaiah 50
Deuteronomy 33, 42, 43, 45-47,
    74, 118
Dienbienphu 129
Diocletian 92, 95
disarmament 129, 130, 162
discrimination 127, 131, 134, 136,
    149, 151, 157, 212, 213,
    214
dissent 171, 172
divine law 158
Donatists 91
Dostoyevsky, Fyodor 203
Dougherty, James 9
Douglass, James 10, 85
Dresden 14, 153
Dulles, Avery 56
Dunne, George H. 210
Durbin 22
Durkheim, Emile 23

E

East Timor 137
Ebenezer Baptist Church 218
Eckstein, Harry 9, 26
Edessa 96
Edict of Milan 7
Egan, Eileen 204, 210
Einstein, Albert 22
Eisenhower, Dwight 27, 206, 225
Ellacuria, Ignacio 55, 69, 247, 252
Ellsberg, Robert 205
Elshtain, Jean Bethke 85, 171,
    172, 248
enemy 34, 38, 42, 44, 46, 48, 58,
    82, 86, 108, 117, 135, 147,
    151, 152, 155, 165, 166,
    167, 179, 180, 189, 190,
    214, 231
Engels, Friedrich 181

Enlightenment 56
enslavement 33, 55, 79, 145, 148,
    230
Enuma elish 44
equality 81, 182, 183, 190, 216
Erikson, Erik 22
eschaton 55, 57-59, 85, 87, 88, 94,
    164, 168, 170, 177, 183,
    186
Essenes 71
eternal law 111, 115, 131, 218
Etzioni, Amitai 9
euangelion 79
Eusebius 7, 85, 97, 98
evil 37, 38, 46, 50, 55, 58, 63, 74,
    75, 77-79, 103, 104, 107-
    110, 112-114, 116, 117,
    120, 122, 124, 128, 132,
    151, 152, 157, 178, 182,
    186, 190, 193, 194, 199,
    201, 212-214, 217, 218,
    221, 224, 225
Exodus 11, 33, 38, 39, 41, 51, 79
exploitation 29, 115, 134, 142,
    147, 158, 187, 198, 208,
    214, 215, 230
expropriation 147

F

Falls, T.B. 80
Falluja 126, 134
Fascist 204
fathers 33, 84, 88, 90, 92, 93, 104,
    105, 158, 233
Fausta 96
federation 35, 36, 40, 48, 52, 230
Fellowship of Reconciliation 207,
    209
first strikes 142
Fisher, Louis 200

Fitzmyer, Joseph 10, 66, 77
Flavius Josephus 10, 72, 73
Foehl, Tucker 173, 254
force 7-9, 15, 17, 36, 49, 61, 68,
    69, 73, 77-79, 86, 91, 92,
    97, 99, 100, 109, 115, 122-
    125, 139, 140, 143, 150,
    170, 174, 184, 185, 189,
    190, 192, 194, 198, 205,
    206, 216, 218, 221, 224,
    225
Ford, John C. 151
foreigner 51
foreigners 11, 45, 51, 52, 80, 93,
    118, 231
Forrest, Jim 203, 248
Franco, Francisco 204
Franks 100
freedom 33, 108, 123, 144, 163,
    170, 173, 183, 189, 192,
    197, 211, 214, 217, 218,
    229, 254
Freud, Sigmund 9, 22

G

Gaius 112, 113
Galerius 7, 92, 95, 105
Gandhi, Mohandas K. 54, 133,
    184, 187-201, 206, 210-
    212, 217-219, 221, 242,
    247-249, 251, 252
Gaudium et Spes 133, 134, 251,
    162, 208, 232
Gautama 195, 249
Genesis 42
Gentiles 61, 63, 72, 82
German Confessing Church 54
Gideon 37, 38
Glover, T.R. 80

good 33, 37, 50, 55, 69, 73, 77-79, 103, 104, 107-109, 111-117, 122, 126, 132, 140, 150-152, 157, 169, 171, 172, 175, 178, 190, 196, 201, 205, 207, 210, 218, 219, 228, 242
Goths 100, 104, 111
Great Depression 180, 204
Greece 25
Guelich, Robert 59
Guatemalan 137
guerrilla 16, 17, 127, 151, 154, 156, 158, 161
guerrillas 154, 155, 156, 216
guerrilla war 151, 155, 156, 158
Gula, SS, Richard M. 16, 111
Gumbleton, Thomas 13, 220

H

Hamburg 135, 153
Hannan, Phillip 209
Harnack, Adolf von 86, 253
Hart, Liddell 184-185
Harvey, A.E. 175, 249
hatred 75, 96, 130, 168, 189, 190, 197, 204, 208, 212
Hauerwas, Stanley 10, 57, 58, 71, 81, 85, 86, 101, 166-176, 249, 252, 253
Hays, Richard B. 9, 10, 59, 68, 79, 81-86, 101, 117, 118, 121, 166-176, 249, 252, 253
Hebrews 5, 8, 9, 11, 31, 32-51, 53, 54, 56, 60, 64, 72, 74, 75, 86, 93, 102, 108, 117, 118, 124, 131, 133, 159, 217, 230, 231, 247, 251
Hebrew Wars 35, 39
Helgeland, John 85, 249, 253

Hemingway, Ernest 28
Hennacy, Ammon 206
herem 43, 45
Herman, A.L. 194, 195, 249
Herodians 70
Hillel 11
himsa 196, 198, 199
Hippolytus 10, 83, 87
Hiroshima 13, 135, 153, 210
Hitler, Adolf 121, 200, 204, 217
Hobbes, Thomas 225, 249
Hobbs, T.R. 9, 34, 37, 40, 41, 48, 50, 53, 249
Holmes, Robert L. 110, 253
Holy War 32-35, 39, 40, 42, 251, 253
Hosea 41, 47
Howard, M. 41
human law 112
human rights 122, 123, 138, 139, 145, 146, 161, 202, 214, 229
Huns 100
Hutchins, Robert Maynard 102, 112, 247
Huntington, Samuel 9
Hussein, Saddam 14, 224
Huxley, Aldous 196, 249

I

immunity 121, 127, 128
impoverishment 23, 163, 181, 204, 214
independence 72, 120, 143, 144, 145
injury 59, 74, 90, 127, 142
international law 18, 153, 154, 230

intervention 11, 38, 40, 136, 138,
    140, 143-148, 152, 169,
    224
Iranaeus 7, 88, 93, 183
Iraq 13, 14, 20, 23, 108, 122, 124,
    126, 127, 134, 137, 142,
    146, 154, 173, 224, 226,
    228, 242, 254
Isaiah 31, 41, 49, 50, 52, 231, 252
Ischyras 96
Israel 32-51, 56, 69, 72, 79, 82,
    118, 124, 146, 147, 174,
    193, 227, 230, 250, 251,
    253
Israelite 33-36, 39, 41, 42, 47, 52,
    71
Isvara 191

J

Jacob 50
James, William 9, 20, 21
Janowitz, Morris 9, 28
Jeremiah 31, 44, 49, 51, 52, 231,
    247
Jericho 32, 42
Jesus 1, 3, 7, 8, 10, 11, 53-71, 73-
    75, 77, 79-86, 88, 89, 91,
    93-96, 99, 100, 101, 103,
    104, 110-112, 115-120,
    122, 125, 133, 134, 156,
    158, 159, 161-172, 174-
    179, 183, 185, 187, 188,
    193, 194, 195, 197, 204,
    205, 208, 212, 218-221,
    224, 225, 230-234, 241,
    243, 244, 247-253
Jews 54, 62, 63, 67, 69, 72, 73, 82,
    118, 163, 166, 193, 200,
    201, 204, 205

John 9, 22, 32, 36, 54, 61-64, 70,
    71, 73, 81, 83, 85, 89, 90,
    118, 161, 162, 163, 165,
    167, 192, 231, 247- 254
John Paul II 122, 162, 167, 224
John XXIII 122, 130, 134, 162,
    167, 207, 208, 250, 254
Johns Hopkins 126
Johnson, Chalmers A. 9, 28
Johnson, Hiram 225
Johnson, James Turner 85
John the Baptist 70, 72, 73, 161
Joshua 11, 31-33, 42, 47, 51, 93,
    231, 250
Judges 11, 31-33, 38, 39, 42, 47,
    51, 231, 248
jus ad bellum 121, 146, 147
jus gentium 113, 183
jus in bello 121, 126, 127, 134,
    149, 150, 157
jus naturale 112, 113, 116, 183
just cause 114, 121, 122, 124
justice 11, 38, 44-47, 49, 50, 54,
    56, 74, 75, 79, 81, 88, 91,
    101, 103, 112, 117, 121,
    124, 130-132, 134, 146,
    164, 165, 167, 168, 174,
    177, 179-184, 190, 203,
    208, 213, 216, 218, 220,
    225, 230-233, 246
Justin Martyr 7, 10, 80
just war 8, 10, 101, 103, 109-111,
    114, 116, 121, 122, 126-
    129, 133, 134, 136, 138,
    140, 141, 143-145, 148,
    153, 154, 156-158, 172,
    173, 179, 205-207, 216,
    231, 233, 234

K

Khan, Ayub 28
Kampuchea 137
Kaufman, Peter Iver 97, 98, 102, 250
Keaney, Peter J. 32
Kennedy, John F. 216
kerygma 79, 82
killing 33, 37, 43, 45-50, 64, 73, 80, 88, 91-95, 103, 104, 114, 117, 118, 120, 122, 124, 136, 151, 152, 155, 156, 233, 242
King, Jr, Martin Luther 133, 184, 195, 210, 211, 214, 215, 217
kingdom 56, 58, 61, 65, 68, 69, 71-73, 81, 84, 86, 119, 120, 160, 162, 163, 167, 168, 170, 171, 173-175, 177, 186, 188, 197, 248, 249
kingdom of God 56, 71, 81, 86, 120, 163, 170, 171, 175, 186
Kings 31, 33, 42, 43, 47
Kosovo 137
Kripalani, Krishna 200

L

Lactanius 10
Lactantius 7, 87, 91, 93
Lakoda, Lake 153
Langan, John 110, 253
Leeb, Field Marshal von 153
Lemay, Curtis 135
Lenin, Vladimir 181
Leviticus 43, 62, 74, 117
Levinson, Daniel 9, 23

liberation 50, 55, 58, 86, 145, 148, 196, 218
liberation theology 55
liberty 79, 138, 141, 143, 146, 147, 193, 221, 230
Lind, Millard C. 9, 35, 37, 40, 164
Logos 83, 84, 97, 98
Lohfink, Gerhard 10, 80, 85
London 14, 16, 27, 48, 86, 150, 191, 196, 247, 249, 250, 251, 252
Lonergan, Bernard 15
Long March 28
Ludlow, Bob 206
Luke 7, 55, 60, 64, 66, 67, 70, 74, 80, 82, 84, 114, 117, 118, 160, 193
Luther, Martin 54, 56, 210, 242, 249, 250

M

MacAlister, Elizabeth 220
Maccabees 71
Malacca Straits 146
Malley, Edward J. 62, 69, 70, 250
Malthus, Thomas 23
Maly, Eugene H. 40
Manichees 103, 110
Mao Tse-Tung 9, 17, 28, 149, 151, 184, 216, 250, 252
Marcion 8, 10, 53, 90, 93
Marcus Aurelius 88
Marduk 44
marginalized 51, 56, 61, 74, 75, 79, 210, 231
Maritain, Jacques 205
Mark 56, 61, 62-64, 69, 70, 250, 252, 254
Marx, Karl 23, 181, 207
massacre 145, 148

Matthew 7, 55, 58, 60, 61, 63, 64,
    66, 67, 70, 73, 75, 82, 84,
    101, 110, 116-119, 125,
    130, 160, 165, 174-177,
    179, 193, 244, 250
Mauriac, François 205
Maurin, Peter 203, 204
Maximillian 92
Maximinus Thrax 95
McCormick, Patrick T. 15, 113,
    248
McNamara, Robert 135
McKenzie, John L. 10, 32, 60, 62,
    63, 71, 210
McSorley, Richard 9, 63, 79, 80,
    89-92, 251
McWilliams, Wilson C. 28
Mead, Margaret 24
Meier, John 10, 56, 62, 70, 72,
    251
Melitene 96
Melito 97
Mennonites 205, 220
mercy 103, 119, 244
Merton, Thomas 220
Mesha 43
Mesopotamia 96, 100
Micah 49, 52, 231
Milan 99, 100, 101
military expedience 153
military necessity 150, 153
Mill, John Stuart 144, 146
Miller, Patrick 9
Milvian Bridge 7
Minucius Felix 10, 82, 83
Mishnah 31
Moltmann, Jürgen 57, 81, 84, 86,
    101, 121, 140, 159-162,
    174, 176, 186, 221, 251,
    252

monotheism 69, 97
Mosaic 69, 72, 77
Moses 36, 41, 93, 101, 103
Mounier, Emmanuel 205
murder 22, 32, 72, 91, 96, 135,
    154, 159, 160, 184
Mussolini, Benito 200
MyLai 14

N
Nagasaki 13, 135, 136, 153
Nagoya 13, 135
Nanking 14
Nasution, Gen. 28
national existence 147
national interests 27, 138, 172
natural law 19, 85, 111, 112, 115,
    116, 125, 130, 158, 162,
    168, 169, 177, 182, 183,
    233
Nazis 14, 54, 153, 171, 184
Niebuhr, Reinhold 59, 120, 121,
    161, 164, 169, 170, 176-
    184, 211, 216, 221, 251
Nehru, Jawaharlal 28
Ne Win 28
Niditch, Susan 9, 38, 43-48, 50,
    251
Niemoller, Martin 54
Nigeria 137
Nolan, Albert 85, 86, 251
non-aligned developing countries
    144
non-aligned nations 143
non-combatants 30, 32, 121, 127,
    128, 134, 149-156, 158,
    232, 233
non-intervention 144
non-violence 8, 58, 72, 87, 89, 93,
    101, 103, 112, 113, 117,

118, 120, 133, 161, 162,
165-168, 170, 176, 190,
192, 195, 197-199, 203,
205, 220, 221
Nordlinger, Eric A. 26, 248
Nouwen, Henri J.M. 220
Numbers 48, 49, 238
Nuremberg 18, 153, 154

O

O'Brien, David 121, 252
oil 124, 146
Ollenburger, Ben C. 33, 36, 42,
251
O'Neill, Eugene 203
oppressed 11, 39, 50, 51, 55, 56,
61, 74, 75, 79, 81, 101,
103, 137, 140, 159, 160,
171, 172, 176, 185, 190,
201, 211, 213, 217, 220,
230, 231
oppression 18, 47, 50, 55, 65, 117,
123, 160, 166, 184, 185,
190, 200, 213, 220, 230
oppressor 60, 185, 212, 217
Origen 7, 10, 83, 87, 89, 93
Orosius 98, 101
Ortega, Daniel 160
Osaka 135

P

Pacem in Terris 207, 208, 232, 250
Pacifism 93
pacifism 92, 94, 101, 103, 120,
133, 172, 176, 204, 205,
206
pacifist 58, 80, 84, 86, 88, 93, 162,
171, 174, 204, 205, 234
Palestine 69, 101, 147, 177
Palestinian 65, 127

Parekh, Bhikhu 188, 192, 196,
199, 251
Park, Robert 9, 24
Parks, Rosa 211
parousia 119, 177, 183
pathos 176
patristic 7, 10, 58, 65, 77, 83, 93,
96, 105, 163
patristics 7, 11
Paul 57, 65, 77, 78-81, 103, 109,
113, 117, 118, 162, 167,
177, 194, 217, 231, 248,
251, 254
Paul VI 131, 134, 208
Pax Americana 48
Pax Romana 48, 98, 166
peace 7, 10, 18, 23-25, 32, 38, 41,
42, 46, 48-52, 61, 67, 74,
75, 77, 79, 89, 90, 96, 98,
102, 108-111, 114, 115,
125, 130-134, 146, 149,
158, 163, 167, 169, 170,
171, 174, 175, 178, 202,
207, 208, 213, 218, 219,
224, 231, 233, 241-244,
246, 253
peacemakers 60, 117, 205, 208,
242
Peacemaking 7, 59, 63, 80, 89, 90-
92, 172, 174, 175, 249, 251
Pedersen, Johannes 9, 37, 40, 48,
251
Pentateuch 31, 40
persecution 7, 21, 50, 60, 70, 94,
95, 97, 99, 102, 103, 118,
120, 165, 184, 205, 217
Peter (Kephas) 7
Pfaltzgraff, Jr, Robert L. 9, 16
Pharisees 70, 72, 166, 175

physical violence 7, 9-11, 33, 53, 62-64, 66, 99, 100, 174, 197, 213, 231, 233
Pinochet, Augusto 137
police 77, 92, 94, 155, 184
Pol Pot 137
Polycarp 88
polytheism 97
poor 49, 50, 55, 56, 60, 75, 81, 101, 117, 125, 132, 203, 211, 214, 215, 243
Populorum Progressio 232
poverty 26, 191, 203, 210, 212-215, 229, 243
Powell, Colin 14, 128
power 7, 11, 15, 17-19, 23, 24, 27, 29, 32, 36, 38, 39, 41, 47, 50, 56, 67-69, 74, 77, 80, 82, 83, 103, 118, 122, 123, 132, 134, 135, 138, 141-147, 155, 159, 161, 162, 164, 165, 168, 170, 173-176, 181-187, 190, 198, 206, 211, 214, 218, 220, 225, 229-231, 238
power politics 138, 144
pre-emptive military strikes 141-143
preventive war 141, 143
Prophets 31
proportionality 121, 126, 127, 129, 149, 150, 152, 157
provocation 142
ptochos 49, 51, 60
punishment 44, 49, 70, 74, 91, 102, 103, 155, 190, 198, 243
purification 47, 49, 62, 63, 217

Q

Q 62, 84, 113
Quakers 188, 205, 220
Qumran 62, 71

R

Rad, Gerhard von 9, 32-36, 38, 39, 41, 42, 48, 251, 253
Rasmusson, Arne 57, 81, 84, 86, 87, 101, 121, 159, 160, 161, 171, 172, 252
Ratzinger, Joseph 122
realpolitik 145, 181
reciprocity 59
reconciliation 60, 74, 75, 98, 120, 125, 169, 174, 213, 231, 232
Red Guard 28
Reed, Jonathan L. 81, 248
reign of God 55, 56, 57, 164
resistance 19, 55, 57, 65, 101, 103, 115, 125, 140, 155, 161, 163, 167, 171, 174, 175, 179, 184, 185, 187, 189, 190, 192-194, 201, 212, 213, 217
retaliation 11, 59, 72, 74, 75, 117, 213
Revelation 80
revolution 9, 17, 26, 28, 67, 72, 121, 123, 148, 160-163, 174-176, 180, 181, 203, 215, 216, 220
righteousness 47, 49, 60, 61, 117, 119, 122, 123, 166, 201
Riverside Church 213-216, 226
Roman 10, 13, 62, 65, 68, 69, 71, 73, 77, 79, 80-82, 84, 85, 87, 88, 92, 94, 95, 97, 99, 100-102, 104, 107, 109,

111, 119, 158, 163, 165, 166, 193, 224, 253
Rome 7, 8, 70, 71, 79, 81, 82, 91, 95-101, 104, 105, 111, 175, 208, 248, 252
Rotterdam 14
Rubenstein, Richard E. 95, 96, 99, 100, 252
Ruskin, John 194
Rwanda 137

S

Saccidananda 191
Salvadoran 137
Samuel 9, 31-33, 39, 42, 47, 51, 231
Sarvodaya 201
sarx 65
Sat 191
Satya 191
Satyagraha 192, 194-196, 199, 201, 206, 212
Saul 32, 39, 41
Schwally, Friedrich 35, 37, 40
secession 145, 148
Segundo, Juan 10
self-determination 144-147, 185, 224
self-rule 190
Sermon on the Mount 57, 59, 60, 103, 117, 158, 162, 164, 205, 231, 253
Sermon on the Plain 117
Shannon, Thomas A. 121, 252
Sicarii 66, 73
Sidgwick, Henry 149, 150, 152, 252
Silvert, Kalman 9
Sinclair, Upton 203
Slattery, William 220

Smend, Rudolf 41, 252
Sobrino, Jon 10, 55, 69, 82, 247, 252
social injustice 189, 203, 210, 214, 217
Soekarno, Pres. 28
soldiers 13, 25, 28, 38, 45, 48, 56, 68, 69, 87, 88, 91, 92, 94, 96, 109, 127-129, 140, 151, 152, 154, 156, 184, 223
Solentiname 160, 248
Somalia 137
Southern Christian Leadership Conference 212, 217
Spain 28, 101, 102, 204
Spanish Civil War 204
Spellman, Francis 208
Spenser, Herbert 9, 27, 252
Stalin, Josef 184
Stolz, Fritz 41, 42, 252
Stuhlmueller, Carroll 10, 50
Sudan 137
suffering 150
  expiatory 50, 59, 118, 148, 163, 165, 166, 185, 186, 194, 195, 197-199, 204, 213, 215, 221, 225, 231, 232, 234
Suharto, Pres. 28
Sumner, William Graham 23, 24
Swaraj 190
Switzerland 24
sword 7, 32, 42, 49, 64, 66, 67, 79, 89-91, 95, 109
synoptic 62, 63, 70
Syria 96

T

Talmud 31
Tanzania 137

Targums 50
temple 41, 44, 61-64, 66, 86
territorial expansion 146
territorial integrity 141, 143, 144, 146
terror 16, 154, 156, 159, 173
Tertullian 7, 10, 80, 87, 90, 92, 93
Theodosius 7, 100, 105
Thomas 13, 23, 62, 70, 74, 247, 249, 251, 252
Thoreau, Henry David 192
threat 16, 24, 29, 69, 78, 81, 82, 100, 113, 138, 141, 142, 144, 159, 165, 166, 184, 199, 204, 206, 208, 229, 240
Tibet 137
Tokyo 13, 135, 153
Tolman, Edward 9
Tonkin Gulf 127
Tocqueville, Alexis de 24, 25, 248
Torah 31, 117
Torres, Camillo 86, 140, 220, 221
Troeltsch, Ernst 85
Trotsky, Leon 26
truth 191, 195, 196, 197, 225
Tubergin, Jon 23
Twain, Mark 223, 232, 252

U

Uganda 137
Ulpian 112, 113, 177, 233
UNESCO 13, 14, 128
United Nations 13, 14, 125, 208
Urban II 108
US 13, 14, 20, 22, 23, 25, 27, 28, 121, 123-126, 128, 129, 132, 133, 134, 137, 138, 142-144, 146, 150, 152--154, 157, 166, 167, 173, 176, 184, 195, 202, 204-207, 210, 211, 214-216, 220, 224-229, 232, 234, 238-240, 246, 252
US military 13, 14, 206, 210, 225, 226
utopia 55

V

Valens 95, 99, 100
Valentinian 95, 99
Vandals 100-102, 111
Vatican Council 10, 56, 208-210
Vawter, Bruce 10, 63
vengeance 17, 44, 74, 117, 179
Vietnam 13, 126, 129, 137, 144, 146, 147, 152, 157, 213, 215, 216, 219
vindication 50, 87, 103, 117
vindictiveness 33, 179
Visigoths 100

W

Waltz, Kenneth 9
Walzer, Michael 10, 136, 138-141, 143-146, 148-157, 185, 253
war conventions 153-156
warfare 15-17, 24, 40, 41, 47, 50, 73, 92-94, 96, 101, 103, 105, 107, 127, 134, 140, 154, 156, 184, 204, 205, 210, 218, 226
Washington, Melvin 211, 250
Weber, Max 9, 36
weapons 66
Wellhausen, Julius 33, 253
White House 202
will of God 55, 60, 71, 74
Wobblies 202, 203

World War 13, 14, 23-25, 134,
        136, 143, 145, 153, 157,
        159, 185, 199, 200, 202,
        206, 234
Wright, Quincy 9, 18
Writings 31, 205, 248, 250

Y

Yoder, John Howard 9, 32, 83-85,
        163-165, 167, 169, 176,
        253
Yokohama 13, 135
Yugoslavia 137

Z

Zabelka, George 135, 136, 253
Zarrella, Joseph 205
Zealots 66, 71, 73
Zwick, Mark & Louis 122, 254